Strategies
for
Brief Pastoral Counseling

Strategies
for
Brief Pastoral Counseling

Howard W. Stone

Editor

Fortress Press

Minneapolis

For Karen Stone

Cover design by David Meyer
Book design by Zan Ceeley

Library of Congress Cataloging-in-Publication Data
Strategies for brief pastoral counseling / Howard W. Stone, editor.
    p.   cm.
    Includes bibliographical references.
    ISBN 0-8006-3299-0 (alk. paper)
    1. Pastoral counseling. I. Stone, Howard W.
    BV4012.2 .S757 2001
    253.5—dc21
                                                          00-066260

The paper used in this publication meets the minimum requirements of American National
Standard for Information Sciences—Permanence of Paper for Printed Library Materials,
ANSI Z329.48-1984.

Manufactured in the U.S.A.   AF 1-3299

Contents

Part I
The Case for Brief Pastoral Counseling

Part II
Brief Pastoral Counseling Strategies

Part III
Pastoral Counseling Theory and Praxis

Contributors

DUANE R. BIDWELL, M.Div., licentiate in spiritual theology and direction; Staff Associate, St. Philip Presbyterian Church, Hurst, Texas; Ph.D. candidate at Brite Divinity School, Texas Christian University, Fort Worth.

BRIAN H. CHILDS, Ph.D., Director of Ethics and Organizational Development, Shore Health System, Easton, Maryland; author of *Short-Term Pastoral Counseling* (Abingdon, 1990; Haworth, 2000); editor of *The Treasure of Earthen Vessels: Explorations in Christian Anthropology* (Westminster/John Knox, 1996); and with John Patton, *Christian Marriage and Family: Caring for Our Generations* (Abingdon, 1988).

HOWARD CLINEBELL, Ph.D., Emeritus Professor, School of Theology at Claremont, Claremont, California; author of *Basic Types of Pastoral Care and Counseling* (Abingdon, 1984), *Growth Counseling: Hope-Centered Methods of Actualizing Human Wholeness* (Abingdon, 1979), *Anchoring Your Well-Being: A Guide for Christian Leaders* (Upper Room Books, 1997), and *Ecotherapy: Healing Ourselves, Healing the Earth* (Fortress Press, 1996).

KATHERINE GODBY, M.Div., Pastor at Rosemont Christian Church, Dallas, Texas; Ph.D. candidate at Brite Divinity School, Texas Christian University, Fort Worth.

NANCY GORSUCH, Ph.D., Assistant Professor of Pastoral Theology and Pastoral Counseling and Director, Pastoral Care and Training Center at Brite Divinity School, Texas Christian University, Fort Worth; author of *Pastoral Visitation* (Fortress Press, 1999).

JAN JAMES, M.Div., Associate Priest, St. James Episcopal Church, Dallas, Texas.

CHARLES ALLEN KOLLAR, Ph.D., Executive Pastor at Glad Tidings Church and Director of On-Trac Ministries, Norfolk, Virginia; author of *Solution-Focused Pastoral Counseling: An Effective Short-Term Approach for Getting People Back on Track* (Zondervan, 1997), and *Mastering Life* (Zondervan, 1999).

ANDREW LESTER, Ph.D., Professor of Pastoral Theology and Pastoral Counseling at Brite Divinity School, Texas Christian University, Fort Worth; author of *Pastoral Care with Children in Crisis* (Westminster, 1985), *Hope in Pastoral Care and Counseling* (Westminster/John Knox, 1995), *Coping with Your Anger: A Christian Guide* (Westminster/John Knox, forthcoming), and with Judy Lester, *It Takes Two: The Joy of Intimate Marriage* (Westminster/John Knox, 1998).

JAMES SHARP, Ph.D., Teaching Fellow, Southwestern Baptist Theological Seminary, Fort Worth, Texas, and Founder of Trucare Ministries, Arlington, Texas.

HOWARD W. STONE, Ph.D., Professor of Pastoral Theology and Pastoral Counseling at Brite Divinity School, Texas Christian University, Fort Worth; author of *Brief Pastoral Counseling: Short-Term Approaches and Strategies* (Fortress Press, 1994), *Crisis Counseling* (Fortress Press, 1993), *Depression and Hope* (Fortress Press, 1998), and *Theological Context for Pastoral Caregiving: Word in Deed* (Haworth, 1996).

FRANK THOMAS, Ph.D., Associate Professor, Family Therapy Program, Texas Woman's University, Denton; faculty member at Brite Divinity School, Texas Christian University, Fort Worth; author with Jack Cockburn of *Competency-Based Counseling* (Fortress Press, 1998), and editor with Thorana Nelson of *Tales from Family Therapy: Life-Changing Clinical Experiences* (Haworth, 1998).

Preface

CONTEXT SHAPES ACTION. It is a potent ingredient in our thoughts, beliefs, feelings, and behaviors. The times and places in which you do things influence how you do them, and circumstances shape your response to the words and actions of others.

Services, products, professions, even avocations need to fit the context in which they are performed or consumed. I would not recommend sushi for a toddler's birthday party menu—nor would I dare serve hot dogs and red gelatin dessert to my wife for an anniversary dinner (but she would be happy with the sushi). A rural general practitioner would require a new set of skills to practice medicine in a large urban emergency ward. A university English professor would need retraining to teach writing for primary school children. Anglers, of course, are accustomed to adapting to their context: jigging for walleye in a Minnesota lake requires different tackle, technique, and mystique from fly-fishing for Atlantic salmon in a Scottish stream or setting out trot lines for monster catfish in a south Texas river.

Pastoral counseling is no exception. Its usual context is not a professional office in a medical arts building or psychiatric hospital. The primary context of pastoral counseling—indeed, its heart—is the congregation.

In the course of pastoral conversation with those they serve, parish pastors, rabbis, and priests daily offer counsel in some form: a late night visit with a worried parishioner in the waiting room of an intensive care unit, guidance given to parents troubled by their son's drug use, help for a married couple at the brink of divorce who have decided to give counseling a try for a session or two, spiritual direction with a widower experiencing an arid prayer life since his wife's death, and an infinite variety of other pastoral moments. Due to their context—the many people they serve and multitude of functions they fulfill, as well as the wishes of their parishioners—ministers rarely see people in counseling for more than a few sessions and often only for one (see chapter 1).

In the congregational context, therefore, counseling inevitably is brief ("brief" in this volume designates a counseling duration of no more than ten sessions, but typically many fewer). Parish pastors have little choice in the matter; it is their reality. Like the doctors, teachers, and anglers in the illustrations above, if they are to minister effectively, they need to adopt strategies to suit that reality.

As early as 1949, Seward Hiltner wrote that the time limitations of the parish suggest that most pastors' counseling be brief. According to him, the principal benefit of brief counseling is to help a parishioner "turn the corner," or change direction: "Even brief counseling can often do just enough to bring a slightly new perspective, hence altering the approach to the situation and giving a chance for spontaneous successful handling of it by the parishioner."[1] Generally Hiltner and his contemporaries favored an insight-oriented, long-term counseling approach. Brief pastoral counseling methods are much more finely tuned now than when he wrote these lines, and they are better designed to help people change direction in a few sessions. Turning the corner, in fact, is a primary goal of brief pastoral counseling, under the assumption that the other ministries of the church will continue to support people as they grow and move into the future.

Strategies for Brief Pastoral Counseling is an attempt to synthesize the thinking of established and up-and-coming thinkers in the area of brief pastoral counseling. It follows up the work I began in *Brief Pastoral Counseling* and, much earlier, in *Crisis Counseling*. The book summarizes the literature in the brief pastoral counseling field and offers a new way, one that addresses the real, day-to-day context of pastoral counseling as it is practiced in local congregations among living, breathing, unique persons.

The eleven authors of *Strategies for Brief Pastoral Counseling* propose an orientation toward pastoral counseling based upon short-term counseling theory and methodology, with the underlying assumption that the vast majority of counselees wish to deal expeditiously with their problems and are unable or unwilling to devote more than a few visits to the task. People seek help from religious professionals because they quickly want to address whatever is troubling them, and not necessarily to achieve insight or delve into their distant past.

While the primary context of pastoral counseling is the congregation, the authors do not intend to exclude pastoral care and counseling specialists; indeed, it is my hope that many of them will read these chapters. Some may find themselves working once again in the parish setting as changes in insurance benefits and health care delivery cause a shift away from long-term therapy for troubled people. Indeed, a majority of the work of specialists, whether they are hospital chaplains, private practitioners in pastoral counseling, or military chaplains, is already brief in nature. Experiences and ideas of these professionals are needed in the conversation. It is my hope that the ministries of parish pastors and pastoral counseling specialists will inform and enrich each other.

Organization of the Book

Strategies for Brief Pastoral Counseling is divided into three sections. Part I focuses on the pastor-parishioner relationship—how we go about establishing or strengthening a bond with individuals enabling them to bring about change in their lives. I begin with a survey of outcome studies that demonstrate the effectiveness of short-term counseling, and an argument for the adoption of brief counseling strategies in parish ministry. Jan James writes about the importance of valuing the parishioner in pastoral counseling, showing how brief counseling methods do just that, and Nancy Gorsuch addresses the collaborative nature of brief pastoral counseling conversation. A distinguishing characteristic of brief pastoral counseling is its attention to our innate temporality and its focus on helping counselees construct new futures; Andrew Lester and I discuss this future orientation as well as methods of helping parishioners to envision a hope-filled tomorrow. Katherine Godby argues that clergy need to recapture the ancient vocation of hospitality, an essential but sometimes forgotten role of pastoral care, examining hospitality from its historical roots in Hebrew and Christian traditions and showing the inherent hospitality within the methods of brief pastoral counseling. Finally, Howard Clinebell speaks from the experience of his nearly fifty years of ministry and teaching about the importance of counseling in the congregation being holistic and brief in nature.

Part II of the book focuses on specific strategies for brief pastoral counseling and discusses how ministers can go about it. I sketch the underlying orientation of brief pastoral counseling. Charles Allen Kollar draws upon solution-focused brief therapy to outline a schema for doing brief pastoral counseling, providing the reader with several clusters of useful and easy-to-remember one-word concepts or "doorways" (based on the principle that we will not use what we cannot remember). Duane R. Bidwell, pointing out that most spiritual direction in the parish is brief in nature, addresses ways in which ministers can learn from brief therapy to enhance the way they guide others in the life of the spirit. Frank Thomas discusses competency-based couple and family counseling, helping people to discover their strengths and capabilities rather than focusing on their problems and weaknesses. Brian Childs presents a style of pastoral counseling that works within specific, agreed-upon time limits, thus using time advantageously to help people reach their goals quickly. Like Kollar, James Sharp draws from the work of solution-focused brief therapy but applies it with his own unique slant to a model for pastoral counseling that addresses the rapidly changing cultural, technological, and social realities of the twenty-first century.

Part III of *Strategies for Brief Pastoral Counseling* goes in a somewhat different direction. It summarizes a study, conducted in 1999–2000, of the major literature in the field of pastoral counseling from the past fifty years. Unlike the previous chapters, the last chapter is less about how to do brief pastoral counseling in the congregational setting and more about how little the field of pastoral counseling addressed the congregational context over the second half of the last century. It offers ways in which the field can speak more directly to the concerns of parish pastors as they offer counsel to those they serve. It is a call, in short, for theory in the field of pastoral counseling to take seriously the context of its practice.

Terms and Cases

Words are important; the terms we use for people influence our perceptions of them and our relationship to them. The authors of this book have chosen their terminology with its audience in mind: while pastoral care specialists will benefit from *Strategies for Brief Pastoral Counseling*, the book was written primarily for ministers (or hospital, military, and other chaplains) who are serving congregations of one kind or another. Throughout the book, therefore, the one who gives care is referred to as a pastoral caregiver, pastor, minister doing counseling, or some variation on those terms, rather than as counselor or therapist. Likewise, the person receiving help in most cases is called a parishioner rather than patient or client. Here "parishioner" refers not only to the immediate members of a congregation but also to those in the wider community who seek the church's help, using a historic understanding of the parish as a community or neighborhood (as opposed to members of a club or people in attendance at a service). "Counselee" is occasionally used for variety's sake but tends to limit the discussion to formal counseling in the minister's office, whereas "parishioner" suggests a broader range of care that includes many informal encounters in the varied course of parish life. Much of the counseling that goes on in ministry falls somewhere between a pastoral care visit and a pastoral counseling session, and the content of the book—while it certainly applies to formal counseling—also covers those many pastoral conversations that occur after committee meetings, at chance encounters, during illness or crisis or family celebrations.

Many of the ideas presented here are drawn from the day-to-day practice of pastoral caregiving. Consequently, the book contains portions of actual case histories. Since confidentiality is essential to pastoral practice, all case descriptions have been altered with respect to names and a number of other identifiers in order to preserve anonymity while not distorting the essential reality of the experience described.

How to Use This Book

The following suggestions will help the reader use *Strategies for Brief Pastoral Counseling* to maximum benefit. First, I recommend that the book be read with a journal or notebook near at hand for recording important points as well as personal reflections. You will find some repetition among the chapters as important themes, ideas, and methods are picked up by one and another of the authors; you may want to note these key points of convergence in your journal.

Since one problem for pastors who do counseling in the congregation is a preponderance of literature that describes a style of counseling (long-term, analytical) that they are rarely able to do in the parish, the citations and bibliographical references throughout the book should provide welcome avenues for further study. Note the sources of ideas and methods that interest you, and read other works by authors you have sampled in this volume. (See also the list of recommended readings in appendix B.)

Case studies are one of the best ways to envision and understand a counseling strategy. As you read the case illustrations in this book, expand your thinking about them. Reflect on similar cases you have encountered. Imagine how you might counsel the (thoroughly disguised) parishioners in the presented case. Think back on your own ministry for other examples that illustrate or connect in some way with the case and the strategies presented on the pages in front of you. Write these reflections in your journal, and follow with applications to your own ministry (in general, or to specific parishioners you know or are seeing in counseling).

Are there areas of the parish context of pastoral counseling, especially its brief nature, that you feel are not addressed in these pages? Then communicate your thoughts and suggestions to one or more of the authors. The burgeoning field of brief pastoral counseling is a corrective to ivory tower theory that got disconnected from congregational ministerial practice; as such, it must be grounded and shaped by the ongoing experiences of ministers such as you, as they counsel and care for their parishioners.

No doubt your reading in *Strategies for Brief Pastoral Counseling* will remind you of many more stories and passages from the Bible than the authors could cite in their limited space. Note these in your journal for future reference; often parishioners find it not only comforting but also empowering to know that there is a scriptural grounding for the efforts they are making toward resolution of their problems.

Finally, as you reflect upon and apply what you have read, do not neglect to look within yourself. You may well find that the orientation and methods of brief pastoral counseling will enrich your own personal relationships and spiritual life so that—as you use them to guide others—you will do so not as a knowing expert imposing advice and wisdom from without, but as a partner sharing their journey.

Thanks

The research for this book was assisted by grants from Brite Divinity School of Texas Christian University, and from The Louisville Institute. For their help, and for making the project possible, I am very grateful. The project would have been difficult if not impossible to accomplish without the help of these two institutions.

Much of the book was written and edited while I was on research leave, during which the burden of my teaching and supervising responsibilities fell to my colleagues at Brite Divinity School, especially Nancy Gorsuch, Andrew Lester, and Frank Thomas, and I am grateful to them for carrying the extra load. I thank Wesley House, an affiliate of Cambridge University in England, for providing a venue for my research, as well as Kenneth Cracknell and Susan White for the use of their comfortable home in nearby Saffron Walden. I appreciate the parish pastors and student pastors, serving congregations large and small both in England and the United States, who gave me invaluable information about their caregiving ministries as well as feedback concerning the usefulness of these strategies.

I am indebted to my colleagues who have helped in the writing effort, especially those who gave their time and energy to read all or portions of the manuscript and share their constructive criticism: Duane R. Bidwell, Shirley Bubar, Howard Clinebell, Nancy Gorsuch, and Andrew Lester. I also thank Duane Bidwell for his work on the appendices and the index. I thank Fortress Press and a long line of editors who have published my works over thirty years' time; theirs is a great and often underappreciated ministry to the church. Finally, I want to express my deep gratitude to Karen Stone, who gave many hours of her time in reviewing the text.

Note

1. Seward Hiltner, *Pastoral Counseling* (New York: Abingdon, 1949), 82.

Part I

The Case for
Brief Pastoral Counseling

1

The Changing Times:
A Case for Brief Pastoral Counseling

Howard W. Stone

TONY HILLERMAN, BEST-SELLING AUTHOR of mysteries set in the American Southwest, tells the true tale of Black Jack Ketchum, the most successful train robber Folsom, New Mexico, had ever known. Black Jack figured out that, while chugging up the old horseshoe curve southeast of Folsom, the Colorado and Southern train had to slow down so much that a horseman could hop out of the stirrups and onto the train without even having to gallop his horse. It was, apparently, like snatching candy from a baby. The system worked for him over and over again, so brilliantly that he saw no reason to change it.[1]

Eventually the Colorado and Southern Railroad management figured out what he was doing. They packed the train with guards. The next time Black Jack rode up in his usual style, they shot and captured him and quickly brought him to trial—after which, Hillerman adds, "he was consequently and subsequently hanged over at Clayton with such enthusiasm that his head came off."[2] Ketchum had a method that worked perfectly for a time, but the times changed.

The times are changing for health care and pastoral care just as they changed for Black Jack Ketchum. Long-term therapy was the underpinning of pastoral counseling in the early days of the twentieth century, and remains so for some practitioners in the twenty-first century. It was appropriate then because it was based upon the best information available at the time. Today new information is available. This new data not only favors brief approaches but suggests that, except in a few select cases, long-term counseling is no longer practical.[3] The medical profession has gotten the word. So have mental health researchers, the United States Department of Health and Education, insurance companies, and mental health providers. If the Colorado and Southern Railroad were still operating today, its managed health care organization most likely would mandate some version of brief counseling (in combination with pharmaceuticals, when appropriate) for the treatment of employees' mental health problems.

The fact is, congregational ministers, priests, and rabbis traditionally have practiced brief counseling for many generations in the parishes they serve. As a variety of other helping professionals "discover" brief counseling with its many advantages—it is effective, enduring, economical, and humane—the time has come for parish pastors to reclaim it as the preferred strategy for helping troubled parishioners who come to them for guidance in resolving their difficulties.

The basic premise of this chapter is that brief pastoral counseling methods should be the primary mode of operation for pastoral caregivers—parish pastors and chaplains as well as pastoral counseling specialists.

Focus on Research

When choosing methods to use in your counseling, what do you take into consideration? Your training? Readings in the field, amply illustrated with individual case studies? Past experience? How we go about counseling parishioners certainly grows out of our own experience, but it also needs to rely on the demonstrable experience of others and the outcomes of their counseling. Well-constructed research documents the work of others in a controlled way and helps to mitigate the unavoidable bias of the helper who is doing the counseling. Pastoral counseling needs to pay more attention to such research, especially to outcome studies, than the field traditionally has done.

My personal physician is a fine family practitioner named Joseph Cappel. When I go to see him, I expect him to have read all of the current journals and bulletins that apply to his area of medicine. If I have a physical ailment, I want him to use state-of-the-art procedures that are based on the best and latest research in the field. Let us say he has two choices of therapy for my condition, and both have been shown in research to be equally effective but one is more invasive, takes longer, and is more expensive than the other. I trust (and my HMO demands) that he will consider those findings when he prescribes my treatment.

Surely clergy have a similar obligation to their parishioners. We have been trained to give heed to revelatory personal experience; however, carefully designed qualitative and quantitative research may be equally revelatory. We need to stay abreast of sound research in our field, and to consider it in choosing how we offer care to those who trust us with their well-being.

Most people who come to us for help are not on a quest for self-discovery. They seek to resolve a specific problem and move on as quickly as possible, not to overhaul their personality.[4] Even though many counselors who are in therapy themselves appreciate and value their personal journey of discovery, for the most part their counselees do not.[5] After the first session, most people do not return for many additional sessions, if they return at all. The pastoral counseling process is—by default if not by design—a short one. People tell us by their actions that, along with alleviation of their troubles, in counseling they want brevity.

There was a time when insurance companies tacitly condoned the long-term therapy bias by at least partially covering its costs. That is no longer the case. Today many health maintenance organizations and insurers reimburse only the more cost-effective brief therapies. The change to short-term modalities has sent ripples throughout the mental health community and set off controversy between proponents of the two approaches.

Is brief counseling a sign of the times? In our fast food, instant coffee, crash diet, microwave age, have people lost their patience to work toward long-term solutions to their problems? Is the desire for a quick fix part of their pathology? Or is it a sign of health, of a willingness to tackle a problem head-on and promptly do what is needed to get on with the business of living?

Any of these motivations may be present in any given case. One individual may be looking for a bromide or the wave of a magic wand; another may need some advice, a strategy, a way to go about breaking out of a harmful pattern of behavior; yet another may be financially unable to afford more than a short series of sessions with a therapist in an independent practice; others may be moving out of the area soon . . . and so on. Whatever the motivation, the fact remains that counselors spend on average only five to six hours counseling most individuals or families, and many encounters are limited to a single session. Even people who have agreed to long-term therapy often stop coming after a few sessions.

This book will not try to persuade pastoral caregivers to practice short-term counseling, because it doesn't have to; recent research has made the somewhat startling discovery that the majority of counseling performed today, irrespective of professional discipline, already is short-term.[6] Instead, the book addresses the dissonance that occurs when one believes in the superiority of long-term counseling but engages primarily in short-term care. The present chapter, based upon documented studies of the value of brief counseling, will make the point that brief pastoral counseling needs to be the model of choice for pastoral caregivers, not only for practical reasons but because it is ethically the proper thing to do.

First, let us look at several cherished misperceptions of brief counseling that seem to rise out of the old, long-term psychotherapeutic model.

Misperceptions about Brief Counseling

As director of a pastoral counseling center some years ago, I noticed that staff members who tended to terminate counselees after shorter periods of therapy appeared to have results equal to those who counseled their clients for longer periods of time. It was an intuitive impression, for at the time I was not aware of clinical studies showing that brief counseling is as effective as long-term therapy. Those who were doing briefer counseling, I observed, seemed especially skilled at concentrating on a single specific issue and quickly shifting the counseling focus from problems to goals and achievements. Those who were engaging in longer-term therapy seemed to be especially good at developing a relationship that directed the counseling focus from the stated problem to some form of personality reconstruction. The long-term counselors appeared more likely to develop relationships in which counselees became increasingly dependent upon them.

To be sure, pastoral counseling professionals who work within a long-term paradigm do so because they believe in the correctness and efficacy of those methods. Unfortunately, the psychodynamic theory that underlies most long-term pastoral counseling practice depends on certain convictions that have not been validated by research. One such misperception is the alleged superiority of long-term counseling; others include the imperative for exposing root causes of counselees' problems, the assumption that the results of long-term counseling are more durable, and the belief that brief counseling ignores the past.

The "Superiority" of Long-Term Counseling

It is a common and cherished belief that short-term counseling methods are inferior to long-term approaches. In this view, brief therapies are regarded as the methods of choice for working with people who are poor, undereducated, and unable to delay gratification, as well as some minorities and individuals who are not insight-oriented. Long-term counseling, in contrast, is often described as depth counseling, insight-oriented, dynamic, and intensive—the therapy that gets to the root of a problem and yields enduring benefits. Believing does not make it so, however, and outcome studies do not support the superiority of long-term therapy.[7]

Stieper and Wiener divided clients into long- and short-term counseling groups, controlling for education, intelligence, and diagnosis. Their work identified no correlation between the time spent in therapy and the degree of improvement.[8] Another study, reported by Garetz, Kogl, and Wiener, using a somewhat different research methodology, also failed to find superior improvement among long-term therapy clients.[9]

Time-limited therapy, a form of short-term therapy in which the counselor and counselee agree to specific limits on how much time will be devoted to the counseling process, was the focus of a study comparing Rogerian client-centered and Adlerian approaches. The study reported that those who received time-limited therapy and those given unlimited time therapy, regardless of the therapeutic approach, showed equal improvement (see chapter 11).[10] The only difference noted between the two groups was that the gains achieved by the time-limited group occurred in about one-half as many counseling sessions.

Munch compared long-term, short-term, and time-limited therapeutic results over a five-year period. The results suggested that significant positive counseling benefits accrued for short-term and time-limited therapy clients, but not for those in long-term care.[11] Reid and Shyne randomly assigned 120 cases, predominantly marriage and family issues, to either brief counseling (defined in this study as eight sessions or less) or unlimited counseling. Using a variety of assessment measures, they discovered that a short-term approach was at least as effective as a long-term approach, and in some categories more effective.[12]

Beck and Jones reviewed over three thousand counseling cases comprised of an assortment of marital, family, and personal problems. In their study brief counseling methods were equally or slightly more effective than long-term methods.[13] Leventhal and Weinberger, investigating over one thousand cases, came up with the same results: short-term counseling was as effective as long-term counseling.[14]

A study by Sloane and his colleagues compared the results of psycho-dynamic therapy, behavioral short-term counseling, and a control group that received no treatment. Extensive evaluation of the counseling was carried out by the counselor, client, family members, and an independent psychotherapist who did not participate in the care. Their research found no differences in effectiveness between the two psychotherapeutic modalities.[15]

Other studies have demonstrated similar results.[16] Most report about a 70 percent improvement rate.[17] Indeed, in a 1994 review of a large number of outcome studies comparing brief and long-term counseling, Mary Koss and Julia Shaing reported that "brief treatment methods have generally reported the same success rates as longer treatment programs."[18]

Root Causes of Problems

Many of us who grew up under the shadow of Freud were taught that to resolve a problem in a lasting way one must get at its roots. According to this school of thought, any difficulty requiring serious attention should be entrusted to an expert who can dig out its underlying causes. The problem is only a symptom; something deeper lurks behind it, and one's past needs to be explored to get to the problem's fundamental causes.

In actual practice, the extensive exploration of a person's history and the discovery of a problem's sources generally are not prerequisites for effective and lasting change. Of course we should not ignore or gloss over a parishioner's history, but in most cases people are able to make remarkable improvements in their lives without spending a lot of time digging into the sources of their troubles—indeed, sometimes, without spending any time at all looking for causes of their problems.[19]

Furthermore, when people gain insight into the underlying causes of their problems, resolutions do not automatically follow (see chapter 13). Even profound insight often proves insufficient; it supplies rich data for reflection and maturation but does not necessarily result in the specific life changes that could bring relief or resolution. Haley writes that most helpers make people more aware of their problems but frequently do not harness their considerable potential for coping with or overcoming them.[20]

Durability of Results

Many caregivers believe that, because short-term methods do not get to the underlying roots of a problem, any resulting changes will not endure. On the surface this conclusion appears to make sense. Crash diets, for instance, tend to result in eventual weight gain. Hasty conclusions are often wrong. If you mow down your weeds instead of pulling them, the roots will remain and the weeds will grow back quickly. But people are not weeds, and this way of thinking is not borne out by research.

Outcome studies are subject to some controversy because of the near impossibility for any two researchers or theoreticians to agree upon a definition of a good counseling outcome. However, research does provide a reliable picture of the effect of time upon counseling results. Several studies have looked at the durability of change in brief counseling by including follow-up assessment methods in their research design.[21] Follow-up evaluations in these studies took place from four months to two and one-half years after the completion of counseling. The findings are surprisingly consistent. Although some minor deterioration of counseling benefits was noted at the time of follow-up for short-term counseling, its deterioration was no greater than that suffered by any other psychotherapeutic modality, long-term included. The durability of benefits from brief counseling methods is equal to that of long-term therapy.

In spite of differing methods, controls, and criteria, not one study of counseling outcomes has found any correlation between length of therapy and degree or durability of improvement. All studies discovered that short-term methods were as effective as long-term methods, and as lasting. The only significant difference was the length of time over which the changes occurred.[22]

Past versus Future

Another misperception about brief therapy is that it ignores the past. You cannot jettison a person's entire history, the argument goes, and that is just what brief counseling is thought to do. Future-oriented it is (see especially chapter 4); but brief pastoral counseling surely uses the past. It does so, however, without giving emphasis to past problems and mistakes. Reframing is one way in which brief therapy redeems the past and neutralizes its painful memories or even views them in a positive and affirming light. Another brief counseling method, looking for exceptions, urges parishioners to scour their history for times when the problem was absent or diminished, looking for clues as to what their future might be like without the problem. It examines those periods of relief for behaviors that can be repeated, therefore building on success rather than paying attention to failure. Both methods are discussed in several chapters to come.

I contend that focusing continually on the misery of the past has no ethical, theological, or practical justification; it even can perpetuate the misery. Reframing the past in positive terms and building on its successes (however small) is the proper use of yesterday as we enable suffering people to move into a hope-filled tomorrow.

Interpretation and Acceptance of Research Findings

Even the most current hard data represents only what research has found to date. New studies are underway, and new findings may result. However, though the results reported here might not be conclusive in an ultimate way, by even the most conservative interpretation the assumption that long-term counseling methods produce better and more lasting results than do short-term methods is not confirmed. (Granted, the American Psychological Association's Task Force on Health Research has claimed that more contact with an individual in counseling means a greater chance that long-term benefits will result—but the only research that justifies this claim is an unpublished work on encouraging tooth brushing.)[23]

As early as 1962, Phillips and Wiener concluded their review of a number of outcome studies on short- and long-term counseling by stating, "Long-termness or interminability of treatment seems most likely to be determined by the dependency and the conceptual needs of the patient and by the personality and theory of the therapist, and it apparently has little direct relationship to improvement in treatment."[24]

This view diverges dramatically from the classic psychoanalytic view expressed by the analyst Bruno Bettelheim when he remarked, concerning the time needed for counseling, "hurrying up the process has more to do with one's own anxieties than with anything else."[25] Such a statement has never been demonstrated by research, even though long-term therapists have promulgated the idea that extensive therapy is superior to short-term care.

Lambert and Bergin, referring to the lack of supporting evidence for the superiority of long-term therapy, state that it "certainly raises questions about the general necessity of long-term treatments for the majority of patients and has clear implications for the practice of psychotherapy."[26] Bergin and Garfield go even further in assessing the equality of results in outcome studies of brief and long-term counseling. They believe that many professionals in the helping fields have refused to accept these results in an attempt to "preserve the role of special theories, the status of leaders of such approaches, the technical training programs for therapists."[27] These are strong words, but for me they have the ring of truth—even in the field of pastoral counseling. Perhaps they explain, in part, why it seems easier for newer helping professionals to embrace brief counseling methods than it is for those who have been at it for a good many years. (See, however, my acknowledgment in chapter 13 of the great difficulty of adopting new methods and ideas that attack the very philosophical base of a lifetime of work—changes that in effect knock out one's underpinnings.)

Yet another reason for seasoned professional pastoral counselors' reluctance to adopt short-term counseling may be that, while their counseling practices most likely began with many short-term encounters, over the years individuals who remained for long-term therapy began to make up an increasingly larger portion of their practice. As a result, their attention to short-term counselees may have receded and led to the illusion that most counseling is a long-term enterprise, even though epidemiological studies demonstrate quite the opposite. It is tempting to view long-term therapy clients as the "real" counselees—even though they actually comprise a small percentage of those who seek help for their problems of living.[28]

Increasingly, brief counseling approaches that were ignored even a few years ago are finding acceptance in a wide variety of therapeutic encounters, not only in crises or for those who are disenfranchised or limited. Along with the other authors in this volume, I maintain that most people who come for counseling do not require lengthy intervention and that short-term methods will be equally effective—hence the premise of this chapter and the book, which is (to repeat) that brief pastoral counseling methods should be the primary method of operation for all pastoral caregivers—parish pastors, chaplains, and full-time pastoral care specialists alike.

Ethics of Long-Term versus Short-Term Methods

The attention given in recent years to the grounding of pastoral caregiving in theology is a hopeful sign of change in the field. Ironically, most of those doing such pastoral theological reflection seem tied primarily to psychodynamic therapy in some shape or form, and most psychodynamic theory generally still assumes the superiority of long-term therapy. The result is that even recently, pastoral theologians have not addressed the embedded ethics of long-term therapy. It seems almost a taboo subject. Yet our attention to ethical issues is essential, not only in relationship to the rights of counselees, sexual harassment, or insurance fraud, but when one method of counseling (long-term therapy) by necessity leaves out many people who, because of financial considerations, time, or lack of educational status, are not able to participate in the enterprise and enjoy its benefits.[29]

This chapter will approach the ethics of short-term versus long-term methods from several perspectives:

- potential conflicts of interests that can arise when the helper who determines how much counseling is needed stands to benefit personally or financially from a longer course of treatment
- overtreatment and the utilization of services
- the issue of justice when financial well-being is a primary criterion for the ministry of specialized pastoral counseling
- the impact of power in the helper-helpee therapeutic alliance that influences how long someone is urged to attend counseling
- a comparison of the embedded theological anthropology in long- and short-term counseling.

Counselee Welfare and Counselor Income

Professional counselors are part of an economic mental health care structure in which the welfare of counselees can conflict with counselors' need for income. Do helpers offer long-term rather than brief care, knowing that brief counseling is as effective and seems to be what most counselees want, because of financial considerations? (Health maintenance organizations, to be sure, sometimes have equally questionable motivations for their support of brief counseling.) Can caregivers in private practice be trusted to determine an appropriate length of treatment for their counselees when their own fiscal interests are at risk in that decision? Austad asks, "Can the fox really be trusted to guard the hen house? Can altruism consistently triumph over greed? Not unless we all are saints."[30]

Most people in the helping professions view themselves as altruistic. Among all of the pastoral caregivers I know, at least part of the motivation for helping others is benevolent. But there are no pure acts. As Luther cautioned, everything we do is tainted with sin. Reinhold Niebuhr warned that any of our acts can be self-serving, that we can deceive ourselves into seeing our selfishness as altruism, that we are liable to cloak or sugar coat our evil.[31] Specialized caregivers' realistic need for income *can* influence what they determine counselees need concerning counseling. Fee-for-service counseling *can* lend itself to inflating the need and extent of counseling.

Naturally, adherents of long-term therapy do not see what they are doing as inflating or extending the need of care; they are living out their theory in practice and believe they are giving counselees what they need. Professional counselors have to make a living; it is only fair. The days when specialized pastoral counseling was one of the best-paying jobs in ministry are gone and unlikely to reappear in the foreseeable future. Nevertheless, the profit motive inescapably enters into the counseling relationship, either subtly or overtly. To what degree does it do so? Pastoral counseling specialists need to ask this question of themselves and each other with honesty and clear vision—for the sake of their own integrity and their counselees' welfare.

Considering the possible conflict between the welfare of those needing help and the legitimate need of helpers to earn a living, one is struck by the natural advantage of pastoral counseling in the congregational context, wherein pastors counsel their parishioners with no fee (or in some instances a nominal fee) as part of their total ministry.

Utilization of Services

In recent months and years there has been a general outcry against the restriction of medical services by health maintenance organizations and other health care providers as a result of cost-cutting in the insurance industry. Undertreatment certainly occurs, and on some occasions, the results are tragic. However, in the United States at least, overtreatment is still vastly more prevalent.[32] The overuse of radical mastectomies, hysterectomies, and cesarean sections are but a few examples of this phenomenon in medicine; such categories of overtreatment have come under public attack and are, we are told, declining.

Fraudulent practices in the field of mental health, such as bogus insurance claims, kickbacks, patient head-hunting, and extending care have become front-page news and raised suspicions about the mental health industry. Investigators have documented abuses by some mental health care providers; in some places the fraud has been deep and pervasive. Counseling professionals have manipulated diagnoses to fit categories that insurance companies would cover. People have called help lines without suspecting that the person answering the telephone was paid a fee for every client gained. Some patients have been held in hospitals against their will—until their insurance coverage ran out, when they were discharged summarily. One might hope, with the exposure and prosecution of many hospitals and practitioners, that these instances have diminished as well.

Quite a lot of overtreatment occurred (and still takes place) as a practitioner's defense against litigation; excessive tests insure that all avenues have been investigated in case a patient should later claim malpractice. Other cases of overtreatment simply line the pockets of the hospitals, clinics, and practitioners providing care.

Professional counselors also may be vulnerable to criticism in this area. Encouraging counselees to return for repeated sessions that are not truly essential for their well-being not only imposes a financial burden upon them—it may damage their autonomy and self-responsibility. It is easy to think: She benefits from the sessions, wants to come every week, and is willing to pay for it—why shouldn't I let her keep coming in? But the real questions should be: Is he working toward the realization of his goals? Is she taking responsibility for her own life? Are they ready to face the daily challenges of married life as a couple without the intervention of a third party?

In the parish, utilization of services is an issue as well. As many authors in this book (especially Childs and Thomas) point out, congregational ministers are extremely busy people with a multitude of functions and responsibilities. Those who choose long-term methods to help parishioners who come to them for counseling do so at the expense of others who also need their guidance, and even at the expense of other areas of their ministry. It amounts to overtreatment of a few parishioners and thus the undertreatment of many.

Love and Justice

To the "real questions" listed above we must add: What about issues of justice that arise when the luxury of long-term therapy is provided for the few who can afford it while so many who need help must go without? Many critics of the mental health delivery system have raised the objection that, in Austad's words, "rationing of care appears to be based upon the patient's financial well-being. Many practitioners concentrate on giving long-term psychotherapy to the 'worried well.'"[33] Don Pope-Davis recently commented at a meeting of the American Association of Pastoral Counselors that "the majority of people needing our help are not middle class and yet our profession is designed primarily for the middle class."[34]

One of the sad facts of mental health care in this day and age is that those with the least need tend to receive the greatest care. Many mental health professionals prefer to treat verbal, educated, intelligent, successful people whose problems are mild—and who pay their bills—rather than people who have severe or chronic problems and are poor as well. Forty-one million residents of the United States lack health insurance and therefore cannot receive counseling from most counselors.[35] Not all of them are technically poor; some are middle class, hard-working people (such as the self-employed) who simply cannot afford to pay the premiums for health insurance. Many of them are in our parishes.

Should not care and counseling be available for the uninsured as well as for the insured? Is it our concern, as pastoral caregivers, that one person's long-term therapy for depression consumes fifty thousand dollars or more, while the uninsured or indigent whose problems are just as severe or worse cannot obtain even basic brief counseling or are subjected to long waiting lists before they can get it?

Social justice based on a group or community ethic was a vital issue for the church in the twentieth century; incomprehensibly, the profession of pastoral counseling has been dominated by an almost exclusively individual ethic.[36] I can think of no other area of ministry in which there is greater conflict between an ethic that primarily values the self and one that recognizes our interdependence with others, than in the therapy provided by specialized pastoral counselors. (For an extended criticism of individualism in modern American Christianity, see Stanley Hauerwas's *A Community of Character*.)[37]

Parish ministry has done a better job of working for the welfare of all members of the community and of recognizing our interdependence as human beings. Although there certainly are some exclusive and elitist parishes, many churches not only open their doors but actively seek out the disenfranchised, the unemployed and working poor, prisoners and addicts, and people living on the edge of society. They offer pastoral care and counseling not only to the "members of the club" who attend church faithfully, but to the whole community—to those who can pay and to those who cannot.

If we truly care about justice in the distribution of counseling services, we need to ensure that every person and family who needs our help receives equal access to equal-quality care.

Power and the Helping Relationship

The helper-helpee therapeutic alliance is a very powerful tool in all psychotherapy. It allows or even causes counselees to do things they would not ordinarily do or would not have done before they sought help. The power of that helping relationship has been well documented in discussions of sexual harassment. That same power has other potentially deleterious consequences as well. It can, for example, influence people to stay in counseling longer than planned and thereby lead them into unhealthy dependence that may even inhibit their ability to make positive changes in their lives. It can lead them into debt, crippling their abilities to pay for life's necessities.

More often than not, long-term psychotherapy tends to focus on the therapist's image of what ought to be rather than the client's own wishes or the needs of the community. Any failures—including the failure of counselees to return for repeated sessions—are seen as insufficient motivation on their part.

All pastoral caregivers, of course, work from an embedded faith-based ethic. In their counseling they sometimes raise moral issues and act in a prophetic and guiding role. At the same time, clergy who embrace brief counseling modalities will seek to determine what parishioners really want for their own lives and how they can faithfully serve the community. Instead of addressing the "underlying problem," brief pastoral caregivers honor what parishioners themselves believe to be their problem and what they consider acceptable solutions. This is a significant paradigm shift; I cannot understate its importance or its implications for the pastoral care and counseling enterprise.

Certainly a strong counseling relationship is critical for helping people bring about change in their lives.[38] Brief counseling achieves the therapeutic alliance rapidly. As a result, many of the abuses of power endemic to therapeutic relationships are less likely to occur—not only because the helping process is brief, but also because the caregiving is based upon the parishioner's strengths and independence rather than upon transference and dependence. Homework assignments to be completed outside the session increase parishioners' responsibility for their own lives and thereby decrease their dependence on the helper. Short-term pastoral counseling thus minimizes the chances for abuses of power and, in the parish context, allows pastors to continue ministering to parishioners after counseling is ended.

A Theological Anthropology of Brief Counseling

Pastoral caregivers whose understanding of persons fails to take seriously our brokenness and the ongoing reality of sin in human lives are likely to be predisposed to many types of long-term therapy. The image of persons implicit in many psychotherapeutic systems compares the individual to an onion. The helper therapeutically peels away the outer layers of the self until the pure inner core is revealed. Long-term therapy would certainly make sense in such a view because it would cooperate with the task of sanctification. Counseling would strive for the emergence of that true self.

In contrast, church reformers affirmed sanctification but assumed that, as the layers continue to peel off, the inner self inside is a person still bound to sin, still accepted by grace. Luther used the Latin phrase *simul justus et peccator* to describe the state of Christians: we are simultaneously saint and sinner, no matter how far we have walked on the road of sanctification and no matter how many years we have spent in therapy.

Many pastoral caregivers do not take seriously the undoneness of life. They fail to recognize that human existence on this side of the second coming is fraught with imperfection, tragedy, and evil. It would be nice to resolve many of the issues that come up in the course of long-term therapy—but people can and do live with them. O'Hanlon and Weiner-Davis point out that

> one of the reasons therapists fail to terminate is because, even when there is no longer a problem, clients offer details of their lives which seem to merit intervention—a fight with a spouse, a bad day at work, a

ravenous departure from a strict diet, and so on. However, we all know
that ups and downs are a natural part of life. Therapy is not meant to
be a panacea for all of life's challenges.[39]

The shocker is that most people resolve their problems by themselves without the intervention of professional helpers. They benefit from the help of family, friends, formal and informal groups in church and community. Studies
indicate that these people deal with the same issues that psychotherapists
address, but they do it on their own.[40] Most people get better without (or sometimes in spite of) the intervention of mental health caregivers. This is not to
diminish the fact that people are genuinely helped by counseling, but to recognize that outside assistance is not necessarily required for change to occur. People have resident strengths and problem-solving abilities. Many times, when all
else fails, they learn to live with their problems and see them in perspective.

The primary goal of brief counseling, once again, is not to bring some form
of change in personality. It is not to resolve all or even most of people's problems. It is not to walk with them all the way through the "valley of the shadow"
or to delve into alleged underlying causes of their problems. Brief pastoral
counseling has a considerably more modest goal: to get people moving in a positive direction of their own choosing and then get out of the way. It aims to help
them see things in a slightly new way, do things a little differently, relate to others in a slightly more appropriate way. That is all. Brief pastoral counseling
starts the process of planned change; it does not attempt to complete it. It takes
for granted that people have many strengths and resources of their own and
will use them to continue the process of change. It trusts that the various ministries of the church will support individuals in their walk through life, and
simply helps them to turn an important corner in their journey.

Brief pastoral counseling takes seriously both the brokenness of humans
and the strengths that reside within them. Its goals are in touch with what
parishioners actually want. Instead of focusing on problems, it helps counselees
to use inner resources that they may have discounted or ignored to envision a
new future and begin moving into it.

Brief Counseling:
The Pastoral Caregiver's First Choice

We can provide care for all who need it because brief counseling methods make
efficient and responsible use of caregiver resources. Those who find it hard to
believe that short-term pastoral counseling works as well as its more esteemed
long-term cousin might ask what accounts for the surprising similarity in

counseling outcomes. Meltzoff and Kornreich discovered one probable cause in an extensive metastudy of the outcomes of existing therapeutic modalities. They concluded that all successful counseling achieves its major gains at the beginning.[41] A *window of opportunity* occurs early in a helping relationship when people are more open to making changes in their lives, and most change takes place in those first few sessions. Brief counseling simply makes use of this phenomenon.

In addition, the abbreviated time that most people are willing or able to give to counseling means that endless sessions of talking without a sharp focus is a luxury they cannot afford. Brief counseling is by necessity more intense than long-term therapy; it requires pastoral caregivers to be more active. It focuses on key issues, develops a plan for change, and helps parishioners take concrete actions. It is not so much a series of newly developed counseling methods as a radically different perspective on the pastoral counseling enterprise as a whole. As such, it forms whatever we do. It shapes how we establish relationships, what questions we ask, how we use time, what counseling methods we choose, and how we use them.

Since pastoral caregivers can expect to spend only a few sessions in a typical pastoral counseling relationship, they need to structure the care they offer around those few sessions rather than on some unlimited ideal. Every session should be regarded as potentially the last one. At each meeting, every effort should be made to provide parishioners with what they require to begin resolving their distress. For a variety of reasons, they may never return.

Brief pastoral counseling reclaims this way of caregiving that has been a part of parish ministry for centuries.[42] The pastor cares for the entire congregation, all of the time. All are saved by grace and accepted by God; sanctification and growth as individuals and as members of the community of faith is an ongoing, lifelong process. During crises or specific difficulties, the pastor offers counsel for one or a few sessions, after which parishioners return to the general ministry of the congregation.

Brief pastoral counseling is more closely related to the parish ministry model than it is to long-term psychotherapy. Parishioners come to the pastoral caregiver for short periods of counseling whenever they face a crisis or difficulty that they have trouble managing on their own. After a few sessions of counseling, they return to their normal life without the weekly sessions. Instead of one protracted period of counseling that continues for many months or years, individuals can avail themselves of counseling episodically; once they gain tools or strategies for working out their problems, they may not return for months, or years, or ever. For this reason alone, brief pastoral counseling is the best choice in a congregational context; its flexibility is well-suited to the comings and goings of parish life.

First choice, however, does not mean the only choice. Even though short-term therapy helps individuals reach their counseling goals as effectively as extended care, long-term methods still have a place.[43] A few counselees will not be helped by brief counseling; others are not good candidates for therapy and will not achieve positive change by any method of care, but may appreciate the comfort that a long-term therapeutic relationship provides. However, long-term therapy (if used at all) should be employed as a last resort only after brief counseling methods have not proven successful, or when a parishioner has requested it and the pastor has time to offer it.

∽

In this chapter I have taken the view that brief pastoral counseling methods, for most people who come to us for help, are not only as good as longer methods but are actually better because they take less time, give equally beneficial and lasting results, respect people's vision and choices for their own lives, and enable the widest possible delivery of effective care to those who need it. It deals with the reality that parish pastors, hospital chaplains, and many other caregivers cannot do anything other than brief counseling because of constraints of their jobs. I also have argued that brief pastoral counseling may be a more ethical, theologically congruent approach than long-term counseling. These reasons alone mandate brief methods as the approach of first choice for pastoral caregivers.

Until recently, the fields of pastoral counseling and psychotherapy have shown little interest in developing strategies for shortening the counseling process, too often investing their energy instead upon engaging counselees so that they would stay in the therapeutic process for longer periods of time. (Crisis intervention is a notable exception.)[44] But change is in the wind, and pastoral caregivers are beginning to take notice. The authors writing on brief pastoral counseling for this book provide background and methodologies that can be applied to a broad range of counseling situations, as befits congregations, hospitals, and specialized pastoral counseling settings. In them you will find strategies to shorten the process of pastoral counseling while preserving and even enhancing the quality of care that you offer.

Notes

1.   I want to thank my colleagues James Duke, Andrew Lester, and Rebekah Miles for reviewing a draft of this chapter. Portions of this chapter were included in modified form in my article "Pastoral Counseling and the Changing Times" in the *Journal of Pastoral Care* 53, no. 1 (Spring 1999): 31–46. A broader presentation of

the ideas in this chapter can be found in my book *Brief Pastoral Counseling* (Minneapolis: Fortress Press, 1994).

2. Tony Hillerman, *The Great Taos Bank Robbery and Other Indian Country Affairs* (Albuquerque: University of New Mexico Press, 1973), 94.

3. M. Koss and J. Shaing, "Research on Brief Psychotherapy," in S. L. Garfield and A. E. Bergin, *Handbook of Psychotherapy and Behavior Change*, 4th ed. (New York: Wiley, 1994), 664.

4. Ibid.

5. G. Pekarik and M. Wierzbicki, "The Relationship between Counselees' Expected and Actual Treatment Duration," *Psychotherapy* 23 (1986): 532–34.

6. D. Beck and M. Jones, *Progress in Family Problems* (New York: Family Service Association, 1973) examined 3,596 cases in family service agencies across the United States for the length of time persons were in counseling. They compared their results to a similar survey in 1960 and discovered a significant shift toward brief counseling. Indeed, in their research, short-term cases averaged five sessions, but even "continued service" cases, which the agencies would consider long-term, averaged only nine visits.

In another study, D. Langsley, in "Comparing Clinic and Private Practice of Psychiatry," *American Journal of Psychiatry* 135 (1978): 702–6, examined 4,072 psychiatric cases seen in both clinics and private practice. It might be expected that psychiatrists would see individuals for considerably longer periods than would other mental health professionals, yet the median number of visits to private practitioners was 12.8, and only 10.3 for clinic psychiatrists.

In another study of counseling that took place in an outpatient clinic, S. L. Garfield and R. Kurtz, "A Study of Eclectic Views," *Journal of Consulting and Clinical Psychology* 36 (1977): 228–34, reported similar results. They considered 1,216 cases and found the average number of sessions to be six, with very few individuals seen for more than ten visits. In fact, they noted that 57.7 percent of the counseling was completed in one to four sessions.

E. L. Phillips, *A Guide for Therapists and Patients to Short-Term Psychology* (Springfield, Ill.: Charles C. Thomas, 1985), reviewed student visits to a university counseling center over a four-year period. He found that about one-half of the students did not return for a second visit. Thus one-half of all counseling cases were of the one-session variety. Bloom (Phillips, 1985) investigated whether those who did not return for more than one session were dissatisfied with counseling. He discovered the contrary, that two-thirds reported "satisfaction" with the counseling but did not return because they either no longer felt a need or, due to practical changes in their lives, felt some sense of resolution.

Garfield reviewed a number of studies of psychotherapy and reported that the average duration of counseling, whether independent practice or a community-based setting, is between four and eight sessions. S. L. Garfield, "Research on Client Variables in Psychotherapy," in Garfield and Bergin, eds., *Handbook of Psychotherapy and Behavior Change*, 4th ed., 190–228.

7. For a discussion of some of the studies, see Stone, *Brief Pastoral Counseling*, 10–12.

8. E. L. Phillips and D. Wiener, *Discipline, Achievement and Mental Health* (Englewood Cliffs, N.J.: Prentice-Hall, 1962), 21.

9. F. Garetz, R. Kogl, and D. Wiener, "A Comparison of Random and Judg-mental Methods of Determining Mode of Outpatient Mental Hygiene Treatment," *Journal of Clinical Psychology* 15 (1959): 401–2.

10. Phillips and Wiener, *Discipline*, 55–56.

11. Ibid., 135.

12. W. Reid and A. Shyne, *Brief and Extended Casework* (New York: Columbia University Press, 1969).

13. Beck and Jones, *Family Problems.*

14. T. Leventhal and G. Weinberger, "Evaluation of a Large-Scale Brief Ther-apy Program for Children," *American Journal of Orthopsychiatry* 49 (1975): 119–33.

15. R. Sloane, F. Staples, A. Cristol, N. Yorkston, and K. Whipple, *Psychothera-py versus Behavior Therapy* (Cambridge, Mass.: Harvard University Press, 1975).

16. P. De Jong and I. K. Berg, *Interviewing for Solutions* (Pacific Grove, Calif.: Brooks/Cole, 1998); A. E. Bergin and S. L. Garfield, "Overview, Trends, and Future Issues," in Garfield and Bergin, eds., *Handbook of Psychotherapy and Behavior Change*, 4th ed.; Koss and Shaing, "Research on Brief Psychotherapy," 664–700; A. J. McKeel, "A Clinician's Guide to Research on Solution-Focused Brief Therapy," in S. D. Miller, M. A. Hubble, and B. L. Duncan, eds., *Handbook of Solution-Focused Brief Therapy* (San Francisco, Jossey-Bass, 1996), 251–71; M. Beyebach, A. R. More-jon, D. L. Palenzuela, and J. L. Rodriguez-Arias, "Research on the Process of Solu-tion-Focused Therapy," *Handbook of Solution-Focused Brief Therapy* (San Francis-co: Jossey-Bass, 1996), 299–334; J. Frank, "The Present Status of Outcome Studies," *Journal of Consulting and Clinical Psychology* 47 (1979): 310–16; S. L Garfield, *Psy-chotherapy: An Eclectic View* (New York: Wiley, 1980); L. Luborsky and B. Singer, "Comparative Studies of Psychotherapies," *Archives of General Psychiatry* 32 (1975): 995–1008; H. Strupp, "Psychotherapy Research and Practice: An Overview," in S. Garfield and A. Bergin, eds., *Handbook of Psychotherapy and Behavior Change*, 2nd ed., (New York: Wiley, 1978), 3–22; and R. Wells, *Planned Short-Term Treatment*, (New York: Free Press, 1982).

17. M. Koss and J. Butcher, "Research on Brief Therapy," in S. L. Garfield and A. E. Bergin, eds., *Handbook of Psychotherapy and Behavior Change*, 3rd ed. (New York: Wiley, 1986), 656.

18. Koss and Shaing, "Research on Brief Psychotherapy," 664.

19. B. Childs, *Short-Term Pastoral Counseling* (New York: Haworth, 2000); S. de Shazer, *Keys to Solution in Brief Therapy* (New York: Norton, 1985); idem, *Clues: Investigating Solutions in Brief Therapy* (New York: Norton, 1988); idem, *Putting Difference to Work* (New York: Norton, 1991); J. Haley, *Uncommon Therapy: The Psychiatric Techniques of Milton H. Erickson, M.D.* (New York: Norton, 1973); J. Haley, *Problem-Solving Therapy: New Strategies for Effective Family Therapy* (San Francisco: Jossey-Bass, 1976); F. N. Thomas and J. Cockburn, *Competency-Based Counseling: Building on Client Strengths* (Minneapolis: Fortress Press, 1998); H. W. Stone, *Brief Pastoral Counseling.*

20. Haley, *Problem-Solving Therapy.*

21. S. Fisher, "The Use of Time Limits in Brief Psychotherapy: A Comparison of Six-Session, Twelve-Session, and Unlimited Treatment with Families," *Family Process* 19 (1980): 377–92; S. Fisher, "Time-Limited Brief Therapy with Families: A One-Year Follow-up Study," *Family Process* 23 (1984): 101–6; D. Langsley, P. Machotka, and K. Flomenhaft, "Avoiding Mental Hospital Admission: A Follow-up Study," *American Journal of Psychiatry* 132 (1971): 177–79; Reid and Shyne, *Brief and Extended Casework;* R. Wells, "Communication Training vs. Conjoint Marital Therapy," *Social Work Research and Abstracts* 13 (1977): 31–39.

22. See Stone, *Brief Pastoral Counseling,* 10–11, for a review of outcome studies.

23. I. Janis and I. Lester, *Short-Term Counseling: Guidelines Based on Recent Research* (New Haven: Yale University Press, 1983), 56.

24. Phillips and Weiner, *Discipline,* 21.

25. W. S. Meyer, "In Defense of Long-Term Treatment: On the Vanishing Holding Environment," *Social Work* 38, no. 5 (1993): 574.

26. M. J. Lambert and A. E. Bergin, "Achievements and Limitations of Psychotherapy Research," in D. Friedheim, ed., *History of Psychotherapy* (Washington, D.C.: American Psychological Association, 1992), 377.

27. A. E. Bergin and S. L. Garfield, "Overview, Trends and Future Issues," in Bergin and Garfield, eds., *Handbook of Psychotherapy and Behavior Change,* 4th ed., 823.

28. C. S. Austad, *Is Long-Term Psychotherapy Unethical?* (San Francisco: Jossey-Bass, 1996), 135–55.

29. H. Stone and J. Duke, *How to Think Theologically* (Minneapolis: Fortress Press, 1996).

30. Austad, *Is Long-Term Psychotherapy Unethical?*

31. Reinhold Niebuhr, *The Nature and Destiny of Man,* 2 vols. (New York: Scribner's, 1964).

32. Austad, *Is Long-Term Psychotherapy Unethical?*

33. Ibid., 93–94.

34. D. Pope-Davis, "Developing Multicultural Counseling Competencies: Do Counselors Really Want to Change?" (presented at AAPC National Convention, Miami, Fla., April 1998).

35. Austad, *Is Long-Term Psychotherapy Unethical?* 44.

36. H. W. Stone, *Theological Context for Pastoral Caregiving* (New York: Haworth, 1996), 161–70.

37. S. Hauerwas, *A Community of Character* (Notre Dame, Ind.: University of Notre Dame Press, 1981); and *Truthfulness and Tragedy: Further Investigations into Christian Ethics* (Notre Dame, Ind.: University of Notre Dame Press, 1977).

38. S. D. Miller, B. L. Duncan, and M. A. Hubble, *Escape from Babel: Toward a Unifying Language for Psychotherapy Practice* (New York: Norton, 1997).

39. W. O'Hanlon and M. Weiner-Davis, *In Search of Solutions: A New Direction in Psychotherapy* (New York: Norton, 1989), 178. Emphasis added.

40. J. Gurin, "Remaking Our Lives," *American Health* (March 1990): 50–52.

41. J. Metzloff and M. Kronreich, *Research in Psychotherapy* (New York: Atherton, 1970), 357.

42. H. W. Stone, *Theological Context for Pastoral Caregiving* (New York: Haworth, 1996).

43. See Stone, *Brief Pastoral Counseling*, 155–66.

44. See Stone, *Crisis Counseling*, 2nd ed., rev. (Minneapolis: Fortress Press, 1993).

2

The Power of Valuing in Brief Pastoral Counseling

Jan James

ALL PEOPLE—whatever their race, nationality, gender, social rank, employment, lifestyle, sexual orientation, appearance, intelligence, beliefs, attitude, morality, skill, knowledge, health, wealth, or any other characteristic—are infinitely valued children of God. There are no exceptions. The valuing of individuals is a distinguishing feature and a central tenet of Christian faith. Christ saw beyond humanity's limited perception of self and gave us the model of persons as beings of eternal worth.[1]

Jesus deeply valued every person with whom he came in contact. Augustine wrote that Jesus cared for everybody he met as if there was none other in all the world to love, and he loved all as he loved each.[2] Such unconditional love has transforming power and therefore is a critical dimension of pastoral ministry. This is doubly the case in brief pastoral counseling, where limited time is available for mere listening to the parishioner's story, and indeed where the whole counseling enterprise is short in comparison to ongoing pastoral relationships or traditional psychoanalysis. Ministers ought never focus so intently on helping troubled people achieve expeditious results that they neglect the importance of valuing and accepting them. (Likewise, counselors doing long-term therapy ought never focus so intently on the problems of a troubled past that they undervalue counselees' strengths and potential for growth.)

To value counselees is to accept and prize them for who they are and, sometimes, in spite of what they do. We represent the love of God by conveying the message: "You are a person of great value, and I will stand with you no matter what." Howard Stone puts it this way: "Probably nothing has a more powerful influence on your life than to know that someone is for you—through thick and thin, whether you act appropriately or not. Such acceptance serves as a center, a home base out of which all of life can flow."[3]

Valuing Self and Spirit

It is a common misperception of brief therapies that their practitioners are mechanical, results-oriented, superficial, and sometimes even uncaring. Nothing could be farther from the actual practice of brief pastoral counseling ministry. Not just the attitudes of the caregiver but the methods themselves support the ultimate value of the person in need. The minister or layperson doing brief pastoral counseling brings to the relationship an attitude of acceptance—of who we are and what we can be. Stone maintains that the mission of pastoral counseling is "not only to affirm the person who is, but also to appreciate who that person can become in Christ."[4] Truly valuing another person also requires that pastoral caregivers be keenly aware of their part in this transforming process.

Brief pastoral counseling, and particularly brief solution-focused counseling, honors and validates people's experiences as well as the context of their experiences, their perceptions, and their life stories. No circumstance of the troubled person's life is meaningless or unimportant. God works through the ordinary events of every life to transform the self into the likeness of Christ. As Lynn Bauman writes, "The spirit presupposes and works with the abilities and attributes we have and enhances them; it does not negate the structures of selfhood, but provides them with a capacity that they hitherto lacked, namely, a certain possibility for life in God's Spirit."[5] This understanding assigns value and significance to everything that happens in people's lives.

The task of brief pastoral counseling, then, is to help people discern how best to value their strengths and abilities, using them in cooperation with this transforming process. One tool for the process of transformation is reason, our unique gift. The ability to reason, according to Reinhold Niebuhr, gives human beings the capacity for self-transcendence. Furthermore, God's image is seen within our potential for self-transcendence:

> The spirit in its depth and height reaches into eternity . . . and this vertical dimension is more important for the understanding of man than merely his rational capacity for forming general concepts. . . . It is the quality of the human spirit . . . to lift itself as living organism and to make the whole temporal and spatial world including itself the object of its knowledge.[6]

Through reason, human beings have the ability to examine experience, to rise above natural processes, and to choose with our limited freedom many of our own actions and outcomes. One important part of self-determination is the ability to exercise control over our perceptions of whatever happens to us.

When we value ourselves, we do not have to react passively or in a reflexive, "knee-jerk" manner; we have the capacity to decide how we will respond to the circumstances and events of our lives.

Every aspect of a person's life is of great worth because it can be used for the transformation of the self into the likeness of Christ. This is the Christian's ultimate concern. Every difficulty and circumstance in life occurs within the context of this ultimate meaning. Bauman writes that when we take this view of our lives, "the meaning of life begins to emerge from the most commonplace things, which we perhaps previously disregarded as meaningless."[7]

Unfortunately, many people remain unknowing or unconcerned that all of life occurs within the context of ultimate meaning, and thus fail to be fully aware and intentional about the way they live their lives. The pastoral caregiver's task is to help parishioners appreciate the meaning and value of their circumstances and discern how God can use those experiences to transform their lives.

Valuing in Brief Pastoral Counseling

In brief pastoral counseling, helpers prize their parishioners' uniqueness, engaging them in dialogue about whatever caused them to seek help. They do not presume to know what changes would be best for parishioners, but rather address what the counselees want to change.

Bringing about the changes that parishioners say they want is a collaborative effort (see chapter 3). The troubled persons themselves, not their pastoral caregivers, will make the needed changes in their lives. Ministers acknowledge the suffering, pain, desperation, and confusion of people in pain, and at the same time affirm and respect their strengths, capacity for endurance, and willingness to see and understand themselves. This is active valuing—not a passive absorption of endless data from the past, but a willingness to join forces with parishioners in working toward their own vision for the future.

Focus on the Future

People often define themselves by their limitations and by what they view as flaws in their nature. They focus on what is not working. Often they do not sense their own value and may even believe they are not good enough to approach God. On a larger scale, humanity's sense of value is often misplaced and misdirected. Our culture fosters the belief that, given an accurate analysis, the right technology, and adequate intelligence, strength, and will, we should be able to fix whatever problems arise. As a result, we think we need to get our lives together (and get it right) before we can be considered good and valuable people.

Even so, all human beings long to experience themselves as good—even if our understanding of good is distorted. Some part of us yearns to become what God means for us to become. God intends that we be transformed into the likeness of Christ. Sadly, our failure to be so transformed may bring us pain and shame.[8]

It is important, therefore, to understand that God does not start with perfect human beings. We go to God with all our flaws and broken lives. Jesus' intimate relationship with his disciples, who were human beings as imperfect and broken as we are, reveals that God is more interested in the future—in what we can become—than in what we used to be. We do ourselves a great disservice, Bauman believes, "if we spend all of our energies lamenting the ways we've done it so imperfectly in the past," forgetting that God's grace draws us to a future and makes more of us than we imagine we could be.[9]

Pastoral caregivers doing brief counseling value parishioners by showing respect for their life experiences and worldview, in all their incompleteness. This does not mean that they approve of all the parishioners' past behaviors, but that they are more interested in the future—in what can be rather than in what was (see chapter 4). When parishioners come to believe that they are valued despite their problems and failures, a deep trust develops in the counseling relationship. This experience of valuing, of love and acceptance, frees parishioners to explore their future in new and creative ways. It allows them to be vulnerable and totally themselves. They are able to bring the circumstances and events of their lives into dialogue with God, the comforter who attends to them, who will never leave them or let them go. It is a nourishing environment where growth and learning can flourish.

In brief pastoral counseling the helper conveys to parishioners—not only through attitude and words but also through methods and concrete deeds—that they are not condemned for their past or doomed to repeat its failures. Little attention is paid to problems and pathology. In this model, pastoral caregivers seek to empower troubled people to gain a realization of their larger selves.

Building on Counselees' Strengths

It may be difficult for counselees to see that they have anything going for them. They may even experience complete hopelessness. In contrast, pastoral caregivers begin the counseling process with the assumption that parishioners have strengths, positive qualities, abilities, and courage that may have been minimized or completely overlooked in their sense of shame and despair.

Working from the assumption of strength, attention is given to *exceptions to the problem*. This brief counseling method, addressed at some length by several authors in this volume, focuses on those previously unnoticed times when the problem was diminished or absent. Even in a painful past, there are strengths to be found. Parishioners may have a hard time at first discerning periods when they are not troubled by the problem. With exploration, however, most will be able to identify at least a few such times. Once exceptions are identified, it is important for parishioners to note what is different about those times when the problem is absent.

It is also empowering for parishioners to note instances when they have successfully dealt with the problem. Again, initially they may not be able to recall any success in coping with their problem, for they most likely have undervalued not only their strengths but also their efforts. A positive accomplishment may have been short-lived or perceived as trivial. But there is no trivial success. It is important to pay attention to even the tiniest victories, because they point to areas of resident strength and skill that counselees may have overlooked. Success breeds success.

In these and many other ways, pastoral caregivers value parishioners by facilitating the recognition of their abilities and courageous behaviors and guiding them to exercise those strengths. When pastoral caregivers use brief counseling methods to convey that parishioners do have the resources necessary to deal with their problems, those individuals often come to prize themselves and even to look creatively at their problems and possibilities.

Brief approaches to pastoral counseling presuppose a deep trust in counselees' potential for change and growth. Pastoral caregivers collaborate with parishioners to find new ways to view, respond to, and experiment with their circumstances in order to begin moving into a future of greater meaning and purpose. Small changes inevitably have ripple effects in other areas of parishioners' lives. They begin to take responsibility for their learning and to be more intentional about the direction of their lives.

Brief pastoral counseling joins parishioners on a journey; it does not travel the whole journey with them. It does not demand that all of their problems be solved. Viewed in this way, small steps taken toward resolving a difficulty have great value because of the assurance that they will have an ever-widening effect. It is the pastoral caregiver's job to point out and amplify the significance of these small steps. The pastoral caregiver acts as a good mentor, best friend, and cheerleader, encouraging parishioners' every positive movement toward change.

The Counselee as Expert

Seward Hiltner once wrote that the pastor doing counseling "needs to guard against being blinded by the immediate situation."[10] To the contrary, brief pastoral caregivers see it as extremely counselor-centered, even arrogant, to dismiss the parishioner's presented problems as unimportant rather than allowing them to set goals. How highly do we value parishioners when we ourselves set the goals and expectations for their progress? When we interpret their experiences and shape their feelings for them? If ministers work with the premise that each individual is a child of God of infinite worth, then who ought to be the expert about that person's experiences and needs? And who decreed that we must delve into the dark secrets of a troubled person's past? In fact, it is not necessary for pastoral caregivers to have much knowledge of the cause of parishioners' problems in order to help them achieve positive outcomes. This is so in part because of the very nature of growth and change and in part because of parishioners' resident strengths and abilities. It is so because we prize them for who they are and who they long to become.

Pastoral caregivers possess knowledge and skills to help people cope with difficulties and make changes in their lives. They have a prophetic role as well and may need to speak out in the face of sin and moral issues. But at no time do they usurp the parishioners' rightful role as experts in their own affairs. The minister who truly values the other is collaborator, not boss; guide, not director.

~

Brief, solution-focused therapy can be effective even in the absence of a theological understanding of valuing as described herein, because the prizing of the counselee is implicit within its methods. Explicitly embracing the theological dimension will further enhance the transformation of lives. Practiced within this Christian understanding of the ultimate value of persons, brief pastoral counseling provides an opportunity for troubled people, with all their limitations and faults, to experience acceptance by God and by another. It gives them a reason to grasp their own inestimable worth.

When acceptance of the other as an infinitely valued child of God underlies the brief pastoral counseling relationship, counseling becomes not only highly effective, but a joyous experience for both parishioner and pastoral caregiver as they journey into the future to which God calls them.

Notes

1.   Portions of this chapter are taken in modified form from my article "The Power of Valuing in Brief Pastoral Counseling" in the *Journal of Pastoral Care* 53, no. 1 (Spring 1999): 81–86.

2.   J. Claypool, from tape of 1995 Perkins Lecture Series, "The Ones Jesus Chose: Reflections on the Disciples," given at First United Methodist Church, Wichita Falls, Tex.

3.   H. Stone, *Theological Context for Pastoral Caregiving* (New York: Haworth, 1996), 116.

4. Ibid., 120.

5. L. C. Bauman, *A Handbook to Practical Wisdom: A Study Guide for a Short Course in Practical Wisdom, a Component of the Centerpoint Parish Pilgrimage* (Cedar Hill, Tex.: Centerpoint Parish Pilgrimage, 1992), 6.

6. R. Niebuhr, *The Nature and Destiny of Man*, vol. 1 (New York: Scribner's, 1949), 157.

7. Bauman, *Practical Wisdom*, 32.

8. Ibid

9. Claypool, "Ones Jesus Chose."

10. S. Hiltner, *Pastoral Counseling* (New York: Abingdon, 1949), 20.

3

Collaborative
Pastoral Conversation

Nancy Gorsuch

PASTOR GORDON DAVIS stopped at the comfortable home of Jean and James Huber one wintry Tuesday evening to discuss the congregation's upcoming stewardship campaign. While he sat with them at their kitchen table drinking coffee, they began to talk about problems with their teenage son, Sam.[1] In their view, Sam seemed to be doing everything he could to disrupt the harmony of the family. Jean and James both expressed frustration at their lack of influence over his behavior, clothing, music, and choice of friends—all of which, they believed, reflected negatively on their family.

> JEAN: Sam used to be such a cooperative child. Now he's defiant and argumentative, or else he's silent and withdrawn. I can't believe this is the boy we raised. (Pastor Davis listened to more of Jean's complaints.)
>
> PASTOR DAVIS: It sounds as though Sam has changed a lot in the past couple years as he has made more of his own choices. I'm wondering how you understand your purpose now, as parents of a teenager who's relying on you in such a different way.
>
> JAMES: He's not relying on us at all! In fact, he's pushing us away so much that we have no choice but to be even stricter. We ground him when he argues with us and is so disrespectful. It won't be tolerated in this house. I just wish he would be more like our nephew who seems to get along so well with his folks. (James went on to describe the model behavior of their nephew.)
>
> PASTOR DAVIS: Well, you certainly are experiencing some of the diversity God creates even within one family, and some of it is hard to take. I can't help thinking there's purposefulness in this kind of conflict sometimes, that somehow God wants you to be a firm and compassionate base for him to launch from, even though it's uncomfortable.

JAMES: Well, I can be firm when I need to be, and there are some things we just won't allow. It's not right for a son to treat his parents that way. You have to set limits and enforce them. (He described a recent incident when Sam was punished for missing his curfew.)

PASTOR DAVIS: I can hear how difficult it is to set reasonable limits and still be respectful of Sam, to demonstrate the behavior you hope he will come to emulate at some point. You are trying to be good parents, faithful parents, and to figure out what differences you can tolerate between you and Sam.

Pastor Davis believed Jean, James, and Sam to be the experts on their problems as well as their dreams and goals as a family. In brief pastoral counseling this attitude is sometimes called the "not-knowing" position. As pastors we acknowledge that those who come to us for help are the authorities on their own problems, and we work within that frame. But *not-knowing* needs to be balanced with *appropriate knowing,* a pastoral perspective that knows and claims the wisdom of faith and its practice and appropriately proclaims the gospel. Notice that Pastor Davis subtly inserted a theological view into the conversation, suggesting a connection between the diversity of God's creation and Sam's defiant differentness.

Not-knowing and proclaiming are paradoxical tasks that are only altered, not eliminated, by the recent trend toward short-term approaches in pastoral care and counseling. In more authoritarian modes of pastoral counseling uninformed by psychotherapy, pastors may impose a particular moral and theological template upon parishioners' experiences and even dictate goals for them. In more non-directive, psychodynamic models of pastoral counseling, pastors often go to the other extreme. In their effort to hear and be with the parishioner, they hesitate to claim what they know and believe, or even to express a word of pastoral guidance. Even in brief pastoral counseling, which is somewhat more directive because of its solution orientation, ministers may work so hard at taking a not-knowing stance that they neglect their pastoral calling and its prophetic dimension.

The danger of imposing one's own perspective looms large in the effort to use pastoral authority. It is very tempting to exercise authority and "run the show" when people seem hopelessly adrift in a sea of troubles, and pastors who offer counseling to their parishioners need to remind themselves constantly (and humbly) of their lack of expertise in the lives of others—the not-knowing position. However, pastors also need to remember that they do possess knowledge in matters of faith and expertise in questioning and guiding parishioners—not only toward resolution of their difficulties, but also toward an increase in faith and service to God. In fact, such knowledge and expertise define their pastoral calling.

Is it possible to do both? If people in need are the experts on what does and does not work in their own lives, as brief models of psychotherapy assert, can pastoral caregivers speak of God or introduce talk of faith in a way that works with parishioners' own authority and agency?[2] Other authors in this book have demonstrated that people typically are willing to spend only a limited amount of time in formal counseling relationships. How can pastors listen to parishioners' pain, discern their understanding of their problems, help them develop their own goals for the future, and at the same time exercise pastoral authority in proclaiming the gospel—confronting, comforting, and guiding them in their practice of faith—all in a few short sessions? It almost seems too much to ask. And yet that seems to be the task of the pastoral caregiver in the congregational context.

The potential conflict between pastors' theological purpose and therapeutic approach, as the two converge in the helping process, is great indeed. But theological reflection on the purpose of pastoral conversation offers guidance through this dilemma. Both theology and psychotherapeutic theory can help congregational ministers to discern an appropriate use of authority without inappropriately assuming an expert or superior position. It is possible for them to hear about and encourage faithfulness, to speak of God, and to be informed by the knowledge and skills of brief, solution-focused, collaborative and narrative therapies in the process.

The following discussion explores three elements of collaborative pastoral conversation. First, it presents a fuller understanding of collaborative pastoral conversation in terms of partnership and working with the expertise of parishioners. Second, more skillful use of a specific therapeutic approach in brief pastoral counseling is suggested and illustrated by inviting change and opening space. Third, attention to "God-talk"—claiming faith and encouraging faithfulness through pastoral conversation—highlights the effect of a brief therapy approach to this pastoral task. In part, encouraging faithfulness means that the broader theological purpose of pastoral conversation can be confirmed by actively addressing human need in the context of the community of faith as well as the culture in which we live.

Pastoral Authority and Appropriate Knowing

In the case described above, Pastor Davis suggested that the Huber family's problem might have a creative, even constructive purpose for the members of this family. Even so brief a comment served to join or collaborate with the family in understanding their difficulty and to suggest a theological view of the purpose of family in the wonder of God's diverse creation.[3] While not dismissing their pain, the pastor exercised authority by offering an alternative view of their situation based on his knowledge of the faith convictions these parents had claimed.

The collaborative approach requires a relationship in which pastoral care-givers use their expertise to structure and focus conversation while encouraging the full participation of the parishioners in the counseling process. When people ask for help in solving problems or attaining a goal, our task as pastors is not to invent a solution to the problem or to define the goal for them, but to converse with them in a way that draws out their strengths and resources to meet the challenge at hand. We use our pastoral authority in a spirit of collaboration, not dominating or overtaking the parishioners' expertise and resources, but understanding what they want to be different in their lives—all from a perspective of faith. It is crucial that we exercise this authority with humility, respecting others' own sense of relationship with God and purpose in life. But it is equally important that we take responsibility for shaping conversation about the problem or goal being addressed to demonstrate that faith makes a difference. Indeed, we are called as ministers to be experts in guiding such pastoral conversation from the perspective of faith.

We have been listening in on a pastoral conversation that shifted from a simple business discussion to an informal counseling session. The Hubers expressed their faith perspectives freely, and Pastor Davis listened. Responding to the pastor's statement about the diversity of God's creation, Jean continued:

> JEAN: I don't think God wants this kind of conflict in families. Children are supposed to honor their parents, and that's what we expect of Sam. You're asking for something that goes against what the Bible says. I mean, you've studied it more than I have, but that's what it says. Honor your father and your mother.

> PASTOR DAVIS: That is one of the Ten Commandments and an important point in God's covenant with us, what God expects of us. I know that's what you would like with Sam—mutual respect, honoring one another, everyone doing their part to make things good for the whole family.

> JEAN: That's right. He just won't cooperate like he used to. I mean, he is a teenager, but really, we're not asking too much.

> PASTOR DAVIS: I guess I think about it as a process. I wish it weren't so hard for all of you in the meantime, but I have a hunch that—with some combination of firmness and compassion, some setting limits with consequences and knowing forgiveness is possible—somewhere in there Sam is learning to honor himself, to find out more of who he

is, who he'll become, and that this is part of his role in the family right now, maybe even his primary task or purpose as a child of God.

JAMES: So you think we need to tolerate all this?

PASTOR DAVIS: Well, some things, not everything. Some differences between what he's doing and what you wish he would do, as long as he's not harming himself, or you. I respect your desire for him to honor you and all you do for him and your belief that this is what God wants. He's probably depending on that expectation and the limits you set even as he pushes against them. Maybe you're providing a safe space for him to explore what he can honor and what he can challenge so he can respect himself too.

As the conversation continued, Pastor Davis worked with the Hubers as they created a list of differences between themselves and Sam that they could tolerate or even encourage. They even agreed—somewhat reluctantly—that Sam's hair color and earrings and other superficial ways of being different could be indulged, if not exactly celebrated. They also heard from each other what support they needed, what specific things they had to do in order to nurture hope in one another as partners in the process.

Pastor Davis knew something about the Hubers' faith and asserted pastoral authority by introducing talk of God's diverse creation. He heard the Hubers' view of what they expect as parents based on God's covenant with Moses. Pastor Davis and the Hubers worked together to address a family problem through these two elements of the belief they share—thus empowering the family to break its impasse in the context of faith, using the resources of faith, and ultimately strengthening faith.

Theologian Letty Russell defines power as the ability to accomplish desired ends.[4] Using a sociohistorical perspective, she notes that authority in Christian churches usually has been thought of as dominance, as power over a community.[5] A different model of authority—koinonia, a freely chosen, mutual partnership—is found in the ministry of Jesus. Russell suggests that this form of authority is a gift of Christ's love, an interdependent relationship of trust and love, which remembers and anticipates the future new creation God brings. Such partnership does not imply complete equality, but "a pattern of equal regard and mutual acceptance of different gifts."[6]

Partnership shifts the focus from paternalistic authority to collaborative efforts. Individuals, pastors, the local congregation, and the wider community work together to address the needs of troubled people who seek help with their problems. Unlike the reciprocity of friendship, pastoral caregivers do not expect to receive the equivalent of what they offer—certainly not in equal measure—but offer their leadership, compassion, and guidance as members of one body.

In this way, pastors take special responsibility to offer direction and guidance, but their authority is attributed based on a trustworthy pattern of behavior, self-awareness, competence, and perception of God's redemptive presence.

The partnership I am describing may be compared in some respects to the collaboration of a graduate student and her mentor on a special research project. Each person contributes effort and ideas, and each respects the contribution of the other. If the mentor is a fair and honorable person, both will receive credit when the results are published. But one partner has authority that the other does not possess. The mentor has a considerable store of knowledge and experience as well as valuable contacts in the field; the graduate student assents to this authority, both for the sake of their mutual work and to further her own professional growth. The student contributes energy, ideas, and a fresh point of view. In brief pastoral counseling, such a partnership preserves the integrity and agency of the person seeking help. The pastor and parishioner do not function in isolation, but as members of a community of faith to which they are accountable and which offers structure, space, and resources for persons to address their needs.

Thus we help people to recognize God's hand in their lives, to pay attention to signs of God's grace in ordinary and even difficult or troubling events, and to answer God's call to love and serve our neighbor and to work for justice. Howard Rice notes that this type of conversation does not happen automatically in pastoral care and counseling. People who seek help or guidance may talk of many other things, and it is up to us to raise questions about the connection between faith and the issues they bring.[7] Even well-intentioned pastoral care and counseling can do harm if the caregiver misuses interpersonal power and pastoral authority. Just as the best teachers are facilitators and co-learners with their students rather than dispensers of information, pastoral caregivers need to understand their expertise in terms of appropriate knowing and pastoral authority in partnership with those they serve.

Inviting Change and Opening Space

Julia, a young woman recently divorced, came to see Pastor Delia Ramone one evening after work. "I don't need counseling or anything like that," Julia began. "I just thought it would help if I could talk with you for a while." Together they discussed Julia's difficulty in dealing with the end of her marriage—she was still in shock, Julia thought, after nearly half a year. Julia expressed her feelings of grief and the many types of loss she had experienced because of the divorce. The conversation continued:

JULIA: I don't understand how he could do that to me. But it's like God let me down too. I thought if I kept my promises, then God would watch over us and bless our marriage. I'm an honest person, a loyal person, and even though Victor was disappointed in me, with my not finishing college or earning much money, I loved him and tried to be a good wife. I still can't believe he left me for someone else.

PASTOR RAMONE: You feel like he betrayed your trust and broke the covenant the two of you had made, even when you were still loyal to it. You've said that you regret some things, that you didn't do more things Victor enjoyed, like hiking and camping, and wish you'd entered his world more fully.

JULIA: That's true. Looking back, I didn't realize what it meant to him. I didn't think it mattered that much.

PASTOR RAMONE: I'm wondering where you are with that in other relationships now, if you see yourself entering into others' lives in the way you want to, like keeping covenant with your friends, or if you're hanging back, too much alone. (They went on to discuss the possibility that Julia was isolating herself and compounding her losses by declining invitations from friends.)

JULIA: I guess I haven't felt ready to go out. It's been easier to just stay home and keep to myself. But I see what you mean that some of my friends have stayed loyal to me through all this, and that's a kind of covenant too.

PASTOR RAMONE: You know, this may sound too simple, but I keep thinking of a line from a catechism in our church where it talks about what the Spirit does in worship—building us up in faith, hope, and love, and sending us out into the world, something like that. I can't help wondering where you are in the process of being built up again and sent out into the world—if more time alone will build you up, or if you're ready for a small step toward your friends, for instance?

The pastor offered an empathic response to how Julia's life had been affected by her former husband's behavior. She went on to inquire about Julia's influence over her current problem of isolation and about her agency—that is, what she could do about it. Framing the problem and Julia's capacity to address it in terms of the Spirit "building up" and "sending out" brought Julia's need to move forward with her life into the perspective of faith and relationship with God. Pastor Ramone, in her brief pastoral encounter with Julia, opened a space for theological reflection and invited Julia to consider God's agency and action on her behalf, as well as her own agency and action on behalf of her goal. In a collaborative effort between pastor and parishioner, Julia remained free to amend or decline the invitation.

In a brief pastoral counseling context, inviting people to cooperate with change means hearing their beliefs about change, about the problem, and about how it can be resolved.[8] In this process of invitation, pastors ask exception-oriented and solution-focused questions. They open up space for new ways of thinking and acting, and they invite people to enter that space. For example, Julia's pastor could have urged her a bit further into the open space by suggesting the image of an open door or gate, inviting her to pass through, with the implication that she has experienced building up and is ready to be sent forth. The open space must allow for Julia's own view of where she is, intersecting with the pastoral image that affirms God's Spirit at work in her life and situation, building her up, sending her forth for a purpose. Further, the doorway image was (and is) a reminder that the goal of pastoral counseling is not only to relieve suffering, but also to restore persons so that they may love and serve God.

Recalling the earlier illustration, Pastor Davis's reminder to Jean and James Huber of the diversity of God's creation, and Jean's reminder to Pastor Davis about the covenant commandment to honor parents, were confrontations of a sort that invited each to view the problem and counseling goal from a perspective of faith. The purpose of a pastor's confrontation in brief pastoral counseling, writes Howard Stone, is to encourage parishioners to consider different perspectives.[9] It invites them to recognize beliefs, attitudes, and behaviors that may harm themselves or others and that hinder love of self, neighbor, or God. It helps them to see the gifts they possess but may have ignored. Jean's confrontation of her pastor clarified another way in which scripture or tradition could speak to their situation.

Listening for and receiving the religious views of parishioners is, of course, easier when the pastor shares their views and a collaborative dialogue can proceed with relative comfort. It is more difficult and sometimes uncomfortable when pastor and parishioner hold different interpretations of a biblical story or seemingly contradictory interpretations of a theological issue. But opening space for conversation about faith can enlist a new perspective (in the Hubers' case, God's diverse creation and God's covenant expectations) or goal (effective parenting and honoring each family member) that frames the interaction in terms of what God may be calling forth (forgiveness, grace, hope). The Hubers, as well as the pastor, gained a clearer sense of what God may be doing in the midst of their family as a result of hearing and coming to understand one another's views.

In a similar vein, Julia's conversation with Pastor Ramone might have gone quite differently if Julia had placed all responsibility for change in her life in God's hands, affirming her dependence on God but unwilling to claim her own influence upon the problem she faced. Such divergence in theological views would have required clarification and collaboration from both pastor and parishioner, perhaps using Julia's own sense of how God's Spirit works in her life, or an image other than worship that she found more fitting with her present circumstance. The point of their collaborative effort, then, would have been to articulate the problem and its potential resolution from a perspective of faith even if, for the time being, that meant Julia was continuing to wait for God to act on her behalf.

God-Talk: Listening for and Talking about Faith

Exploring a person's sense of what would constitute faithfulness in a given situation is part of the pastoral task in brief pastoral counseling (as well as other arenas of ministry). Finding ways to do so without being intrusive or presumptive is a matter of timing and tact. Confrontation that introduces a theological view is collaborative when it doesn't change the subject but expands a point of discussion in a particular direction. What I call "listening into" the conversation for the right occasion, and discerning an appropriate question or comment to explore a connection with faith, requires some skill. It may be a gentle confrontation or an invitation, but it is the point at which collaboration is crucial.

When using biblical stories, images, or theological themes in brief pastoral counseling, pastors must be willing to hear interpretations they did not have in mind. Themes of faith have a way of resonating with a wide variety of experiences beyond our own. In the process, the status quo of both pastor and parishioner may shift, opening spaces for new stories in ways that cannot be predicted. Biblical stories inform the construction of meaning. In brief pastoral counseling, collaboration entails openness to the intertwining, mutual influence of biblical stories, the pastor's perspective, and the parishioner's experience.[10]

God-talk is not always a requirement of brief pastoral counseling. It can even be presumptive or intrusive in situations where another agenda needs attention, or when a safe interpersonal space and mutual trust do not exist. Introducing a new perspective in the pastoral counseling process can oppress rather than liberate if the caregiver imposes it in an authoritarian rather than collaborative manner. Opening space has a tentative quality; it does not impose a set of beliefs too far afield from the parishioner's own convictions, nor does it intrude into areas that are not open for discussion. There is no doubt that religious ideology can potentially serve a dominating, oppressive function in the lives of those we are trying to help through a misuse of pastoral authority that is far out of touch with the new creation God is bringing forth. Even so, as Freedman and Combs point out, caregivers who fail to take a stand, who do not open space for difference and change, end up fostering the status quo.[11] Inviting the consideration of theological themes is not necessarily oppressive and actually can be liberating. The great difference of the gospel is that we are given freedom to resist whatever is harmful, and to act with courage in the face of what is oppressive.

Some pastoral caregivers may be reluctant to introduce biblical stories and God-talk into their counseling ministry because of their training. Pastoral conversation has long been based on empathy in relationship and on unconditional positive regard for and acceptance of the person seeking care. The genuineness of the caregiver has been paramount, communicating openness and a warmth that invited trust and disclosure.[12] This understanding of pastoral conversation involves the basic helping skills of attending and listening, communicating understanding through empathic responses, and helping persons to identify and clarify problem situations, implement their goals, and create a better future.[13]

To offer no direction and to leave talk of faith out of our counseling ministry, however, is to sidestep our calling. Pastoral theologian Gaylord Noyce points out that many aspects of ministry—preaching, teaching, and pastoral care and counseling—include responsibility for proclaiming and interpreting faith "unfulfilled by Rogerian habits of empathic listening alone." He refers to the over-reliance on empathic listening so commonly found in pastoral counseling literature of the past fifty years as the "nondirective handicap."[14] Collaborative conversation within the framework of brief pastoral counseling listens for and inquires about how people view their experience from a perspective of faith.

Nondirective psychodynamic theory is not the only impediment to active proclamation and interpretation of faith in brief pastoral counseling. Our highly individualistic society, with its emphasis on privacy, makes many of us fearful of imposing our views upon others. Furthermore, what Noyce calls "cheap religious talk" that proliferates on billboards, television, radio, bumper stickers, and T-shirts, dilutes the name of God so that all sense of God's holiness is lost. Religious language may even be a red flag that alienates those who associate it with a style of religion they find oppressive or disagreeable. Avoiding God-talk, however, may become such a habit that in our pastoral counseling we do not listen for or inquire about faith at all. Sharing different views about faith can move a relationship forward in ways we cannot foresee, provided we are collaborating with and not working against each other's views.

It is one thing to speak of faith in general terms, but quite another thing for people to know what faithfulness would look like in their particular situation. Making connections with the daily, ordinary faithfulness of other Christians helps us to better understand the mystery of God's presence (or, at times, our sense of God's absence). In biblical stories, this mystery was often explored through telling a story or parable in two different ways. In one version, we hear of human adventures and foibles without any mention of God; in the second version, we hear God at least just offstage if not directly involved in the action.[15] Who would know, on first hearing, that a seed in rocky soil (Matthew 13) has anything to do with a person hearing but failing to understand a word about the new creation? Who would guess, as the parable of the unforgiving servant begins with talk of transactions and business accounts (Matthew 18), that we are to show mercy to others because God has been merciful to us?

Listening to one version of a story as told by troubled parishioners—usually the version with human challenges and limits—pastors often do not hear anything about God. But, collaborating with the teller and listening "into" the story for its faith dimension, we may discover God just offstage within the narrative. We may hear echoes of biblical and theological themes: confession and repentance, grace and reconciliation, doxology and thanksgiving, blessing and joy, presence in lament and suffering, comfort in loss and grief, healing and wholeness, injustice and oppressive circumstances, freedom and liberation, community and companionship, alienation or isolation, generativity and caring for others, covenants, commitments and sexuality, vocation and work.[16]

Most counseling done in the parish context does not afford a leisurely exploration of biblical and theological themes within the short duration of the counseling relationship. (There is ample time for that in the broader ministry of a local congregation.) However, pastors doing brief pastoral counseling can help counselees to relate themes of faith to their own experience by skillfully raising questions and observations that elicit rather than tell, thus stimulating collaborative conversation. To give a variety of examples:

- You seem to be so thankful for this change in your life, as if it's a real blessing to experience things in this new way.
- You've spoken so much of your responsibility for your problems, but how do you imagine God's grace could show forth to be demonstrated in this situation? How would you go about accepting that grace?
- So you're needing a much fuller sense of God's presence and comfort right now. How have you experienced that before in a way that you're hoping for again? Where were you, what were you doing, what people were around you, what did your day look like?
- You're telling me that the healing you most want is to be at peace with yourself and with God, not so much a cure for your illness— you want God to restore your sense of purpose in life and to give you hope again. What things do you think you can do to participate in God's process of restoration?

- It sounds as if this is a matter of enduring a bad situation and trusting that God will sustain you until circumstances change.
- You seem to be seeking more freedom from your fears in order to be able to take appropriate action when your circumstances improve a little bit. What are some of the ways in which you see God calling you forth from your fearfulness? How is God acting on your behalf?
- Perhaps this is a time to reconsider the covenant you two have made with one another. What things have changed for each of you over the years? What is God inviting you to do (or stop doing) in order to be faithful to your covenant?
- I get the sense that you feel discouraged and isolated, and probably even God seems far away. If God drew closer somehow, what specific things might be different in your daily life?

Introducing a biblical image or theological theme links the ordinary narrative with the extraordinary story of God's faithfulness to us. An imagined dialogue with Jesus or a familiar biblical figure may help people to view themselves and their situations from a different perspective. "What if Jesus were sitting in this empty chair," you might ask; "what would he have to say to you about your family's constant fighting? What would your home life look like to him? How would he talk to you—kindly, gently, harshly, judgmentally? What do you think he would encourage you to do?" (For those willing, this could take the form of a role-play in which the pastor takes the role of the parishioner, and the parishioner speaks the imagined words of Jesus or the chosen biblical figure.)

In a counseling group focusing on women's spirituality, one pastoral counselor used stories from the Bible (the woman who anointed Jesus, the woman with the issue of blood, Mary and Martha, the woman caught in adultery, and the woman at the well) for imagined dialogues in which counselees interacted with the stories and imagined their own interaction with Jesus.[17] With experience, effective pastors will create similar ways to use their authority in collaboration with, rather than over, the parishioners they counsel, trusting God's active presence and influence in the shape and meaning of change in their lives.

One of the benefits of brief pastoral counseling is that it is only one part of a larger ministry and that a community of faith exists outside the specific (and short-lived) counseling relationship to offer nurture, support, and a sense of belonging to all who enter into it. The very brevity of pastoral counseling, in fact, becomes an asset when ministers encourage persons to move forward, beyond the counseling relationship, and into a wider culture better prepared for faithful service. Such movement can be an antidote to the cultural confusion of our time. As Larry Graham writes,

A culturally sensitive ministry of care recognizes that persons are adrift, without moorings, and that the communities which nurtured their visions of reality often no longer sustain or support them. It is sensitive to the conflicting pulls upon individuals and communities from a radically pluralistic world order. It seeks to reconnect persons and communities with their traditions, while at the same time assisting with the construction of new traditions that are responsive to the personal needs and historical realities of our time.[18]

Brief pastoral counseling provides alternatives to a culture in which forces contend for power and influence, extreme individualism undermines social forms of faithfulness, and a focus on the present moment clouds our awareness that things have been and could be different than they are. Pastoral caregivers must ask themselves what constitutes their faithful response to such need, equipped with appropriate knowing balanced with not-knowing, and encouraging faithfulness in others who also extend the ministry of Jesus Christ.

Pastors engaging in collaborative conversation with parishioners discern an appropriate therapeutic approach that informs their counseling, but the larger theological purpose of the dialogue is to enhance the faithfulness of all involved. The individual and family problems pastors hear often reflect larger social and cultural patterns of need, patterns that beg for conversation resulting in action, collaboration leading to influence, and the gathering of the faith community's resources to address a larger need. Brief pastoral counseling may include conversation that encompasses the prophetic dimension of pastoral care by identifying areas for social action and advocacy.[19] It could include such activities as lobbying for funding and recruiting a chaplain in a community hospital, working with local police for a more effective response to domestic violence, establishing a central location for a food and clothing bank, advocating for improved after-school opportunities at a school board meeting, and many more. In many instances, furthermore, collaborative pastoral conversation may serve as a significant contradiction to social and cultural patterns that ignore, perpetuate, or exacerbate individual suffering.

∽

Congregational ministers offering brief pastoral counseling collaborate with parishioners' understanding of their problems and goals for the future, invite change, and open space for new meanings and more faithful action. The not-knowing therapeutic approach toward parishioners' expertise in their own experience and goals, an essential element of brief pastoral counseling, is balanced with appropriate knowing and the claiming of faith perspectives. As collaborators, pastoral caregivers shape the content and direction of pastoral counseling encounters through brief references to faith, biblical images, or questions and comments concerning parishioners' sense of who God is and how God is acting in relation to the problem they face. In this way, congregational ministers doing brief pastoral counseling participate in what God is calling forth within their troubled parishioners' lives. They anticipate the new creation as, together, they speak of it, look for it, and respond in faith. A new story begins.

Notes

1. Illustrations are drawn from composites of persons encountered in pastoral care and counseling and do not represent any particular individual or family.

2. Glenn Boyd, a pastoral counselor and marriage and family therapist, has written several very helpful discussions concerning the relation between postmodern and constructionist therapeutic perspectives and pastoral conversation. Boyd offers an overview of postmodern thought and the Collaborative Language Systems Approach of family therapists Anderson and Goolishian and develops the notion of "agape-listening" as a fuller integration of postmodern thought and pastoral conversation. See Glenn E. Boyd, "Kerygma and Conversation," the *Journal of Pastoral Care* 50, no. 2 (1996): 161–69; "Pastoral Conversation: A Postmodern View of Expertise," *Pastoral Psychology* 46, no. 5 (1998): 307–21; "Pastoral Conversation: A Social Construction View," *Pastoral Psychology* 44, no. 4 (1996): 215–55.

The issue of "expertise" in how a client and counselor work together is discussed in Boyd, "Pastoral Conversation," and in several therapeutic theories that have emerged from family systems theories of psychotherapy. One notable discussion is that of Harlene Anderson and Harold Goolishian, "The Client is the Expert: A Not-Knowing Approach to Therapy," in Sheila McNamee and Kenneth J. Gergen, eds., *Therapy as Social Construction* (London: Sage, 1992). Lynn Hoffman has discussed the notion of reflexivity in therapeutic relationships using the ideal of partnership, "an equity in regard to participation even though the parties may have different positions or different traits." See McNamee and Gergen, "A Reflexive Stance for Family Therapy," 7–24. Other therapeutic theories that address the issue of expertise are solution-focused therapy, exemplified in Bill O'Hanlon and Michele Weiner-Davis, *In Search of Solutions: A New Direction in Psychotherapy* (New York: Norton, 1989), and John L. Walter and Jane E. Peller, *Becoming Solution-Focused in Brief Therapy* (New York: Brunner/Mazel, 1992); and narrative therapy based on a social constructionist approach, exemplified in Jill Freedman and Gene Combs, *Narrative Therapy: The Social Construction of Preferred Realities* (New York: Norton, 1996), and Michael White and David Epston, *Narrative Means to Therapeutic Ends* (New York: Norton, 1990).

3. Herbert Anderson, *The Family and Pastoral Care* (Philadelphia: Fortress Press, 1984).

4. Letty Russell defines partnership as "a new focus of relationship in which there is continuing commitment and common struggle in interaction with a wider community context . . . a new focus of relationship in a common history of Jesus Christ that sets persons free for others." *The Future of Partnership* (Philadelphia: Westminster/John Knox, 1979), 16. See also Letty Russell, *Growth in Partnership* (Philadelphia: Westminster/John Knox, 1981).

5. Letty Russell, *Household of Freedom* (Philadelphia: Westminster/John Knox, 1987), 87–99.

6. Ibid., 92.

7. Howard Rice, *The Pastor as Spiritual Guide* (Nashville: Upper Room Books, 1998), 87–88.

8. John L. Walter and Jane Peller, *Becoming Solution-Focused in Brief Therapy* (New York: Brunner/Mazel, 1992), 204–13.

9. Howard W. Stone, *Brief Pastoral Counseling: Short-Term Approaches and Strategies* (Minneapolis: Fortress Press, 1994), 113.

10. Recent works in pastoral theology that draw upon narrative theory more generally include Donald Capps, *Living Stories: Pastoral Counseling in Congregational Context* (Minneapolis: Fortress Press, 1998); Charles Gerkin, *The Living Human Document: Revisioning Pastoral Counseling in a Hermeneutical Mode* (Nashville: Abingdon, 1984); idem, *Prophetic Pastoral Practice: A Christian Vision of Life Together* (Nashville: Abingdon, 1991); and Andrew Lester, *Hope in Pastoral Care and Counseling* (Louisville, Ky.: Westminster/John Knox, 1995); and Edward Wimberly, *African American Pastoral Care* (Nashville: Abingdon, 1991).

11. Freedman and Combs, *Narrative Therapy*, 57–58.

12. Heije Faber and Ebel van der Schoot, *The Art of Pastoral Conversation* (Nashville: Abingdon, 1965); and Carl Rogers, *Client Centered Therapy: Its Current Practice, Implications, and Theory* (Boston: Houghton Mifflin, 1951).

13. See, for example, Gerard Egan, *The Skilled Helper: A Problem Management Approach to Helping*, 5th ed. (Pacific Grove, Calif.: Brooks/Cole, 1994).

14. Gaylord B. Noyce, *The Art of Pastoral Conversation* (Atlanta: John Knox, 1981), 45ff.

15. Frederick H. Borsch, *Many Things in Parables: Extravagant Stories of New Community* (Philadelphia: Fortress Press, 1988), 4.

16. Thematic listening in theological terms is discussed in numerous works in pastoral theology and pastoral counseling. See, for example, Howard Clinebell, *Basic Types of Pastoral Care and Counseling* (Nashville: Abingdon, 1984), 74–78; Wayne Oates, *The Christian Pastor*, 3rd ed. (Philadelphia: Westminster, 1982), 167–89; Paul Pruyser, *The Minister as Diagnostician* (Philadelphia: Westminster, 1976); and previously cited works by Capps and Lester.

In another work, I have explored three biblical images of the new creation that offer means for reconsidering the purpose of pastoral conversation in visitation and the type of relationship caregivers have with those whom we counsel. Seed growing in soil (Luke 8:4-8), yeast mixing in with flour (Luke 13:20), invitations to a great dinner already begun (Luke 14:15-24) help us to imagine our part in the work God accomplishes, neither over- nor underestimating our role in pastoral care. These images help to recover and strengthen pastoral care as a collaborative use of authority on behalf of what God is doing in our midst. See *Pastoral Visitation* (Minneapolis: Fortress Press, 1999), 33–38.

17. Mitzi Ellington, "Women's Self-Esteem and Spirituality: Narrative Approaches in Pastoral Counseling" (D.Min. paper, Fort Worth, Tex.: Brite Divinity School, 1997).

18. Larry Kent Graham, *Care of Persons, Care of Worlds: A Psychosystems Approach to Pastoral Care and Counseling* (Nashville: Abingdon, 1992), 59.

19. Illustrations of social action based in pastoral care and counseling are discussed in Katherine Billman, "Pastoral Care as an Art of Community," in *The Arts of Ministry: Feminist-Womanist Approaches,* ed. Christie Neuger (Louisville, Ky.: Westminster/John Knox, 1996), 10–38; Pamela Couture, *Blessed Are the Poor: Family Policy and Practical Theology* (Nashville: Abingdon, 1991); Pamela Couture and Rodney Hunter, eds., *Pastoral Care and Social Conflict* (Nashville, Abingdon, 1995); Gary Gunderson, *Deeply Woven Roots: Improving the Quality of Life in Your Community* (Minneapolis: Fortress Press, 1995); Christie Neuger, "Pastoral Counseling as an Art of Personal Political Activism," in *The Arts of Ministry: Feminist-Womanist Approaches,* ed. Christie Neuger (Louisville, Ky.: Westminster/John Knox, 1996), 88–117.

4

Helping Parishioners
Envision the Future

Andrew Lester and Howard W. Stone

> For in hope we were saved. . . . if we hope for what we do not see,
> we wait for it with patience.
>
> —Romans 8:24-25

BRIEF PASTORAL COUNSELING engenders hope. It is not so much a new way to do counseling as it is an orientation to the helping process, a perspective that the pastoral caregiver carries into each care or counseling encounter. One of the key elements in this form of pastoral counseling is the minister's orientation to the future, for it is in the future that hope exists.[1]

Our understanding of hope is influenced by Søren Kierkegaard's understanding of persons. He describes persons as possessors of actuality, freedom, and possibility. All three are part of the self, and a good relationship among all three is necessary for authentic existence.

Actuality refers primarily to the past; it includes our context, our physiological predisposition, and choices we have made.

Freedom is what we have in the present. It is a finite freedom, exercised within the limits of our situation and abilities, our givens and past choices. Because of our actualities, we cannot become whatever we want to be—not even "if we only try hard enough." We make choices, and act, from the range of options available to us.

Possibility addresses the future. It is what we can become as we use our freedom. In this respect, our possibilities are not predetermined. We can imagine and—within the givens of life—we can become something new. Living as an authentic self, according to Kierkegaard, means looking beyond our immediate necessities and past liabilities. We anticipate the future with the awareness that we are free—within our limitations—to realize who we ought to become as faithful Christians; we take responsibility to some extent for shaping that future.[2]

In short, faithful Christian living requires that we recognize givens from the past and exercise finite freedom in the present so that we can imagine and bring into being positive future possibilities. Our hope rests in those future possibilities.

Some people, viewed from Kierkegaard's understanding of persons, allow their actuality (past) to limit and dominate their possibility (future) by not exercising their freedom in the present. Their anguish comes not only from dwelling on a negative past, but also from the loss of a positive future. Unfortunately, much of the counseling offered to such individuals focuses primarily on actuality, or the past, and ignores the future.

Ministers offering brief pastoral counseling need to focus on agency in the present to foster a kind of hope that recognizes actuality but also steps directly into the future by exercising freedom in the present—by taking action. To do so, they must grasp the central importance of thinking about the future and of envisioning hopeful outcomes to human well-being. They also need specific care and counseling methods that will nourish hope in their troubled parishioners. In the pages that follow, we will attempt to address these issues.

The Future

In *Hope in Pastoral Care and Counseling,* I (Lester) identified the future as the primary dimension of time-consciousness in which the struggle between hope and despair plays itself out during the human pilgrimage. The attitude we take toward the future can be placed on a continuum between despair and hope. In the future that is coming toward us, we find possibilities. The visions, vocations, and commitments that give our lives meaning and fill us with hope are connected to our images of the future—what I call "future stories."

In these future stories, the temptation to despair is most dangerous. To nurture hope, therefore, effective brief pastoral counseling must attend to the stories that humans create about this future dimension of time. How people consider the not-yet is crucial to their physical, emotional, and spiritual well-being.

The noted psychoanalyst Viktor Frankl learned about the importance of people's attitude toward the future from his experience as a prisoner in a concentration camp during the Second World War. He discovered that hope was a primary ingredient in the survival of his fellow prisoners. Frankl disagreed with psychological theorists who held that human beings are determined primarily by drives and instincts. He took the future orientation of humans seriously, developing concepts such as the "will to meaning" that describe human beings as reaching toward the future for meaning and fulfillment. To Frankl, this will to meaning is the basic striving of all human beings.[3] Irvin Yalom provides a concise summary of Frankl's perspective:

> Frankl is careful to distinguish between drives . . . that push a person from within . . . and meaning . . . that pulls a person from without. . . . The difference is between drive and strive. In our most essential being, in those characteristics that make us most human rather than animal, we are not driven but instead actively strive for some goal. "Striving" conveys a future orientation: we are pulled by what is to be, rather than pushed by relentless forces of past and present.[4]

Indeed, time-consciousness is the foundation stone of our existential context. Human beings live in three dimensions of time; we have a past tense, a present tense, and a future tense. Existence includes *accepting the givens imposed by the past, living with the freedoms provided in the present, and shaping the possibilities of the future.*

Theology views time not only in the historical sense of past, present, and future but also in relation to the activity of God. Past promises and future fulfillment came together in the person of Jesus the Christ. God acted in a present moment of real time (the Christ event), which now lies in the past but has changed the course of human possibility. Our future is open in a new way because of the advent of the Christ. Even though the realm of God was activated in the past and is here in the present, its completion is out in front of us, in the not-yet.

Jürgen Moltmann, the central figure in the eschatological theology movement heavily influenced by Ernst Bloch, calls attention to the importance of the future dimension of time-consciousness. He argues that human beings learn of their basic nature not from their present perceptions of selfhood but from the future. Humans are grounded in history, a history that is "open to the future, open for new, promised possibilities of being."[5] Moltmann takes the stance that the basic identity of a person is hidden and can be revealed only by those unseen possibilities that lie beyond the future horizon. Basic to the nature of humans is their being "always on the way towards some . . . expected future whole." This future is the stage on which persons can become what they are not yet.[6]

The impact of future consciousness upon present actions has been underestimated. Until recently, the human sciences largely have neglected the future dimension of human existence in personality theories as well as methodological strategies. The field of pastoral care and counseling, under the spell of the behavioral and social sciences, also has largely omitted the future tense in its formulations about the human condition. But human beings are shaped by images of the not-yet just as powerfully as they are influenced by their past and present. It is our hope that pastoral caregivers will increasingly ground their theory and practice on a more complete theological anthropology that pays careful attention to the future.

Hope

Hope presents a future filled with possibilities, and it offers a blessing. Used theologically, the word *hope* is a recognition of possibilities that lie ahead, a trusting anticipation of a time when troubles lessen or end, an investment in a tomorrow that holds promise. It is based upon a trustworthy God who calls us into an open-ended future, who promises deliverance, liberation, salvation.

How does hope relate to our experience of the future? In each present moment, hope anticipates the next moment and responds to the thought of tomorrow with expectation, even excitement. Theologian William Lynch describes hope as

> the fundamental knowledge and feeling that there is a way out of difficulty, that things can work out, that we as human persons can somehow handle and manage internal and external reality, that there are "solutions" in the most ordinary biological and physiological sense of that word, that above all, there are ways out.[7]

Since hope is future-oriented, caring for persons who feel hopeless means helping them to *imagine*. Those who lack the capacity to fantasize, to imagine, to picture in their mind's eye events that have yet to occur, cannot hope. Despairing people tend to envision a pessimistic outcome. They communicate it with phrases such as: "That's impossible." "That will never work." "I can't do that." "I don't know where to go from here." "There is nothing else to do." They are blind to the many possibilities inherent in their situation.

Alternative, hopeful future stories allow space for creation's inherent potential to develop. They free persons to explore options, to experience new things, to imagine change, to expect surprises, and to anticipate growth. In contrast, hopeless future stories imprison the future; when people feel trapped by life, their future stories lose power to open the way.

The good news is that brief pastoral counseling methods can bring about hope where hope was lost. In the following pages, we will present some ways of helping parishioners and counselees to envision new futures.

Methods for Envisioning a New Future

During the initial phase of a pastoral intervention—such as a pastoral counsel-ing session, a hospital visit, or a pastoral conversation with a young man after a youth group meeting—it is important to heed and help open up images of the future. From the beginning of the first visit, we need to communicate that talk-ing about the future is as natural and important to the helping process as talking about the past and the present. Particularly in the context of a pastoral relation-ship, where spiritual issues are a natural topic, establishing the centrality of hope is not only appropriate, but essential.

In the first encounter with those who seek our help, it is wise to find the earliest possible time to introduce the future into the conversation in order to assess how their future stories shape and are shaped by the current situation. Urge parishioners to tell what they imagine life will be like in times to come. Invite them to tell the "out there" as well as the "back when" and the "right now" by saying something like:

> *Mary, you've told me about your past and about your present situation. But I don't know much about what you imagine lies ahead of you. Tell me about your future.*
>
> *What do you think life will be like for you in three months?*
>
> *What do you anticipate if things do not change?*
>
> *What will you do when . . . ?*
>
> *Tell me what you dream about in the future.*

Parishioners may respond with surprise and uncertainty, with comments such as "What do you mean, tell about the future?" or "How can I tell you about what hasn't happened yet?" If so, take a minute to teach them about temporal-ity, pointing out that all people harbor images about the future. Even though they may still wear a puzzled look, most people then will at least attempt to describe their future. If they ask how to begin or what to say, suggest that they tell about something they anticipate or something they wish would happen.

The following are a series of methods that caregivers doing brief pastoral counseling can use to help parishioners focus on the future and thus en-gender hope.

Reframing Hope

An important task early in all pastoral counseling, and especially brief pastoral counseling in which people are seen for only one or a few sessions, is to help individuals frame hope where they are now framing hopelessness.

Frames are the ways we perceive events or circumstances; they shape our reality. *Reframing* changes those perceptions. It constructs for people a new way to organize and view their experiences and turns liabilities into strengths. "I'm a total failure at classroom management; my students interrupt and talk all at once" changes to "I encourage a free give-and-take of ideas in my classroom; how can I learn to channel our discussions into even more productive outcomes?" As meanings change, individuals react to similar situations with very different feelings, thoughts, attitudes, and behaviors.

The reframing method comes from neuro-linguistic programming[8] and family therapy theory.[9] To reframe is to reshape perceptions, to change the cognitive sets by which individuals, families, or groups interpret events or relationships, to transform the way in which they conceptualize a life situation. Once they entertain even the slightest doubt about any portion of their frame—once they consider that there may be another way of looking at events—they find it hard to return to their previous point of view. They begin to visualize a future without the problem. Reframing also helps people to rearrange the furniture and change the decorations in a certain room of their memory—that is, to change their understanding of the past.

For our purposes, reframing also encourages people to develop a new perception of their present situation and to reshape their ideas about the future. When they reveal to the pastoral caregiver a negative frame composed of images that contradict hope, shifting to a positive frame will help them envision a hopeful future.

Certain events are more difficult than others to frame positively. They may appear to offer little that is good. (For example, a couple who have recently lost their home and nearly all their possessions in a fire might have trouble putting a positive spin on the discovery that their homeowner's insurance had been allowed to lapse.) However, it is vital to let in some positive information, even if one has to work hard at believing it. Try urging those who have difficulty believing any positive frame to act temporarily as if the reframed way of viewing a situation is true. Strike a deal with them, if necessary, or ask them to humor you. If they object that it would be hypocritical, agree with them; propose that they be a "hypocrite for a day" (or longer). If in doing so they experience any positive change in feelings or behavior, encourage them to continue acting as if the frame is true.

One study of counseling conversations discovered that most people tend to overlook positive changes they have made in their lives, preferring to dwell on what is undone.[10] (The man who insists that he is hopelessly shy and withdrawn, for example, may fail to note that in one day's time he returned the greetings of two strangers who said "Good morning" and offered his seat on the subway to a woman carrying a baby.) When helpers in the study focused on past or current instances of positive change, counselees reported becoming more aware of other positive changes that they had previously forgotten or ignored. They recalled past situations in which they had solved a problem, or even ways in which they were addressing some present difficulty.

Because many troubled people have a negative view of events, pastors who care for them have to promote different perspectives, help them reframe what is happening so that hope grows and positive change appears possible.

Storytelling

One strategy for helping people to envision a hopeful future in brief pastoral counseling is inviting them to identify or create stories about specific future events. Using the imagination to spin a tale gives particularity to what was previously unspeakable. Narrative theory demonstrates the power of stories for affecting the way in which people construct their worldview.[11]

Using storytelling, pastoral caregivers invite parishioners to imagine a future that is hopeful, to reach for positive values, to experience a joyful life. For example, they may begin with questions such as:

> *If your life was made into a movie with a happy ending, tell me what the ending of the movie would look like.*
>
> *If you wrote me a letter in a few years and it was filled with good news about your life, what would the letter say?*
>
> *If I read a story in the newspaper next year about some wonderful thing that happens to you, what would it be?*

Next ask them to add details—people, places, scenes, and events—until they describe a fairly clear and concrete future story that could serve as a basis for choosing creative behaviors and adopting a more hopeful stance toward the future.

Richard Gardner's mutual storytelling method can help people form more hopeful future stories. Gardner, a child psychiatrist, invites children to tell stories for his "Make-Up-A-Story Television Program,"[12] informing them that he, too, will be telling stories. He instructs them to make up a story that has a beginning, a middle, and an end. After they finish the story, Gardner asks them to tell what the story means. He decides what part of the story needs to be challenged in order to provide an alternative frame of reference and then, using the same characters and story line, retells the story with a different outcome. Pastoral caregivers can adapt Gardner's guidelines for retelling adult parishioners' stories about the future. In particular, they look for places where a liability can turn into an asset, a disappointment into an opportunity, a crisis into a chance for growth, thus leading to a positive or hopeful dénouement.

Family members or friends often contribute to the development of the new future story. If they are not present, ask parishioners to share the future story with significant others and solicit their responses, thus benefiting from different perspectives. ("I've been thinking about going back to college now that Prinella is in high school; what do you think?") When people begin talking about possible future scenarios, it is amazing how much energy they generate, not only in themselves, but also in their families.

In cases where people find it difficult or impossible to speak about the future, pastoral caregivers can create and tell the stories for them (a variation on Gardner's method). It is a powerful strategy. Hearing their own future narratives from a trusted and respected caregiver extends the limits of their imagination, and is likely to influence how people reframe or reconstruct their future. To be useful, the story must be connected to reality but filled with possibilities that extend horizons and offer hope.

Tracking and Expanding Future Stories

As people tell stories about their future, we can ask them to expand and elaborate in the same way that we pursue stories about their past and present. Frequently they will offer only a brief outline of events. Caregivers must ask for more information in order to fill out the story, inviting elaboration and asking for specifics:

> *Tell me more about . . .*
> *Suppose that . . .*
> *Where does your husband (wife, father, etc.) fit into that picture?*
> *How would that be different when you . . . ?*
> *Have you considered how your future will change when (your mother dies, you graduate, the baby comes)?*

Since future stories are so important to understanding people's lives and bringing about wholeness, attending to the future tense during the entire helping process is critical. Use various storytelling methods to invite and even challenge people to make the future dimension of their lives explicit, to become aware of whatever they anticipate or dread. Questions such as those suggested above and in the following paragraphs are good story-starters. Other storytelling methods will follow. Above all, encourage parishioners to get curious about their future.

Envisioning the Future without the Problem

Parishioners in need of counsel often focus on a particular problem that appears unsolvable and keeps them from re-visioning the future. In such cases,

William O'Hanlon and Michele Weiner-Davis pursue counselees' images of the future by asking what they call "fast-forward" questions, challenging them to envision a future without the problem. They hold that, having described the future without the problem, counselees also have described the solution to their problem.[13] The process of imagining a time weeks, months, or years hence without the trouble(s) of the past and present is itself a creative task.

Using a similar approach, Ben Furman and Tapani Ahola ask counselees to imagine a time in the future when their problem no longer exists.[14] They talk about that imaginary future time, asking questions such as "How is your life these days?" Discussion revolves around statements such as "Tell me about your (work, marriage, parents, problems)." After a while they ask, "What made all these changes possible?" Usually counselees are able to describe what would have changed in themselves and others in order for the imagined future to occur. The seeds of change lie within those descriptions.

Establishing Future Goals

When people feel hopeless, they need future stories that offer security, excitement, and joy in the moment. Caregivers doing brief pastoral counseling must enable their parishioners to summon their courage, to lean into tomorrow, to compose future stories that capture hope rather than hang onto despair.

In order to help parishioners to construct positive futures, pastoral caregivers first need to help them develop a vision for how their lives might be, as well as specific goals toward achieving that vision. Establishing goals is a critical but sometimes difficult task because so many people seem frozen in the unchangeable past—in Kierkegaard's term, their actuality—and experience little or no freedom.

In brief pastoral counseling, pastors help their troubled counselees to identify objectives that are achievable in a short period of time and to determine how they will reach them. Of course caregivers must challenge any goals that are unethical or superfluous.

The *future question,* a method that I (Stone) find useful in helping people to form goals that express their vision,[15] often teases out peoples' embedded eschatology. It goes like this: "How do you want your life to be different one month (three, six, nine months) from now? Be realistic—take into account your job, family, and finances. Also be very concrete and specific."

So challenged, counselees may respond in any number of ways, such as: "I will sign up for a painting class so I can explore my interest in art and be more involved with other people" or "I will join Al-Anon and learn how to live with my wife's drinking problem" or "I'm going to upgrade my computer skills so I will be eligible for a promotion at work."

There is good reason for encouraging the hope-deprived to choose a specific objective and to work solely on that one task. Change, as Wells noted, "is most likely to ensue from a concentrated focus on a single but significant problem in living (and, conversely, the belief that much natural problem solving is weakened by attempting to deal with too many difficulties simultaneously)."[16] The pastoral caregiver helps parishioners who face an assortment of problems to choose one goal as their highest priority. Since most pastoral counseling is by nature time-limited, its goals also must be modest. Narrowing the focus to one small objective increases the likelihood of positive change.

Imagining a Miracle

Throughout time, human beings have fantasized about changing their lives with the wave of a wand, a magic word, a genie in a bottle, a winning lottery ticket, a stroke of good luck, a miracle. Steve de Shazer and his group take advantage of this human desire and use it for therapeutic purposes. They employ what they call the *miracle question* to spark images about the future,[17] asking counselees to imagine waking up one morning and finding their problem vanished:

> *Your husband no longer uses alcohol.*
> *You and Susan are remarried.*
> *Your depression has lifted.*
> *You weigh only 130 pounds.*
> *You and your mother rarely argue.*

The miracle question may go like this: Suppose you awakened tomorrow morning and your problem was miraculously gone. How would you know? What would be different in your life?

As pastoral caregivers, you can track this new future story with questions that lead to more details: How will life be different? How will your (husband, child, parent, friend) be different? How will you (act, feel, use money) differently? Where will you live? What will you be doing? Finally, they ask what would be necessary to maintain life as described in this new image of the future without the problem. After enabling parishioners to elaborate on these ideas, use their responses to guide counseling interventions and shape revised future stories.

I (Stone) sometimes ask this variation on the miracle question: "Let us suppose that Jesus came to you in the middle of the night and told you that when you awoke your problem would be resolved. How would you know that it was gone? What would you be doing differently? How would you think differently?

How would it change your understanding of God? How would your family or friends know? How would they say that you had changed? How would I recognize the change?"[18]

Furman and Ahola point out that imagining a miracle can transport people beyond their despairing images of the future. For those who contemplate suicide, pastoral caregivers may raise the future issue by asking them to imagine that, having died, they are met at heaven's gate by an angel who announces a reprieve and sends them back to earth with all their problems solved:[19] "What will life be like for you with your problem solved and a chance to start over?" Working with those possibilities, they can begin to construct a future that is workable in the present. (Of course all mention of suicide must be taken seriously, and in such cases the pastor should consult with another professional without delay.)

When parishioners begin to describe a specific problem, often others come tumbling out. Some people misinterpret this "snowball" effect as a sign that long-term therapy or referral is necessary. In fact, it is nothing more than an example of a negative mind-set that dwells upon what is not done rather than on what is done.

We facilitate hope by encouraging individuals not only to envision a new future, but also to develop specific objectives that can move them toward that future.

Guided Imagery

Guided imagery takes advantage of the human capacity for imagination and the ability to project pictures in the mind's eye.[20] It can help people to discover their own future stories and also to reframe, or reconstruct, a new future story.

Counselees first close their eyes and establish a calm, meditative attitude. Once they are relaxed, ask them to choose a time frame and form a mental picture while describing future possibilities. Next, lead them through various images or fantasies that suggest creative new ways of seeing the time to come, and provide further ideas for alternative futures.[21]

Many people find that this exercise facilitates their efforts to project into the future; the resulting narrative will reveal their own visions of the future.

"As If" Conversation

"As if" conversation bypasses the uncertainty of the moment. It assumes certain possibilities that could be true for the sake of postulating how one's future might play out if those possibilities were to occur. It allows the safe consideration of potentially threatening events that may loom on the horizon. Often this method applies when counseling people who are anxious over some uncertainty in their future. Whether they face a threatening diagnosis, bad news from an employer, or significant conflict with an adult child, they fear even thinking about it. Such threats generate less anxiety when discussed as possibilities rather than actualities in a "let us suppose" context.

Some parishioners may ask what you mean by "as if" conversation. Explain that you will set up an imaginary situation related to an issue they face; then the two of you will talk "as if" the simulation is real. Most people are curious enough to participate. To illustrate this (leaving gaps between sentences for responses):

> *Let's suppose that the doctor comes in tomorrow and says that you need open-heart surgery. Now you and I are going to talk. We will assume that it is happening. What will we say to each other after the doctor leaves the room? What will be your response? How will it affect your faith? Your future? Your relationship with your family?*

In this manner, we address a scary future story as a mere possibility, giving counselees the opportunity to explore their responses in advance and discuss possible ways of acting as if the scenario were to become reality.

"As if" conversation also helps people to envision new future stories. It allows pastoral caregivers to dis-empower threatening realities by helping their parishioners create stories based upon additional data, both factual and imaginative. Parishioners can review their future images, add new characters, bring a different twist to the plot, and arrive at different interpretations of the event's meaning for their lives.

Staying in the Future Tense

When working with parishioners who are stuck in the past, bound by the present, or having trouble exploring the future, at some point pastoral caregivers can suggest that for a specific time the conversation be limited to the future tense. For example:

> *Juanita, when I ask you to talk about the future, we seem to end up talking about what has already happened or what is happening now instead of what is yet to happen. For the next twenty minutes, I would like to limit our conversation to the future. Would you agree to that condition?*

Most individuals readily agree. Arrange a signal to cue them, such as: "If you switch to past or present situations, I will hold up my hand to alert you that we have abandoned the future."

At other times the entire session can be reserved for the future tense:

> *During our next session I want us to do something different. I want us only to focus on your future, not your past or the present. Everything we talk about will refer to what is ahead of you and your part in it, not what is behind you and not what is upon you. So you might want to think this coming week about how you want to see your future.*

Exploring the future is in itself a hopeful exercise for brief pastoral counseling. We find that as we nudge parishioners into a discussion of the future, thereby open that dimension of life to exploration, it contributes positively to hope. Even when we discover frightening future stories, the act of making them speakable seems to move the conversation from supportive pastoral care to pastoral counseling.

God's Call to an Open-Ended Future

We proclaim the good news that God brought into existence a world that is "on the way," in Gabriel Marcel's words. Creation is in process toward an open-ended future. As pastoral caregivers we represent the God who is both with us and out in front of us calling, inviting, even challenging us to move into this future. As Jürgen Moltmann put it, "God is the one who accompanies us and beckons us to set out. And it is God who, so to speak, waits for us around the next corner. . . . Even on the false paths we take in life God continually opens up surprisingly new possibilities to us."[22]

The living God does not beckon from behind, trapping us in history, but pulls us toward the horizons of promise and fulfillment. Authentic existence means looking beyond our immediate necessities or past liabilities, anticipating the future with the awareness that we have freedom—however limited—to actualize who we ought to become as faithful Christians. As such, we bear responsibility for shaping that future.

~

Ministers offering brief pastoral counseling to troubled people need to ignite hope—a hope that recognizes the past, takes action in the present, and moves into the future. Through the use of specific caregiving methods such as reframing, establishing goals, storytelling, tracking and expanding future stories, guided imagery, the miracle question, "as if" conversation, staying in the future tense, and envisioning the future without the problem, we can help those who seek our counsel to create a new outcome.

To act is to recapture hope and thereby to revive faith.

Notes

1. This chapter is based on Andrew D. Lester, *Hope in Pastoral Care and Counseling* (Louisville, Ky.: Westminster/John Knox, 1995); and Howard W. Stone, *Depression and Hope: New Insights for Pastoral Counseling* (Minneapolis: Fortress Press, 1998).

2. Howard W. Stone, *Theological Context of Pastoral Caregiving* (New York: Haworth, 1996), 115–24.

3. Viktor E. Frankl, *Psychotherapy and Existentialism* (New York: Washington Square, 1967), 5–14.

4. Irvin D. Yalom, *Existential Psychotherapy* (New York: Basic, 1980), 445.

5. Jürgen Moltmann, *Theology of Hope*, trans. James W. Leitch (New York: Harper & Row, 1975), 286.

6. Ibid., 286–87.

7. William F. Lynch, *Images of Hope: Imagination as Healer of the Hopeless* (Baltimore: Helicon, 1965), 24.

8. Richard Bandler and John Grinder, *Reframing: Neuro-Linguistic Programming and the Transformation of Meaning*, ed. Steve Andreas and Connirae Andreas (Moab, Utah: Real People Press, 1982).

9. For a summary, see Donald Capps, *Reframing: A New Method in Pastoral Care* (Minneapolis: Fortress Press, 1990).

10. Michele Weiner-Davis, Steve de Shazer, and Wallace J. Gingerich, "Building on Pretreatment Changes to Construct the Therapeutic Solution: An Exploratory Study," *Journal of Marital and Family Therapy* 13, no. 4 (1987): 359–63.

11. Lester, *Hope in Pastoral Care.*

12. Richard A. Gardner, *Psychotherapy with Children of Divorce* (New York: Jason Aronson, 1976), 58–59.

13. William H. O'Hanlon and Michele Weiner-Davis, *In Search of Solutions: A New Direction in Psychotherapy* (New York: Norton, 1989), 106–10. Also see Steve de Shazer, *Clues: Investigating Solutions in Brief Therapy* (New York: Norton, 1988), 51.

14. Ben Furman and Tapani Ahola, *Solution Talk: Hosting Therapeutic Conversations* (New York: Norton, 1992), 91–106.

15. Howard W. Stone, *Depression and Hope: New Insights for Pastoral Counseling* (Minneapolis: Fortress Press, 1998), 57.

16. R. Wells, *Planned Short-Term Treatment* (New York: Free Press, 1982).

17. See Steve de Shazer, *Putting Differences to Work* (New York: Norton, 1991); Howard Stone, *Brief Pastoral Counseling* (Minneapolis: Fortress Press, 1994), 26.

18. Stone, *Depression and Hope*, 57.

19. Furman and Ahola, *Solution Talk*, 102–3.

20. See Joseph E. Shorr, Gail E. Sobel, Pennee Robin, and Jack A. Connella, *Imagery: Its Many Dimensions and Applications* (New York: Plenum, 1980).

21. Some creative techniques can also be gleaned from Ira Progoff in *The Dynamics of Hope: Perspectives of Process in Anxiety and Creativity, Imagery and Dreams* (New York: Dialogue House Library, 1985).

22. Jürgen Moltmann, foreword to *The Origins of the Theology of Hope* by M. Douglas Meeks (Philadelphia: Fortress Press, 1974), x.

5

Extending Hospitality in Brief Pastoral Counseling

Katherine Godby

IN A RARE QUIET MOMENT at her desk one Sunday afternoon, Pastor Mary Taylor took a moment to reflect on the couple just leaving. She felt vaguely disturbed about what she had heard during their short meeting. Karen and Steve Jones had approached her during the coffee hour because of problems with their eighteen-year-old daughter, Laura. Pastor Taylor had told them she had about fifteen minutes and invited them to her office to hear what was going on.

"Laura's stubborn. She's lazy. She's a totally unmotivated, smart-mouthed brat," Steve had sputtered angrily, an assessment of Laura completely at odds with Pastor Taylor's impression of her as a fairly quiet, but active and friendly young woman. "She's three months from graduation—*if* she can pull that off—and not a plan in her head about anything!"

Karen's concern seemed to center on the increasingly bitter feud between father and daughter. "They fight all the time, Pastor. Steve is constantly on her case—well, we both are, really," Karen had remarked. "She's intelligent, of course, but she refuses to study. She tells me one thing and then turns right around and willfully does the opposite—just to spite me, I know."

After hearing their complaints for a few more minutes and determining to her satisfaction that Laura's behavior was not physically dangerous to herself or anyone else, Pastor Taylor found an hour in her schedule on Thursday and arranged for the family, including Laura, to meet with her then. As Steve and Karen left her office, she wondered about family relationships in light of her sermon on hospitality that morning. Preparing the sermon had opened her eyes about the need for relating to others with respect. It seemed to Pastor Taylor that Steve and Karen were judging Laura harshly and certainly not "creating space" for her with an "attitude acknowledging their own poverty," as she had preached only hours earlier.

61

Gathering her things and leaving the office in a suddenly grouchy mood, Pastor Taylor wondered how in the world to approach her meeting with the Jones family next week. "It sounds like more than I can handle," she thought. "Maybe I'll refer them."

Although most ministers want to offer pastoral counseling, like Mary Taylor they may find themselves hesitant. One reason is that, even though parishioners frequently approach them for help,[1] pastors may refer all but the simplest problems to outside therapists because they doubt their own training or ability to counsel. However, pastors can learn and make use of brief pastoral counseling methods to address the vast majority of parishioners' counseling issues without referral.[2] Like anything worthwhile, brief pastoral counseling requires effort and commitment, but most ministers find it to be within their powers when they adopt its underlying epistemological and attitudinal assumptions.

Pastors also may feel that they lack the time to counsel, under the mistaken impression that effective counseling requires a long-term commitment. Yet research consistently shows that parishioners want counseling to be brief (for our purposes, fewer than ten sessions), and that short-term counseling is just as effective as long-term approaches.[3] Pastors use brief methods successfully in marriage and family counseling as well as cases involving grief, stress, problem drinking, depression, anxiety, and more.

Many pastors assume that brief pastoral counseling is somewhat at odds with their calling—that it is not particularly pastoral. This was once true for me. My inclination to help people slow down and pay attention to what really matters did not seem a particularly good fit with brief pastoral counseling. I thought that short-term counseling would contribute further to our culture's overemphasis on the value of speed and efficiency. Becoming acquainted with the church's tradition of hospitality changed my mind.

Hospitality

In the historic notion of Christian hospitality, I found a bridge that links brief pastoral counseling to a truly pastoral way of thinking about it and prevents it from becoming mechanistic. Hospitality has played an important role in the history of the church. It is an important sub-theme in the Bible. Scriptural hospitality is a relationship in which host and guest alike have something to offer; one can easily bring to mind stories in the Hebrew Scriptures when the graciousness of a host was richly rewarded. The host offers shelter, safety, and succor, but the guest also offers gifts of one kind or another. The New Testament builds on those ancient traditions as its writers forge an understanding of Christian community. Our obligation to welcome the stranger has continued to play a role both pastorally and in the Christian moral life.

Unfortunately, in the past century hospitality has lost much of its significance not only in our culture but in the church as well. Henri Nouwen writes of a society "increasingly full of fearful, defensive, aggressive people anxiously clinging to their property and inclined to look at their surrounding world with suspicion, always expecting an enemy to suddenly appear, intrude and do harm."[4]

Clearly it is time to renew our attention to Christian hospitality, especially in the field of pastoral care. As Nouwen points out, it is our vocation. A particularly helpful and practical way for pastors to do that is to integrate into their ministry the principles and methods of brief pastoral counseling, for its assumptions lend themselves to a renewal of hospitality in ministry and in Christian life.

This chapter will link brief pastoral counseling and Christian hospitality by exploring four areas: epistemology, attitude, power relationships, and eschatology. In relation to these areas, I will examine Pastor Taylor's initial reflections on the presented case, explore the applicable assumptions inherent in brief pastoral counseling,[5] and touch upon ways in which pastors can use brief pastoral counseling methods in the perspective of Christian hospitality. (The reader is referred to other chapters in this book for more complete discussions of these brief pastoral counseling methods.)

We begin with the notion underlying any understanding of hospitality and of counseling: that it is important to maintain a degree of uncertainty about what we can know.

Epistemology

As the Thursday appointment with the family approached, Pastor Taylor spent some time reflecting on their initial meeting. It occurred to her that Steve and Karen felt they knew Laura completely. Their certainty seemed to justify an insistence that she conform to their notions of what was best for her future. Pastor Taylor wondered if they had heard her sermon at all. She had spoken of hospitality's requirement of living life as an adventure, uncertain of how the stranger at your door might change your world.

Thinking and knowing are important to pastors. It is part of our role and, quite often, even our identity. The *Herr Pastor* of another age may have become "Pastor Barb" or "Pastor Bob," approachable and casually dressed, but still speaking with authority on matters of faith.

In seeming contradiction to that role, pastors doing brief pastoral counseling (like hosts offering hospitality) take a not-knowing stance. They remain open to the myriad ways in which parishioners will surprise them. This stance arises from brief pastoral counseling's roots in the postmodern theory of social constructionism in which we cannot know what is objectively real but construct a social reality as we relate to others and engage them in conversation. Radical constructionists maintain that there are no external verities, that no reality exists outside of our own subjectivity. Most pastoral counselors using brief therapy modalities shy away from this radical position. They believe that reality does exist—that there are absolutes—but they recognize the wisdom in the social constructionists' view. People bring us their perceptions of experiences and problems, not concrete and measurable facts. Their interpretation of reality is hugely skewed by their chemistry, biology, beliefs, past experience, and chance, to name only a few of the infinite, variable influences on human perception.[6]

The assumption that we know the meanings that others attribute to their experience carries within it a kind of hidden violence. It is a refusal to acknowledge that God has bestowed the gift of life on them in unique ways that may be invisible to us until they emerge in conversation. In adopting a not-knowing stance, pastors do not discount their own knowledge and experience. Rather, for a short time they bracket or set aside their assessment in order to listen more fully to what an experience means for this unique person. The effort to cultivate genuine curiosity struggles against the ubiquitous pressures of a culture in which smart people categorize, diagnose, and predict. Like everyone else, pastors want to appear knowledgeable and authoritative. Adopting the not-knowing stance, and the genuine curiosity it entails, challenges our desire to look proficient and our need for control.

Henri Nouwen beautifully articulated the not-knowing stance when writing about the movement from hostility to hospitality as one of the basic tenets of the spiritual life. Often masquerading as hostility, fear of the Other is something we all experience. Yet it is obligatory for Christians to provide an environment (physical and emotional) in which the Other ceases to be a stranger.[7] Hospitality creates space in which guests freely come and go on their own terms. To provide this freedom, however, requires hosts to be at home with their own poverty of mind:

> Someone who is filled with ideas, concepts, opinions and convictions cannot be a good host. There is no inner space to listen, no openness to discover the gift of the other. It is not difficult to see how those who "know it all" can kill a conversation and prevent an interchange of ideas. Poverty of the mind as a spiritual attitude is a growing willingness to recognize the incomprehensibility of the mystery of life.[8]

Another ally in the struggle for genuine curiosity and a not-knowing stance appears in the New Testament view of hospitality. According to John Koenig, Luke portrayed house church communities as the "creative hub" of God's redemptive work, "lively and winsome, filled with the Spirit and ready for adventure."[9] Luke prepared his readers for mission by urging partnership between the itinerant prophets (guests) who followed Jesus in the world, and the residential believers (hosts) who focused their lives and faith in the house church communities.[10] Living their lives as an adventure in hospitality, these early Christians welcomed strangers during a time of persecution. Opening the door to welcome others was a daring act of saying yes to what they could not know in advance, to the unfamiliar and new. From our forebears in the faith we learn that to offer true hospitality requires a curiosity born of excitement at the bold prospect of adventure.

In the case of the Jones family, their pastor thought that the parents were taking a knowing stance toward their daughter and closing the door to the new and unfamiliar. From her work in preparing the sermon on hospitality, Pastor Taylor assessed that Steve and Karen's certainty about Laura lessened the possibility of discovering their daughter's unique world of meaning. It is important to note, however, that Pastor Taylor does not easily apply the lessons of hospitality to herself and generally opts for a knowing stance toward her parishioners. This made it difficult for her to understand what parenting really means to Steve and Karen. She overlooked the possibility that her impression of their daughter as "quiet and friendly" might bear little resemblance to Laura's behavior toward her parents. Bracketing her judgments, at least for a while, would enable Pastor Taylor to cultivate genuine curiosity about this family's perceptions and meanings.

An all-too-human need to appear proficient in front of her parishioners might have contributed to Pastor Taylor's initial move into the knowing stance. Coupled with the fear that she lacks knowledge and skills in counseling, her need might well have caused her to consider a too-hasty referral of the Jones family to professional therapists. Instead of feeling their lack of qualifications and rushing to refer, hosts who are at home with their own poverty more easily set aside their personal concerns and take time to indulge a genuine curiosity about their parishioners' experience.

Pastors endeavoring to combine brief pastoral counseling with a sense of themselves as hosts, comfortable with their own poverty, might wonder what it is really like for Steve and Karen to be parents. They recognize that there is much they do not know, and therefore might raise specific questions such as: What are your dreams for Laura? What are your fears for her? When you argue, what are your exact words? What does she say in reply? How often does this happen (three times a day, three times a week)? Is there any way in which Laura is realizing your dreams for her, such as grades in at least one class or work performance at her part-time job? What would you like to be different about your relationship with Laura? How will you know when the problem is solved? How are you already experiencing a tiny bit of what you want?[11] Rather than imposing their own knowledge and ideas of what family life ought to be like, ministers doing brief pastoral counseling genuinely want to know what their parishioners expect from pastoral counseling. They ask questions such as: Tell me more about exactly what you want from counseling. What is your goal for coming here? When would you like this to happen?

Attitude

From their tones of voice as well as from their words, Pastor Taylor suspected that Steve and Karen had been worrying about Laura and arguing with her for so long that their attitudes had become closed, fixed, unnecessarily pessimistic. In her sermon that Sunday, she had preached that the attitude of hospitality is one of openness and trust, and that it carries within it an expectation that strangers have gifts to bestow. "I wonder what gifts Laura and her parents offer each other? For that matter," she realized with a start, "what gifts do I offer this family, and they to me?"

Along with the not-knowing stance, adopting an open and optimistic attitude is important for offering hospitably and to the overall effectiveness of brief pastoral counseling. Cultivating this attitude means trusting that God is already at work in our parishioners.[12] In doing so we naturally look for signs of what God has already accomplished in them, and we listen for clues that tell us how God is now inviting them into a new future. When we trust that God calls people toward what is best for them in each situation and provides unique gifts and talents that empower them to move forward, we find ways to assist that movement, for example:

Look for exceptions to the problem. People tend to perceive that the problem never lets up. "They fight all the time, pastor," Karen said. Yet ministers using brief pastoral counseling understand that people filter experience and choose what they pay attention to. Sometimes exercising curiosity about those times when the problem is absent or abates a bit will open up new vistas. In the first fifteen-minute conversation with Steve and Karen, for example, Pastor Taylor might have suggested that, as a homework task to do before the first counseling session, they simply notice when the problem lessens or is not present. Thinking about times when peace reigns in the household would move the couple toward a more open attitude.

Sometimes parishioners have difficulty remembering any exceptions to a problem. When that happens, I often invite them to tell me about times when the problem is less severe or has a different quality to it.[13] Any chink in the wall, however small, opens a view beyond.

Look for strengths and competencies. Because we are curious to know how God has already empowered people to move forward, we focus on their resources and abilities instead of their deficiencies and pathologies. A good time to inquire about strengths and competencies occurs right after parishioners have identified an exception. I might say something like, "Given the magnitude of the problem as you've described it, I'm curious about how you were able to stand against it like that." This often elicits a forgotten talent or resource that we then talk about at length. I also invite parishioners to reflect on the meaning of their ability to defeat the problem. "What does it say about you that you were able to do that?"

Assume that change is always happening. People tend to perceive themselves and others as possessing fixed qualities or being a certain way. "I am short-tempered." "She is lazy." Pastors using brief pastoral counseling resist such labeling because they understand that change is inevitable. Even though people may exhibit certain tendencies, is it not a denial of God's influence in the world and of our own human agency to assume that they remain the same forever? One effective way to subtly challenge parishioners' restrictive, problematic labeling of themselves or others is to substitute forms of the verb "to be" with more active verbs.[14] When Steve said, "She's totally unmotivated," the pastor might respond, "So, you say Laura acts as if fewer things interest her." "She is lazy" might be restated as "She seldom helps with household tasks and rarely finishes her homework."

When we remember that change is inevitable, optimism flows more easily. God has built healing into the very nature of things. Moshe Talmon explains "the natural process of change" as "what is already there (natural), the healing role of time and movement (process), and the inevitable change that is already well under way. . . . There is an incredible therapeutic power hidden in these processes."[15] Taking natural healing into account means that pastors will not overlook the value of uncomplicated suggestions like getting regular exercise or taking a few extra breaks during a hectic day.[16] Since change is inevitable and God constantly seeks to influence us, these simple acts may have great impact even in the face of a seemingly huge problem.

Adopting an optimistic and open attitude fits the Christian view of hospitality. It requires that we empty ourselves of things like pessimism, fear, and defensive attitudes. By so doing we free up space for others. When we allow the creation of space for others, the promise and gifts they offer delightfully surprise us.[17]

Biblical narratives beautifully demonstrate this attitude of openly and optimistically seeking to discover the promise and the gifts of strangers. The story of Rebekah's brother Laban inviting Abraham's servant into the house before knowing his purpose comes to mind (Gen. 24:29-33), as well as the story of

Jesus meeting the two disciples on the road to Emmaus (Luke 24:13-35). In perhaps the most commonly cited story of hospitality in the Hebrew Scriptures, the Lord appears to Abraham and Sarah by the oaks of Mamre in the form of three strangers (Gen. 18:1-21). Abraham runs to meet them, bows down to the ground, and invites them to rest and refresh themselves in the shade of the trees. He offers them water to wash their feet, then asks Sarah to prepare cakes while he runs to the herd and chooses a calf, tender and good. As he stands by them while they eat, having performed the duties of hospitality with obvious openness and trust, they promise him the gift of a son. According to Rabbi Daniel Wolk, this story makes it clear that when we offer hospitality to others, anything is possible. "For Abraham, the son Isaac was a harbinger of a great nation, of a father's future. Be open to the world and rewards will follow, rewards more wondrous than dreams. Close yourself off and the future is barren; open yourself and the future will be born."[18]

Throughout ancient notions of hospitality lies the idea of the stranger as a divine being in disguise. The guest receives the best the host has to offer, and plenty of it—not just water and cakes, but the calf, tender and good, as well. The host acts out of trust that God has built a "secret abundance" into the heart of reality that will amply fulfill everyone's needs.[19] Metaphorically as well as literally, trusting in God's abundance allows us to empty ourselves of fear and rigidity and to move into life with open arms.

Emptying ourselves of pessimism and defensiveness can sometimes be a difficult task. The practice of brief pastoral counseling can hasten the task because of its underlying assumptions: that God is already at work in the parishioner, that there are exceptions to the problem (however small), that change always occurs, and that natural healing is a real phenomenon present in every human situation—assumptions that reflect God's secret abundance, built into the heart of reality. Furthermore, brief pastoral counseling assumes that all people possess resident strengths and competencies—thus fostering our expectation that all people bear the gift of Christ as well as our curiosity about how that gift is uniquely manifested in each person.

Power Relationships

Pastor Taylor found herself curious about the meaning of the arguments between Laura and her father. She mused, "I wonder whether Steve believes he has a moral responsibility to use his power to push her toward certain avenues in life." This led her to wonder about her own use of power in counseling situations, especially since she had just preached about violating God's hospitality in the seemingly endless human quest for power and control.

Colonialism

Pastors using brief counseling assume that the parishioner is the expert, not the pastor. This assumption is a necessary one if the power dynamics in the room are to contribute to mutuality and not to a subtle oppression of the parishioner. Therapists Amundsen, Stewart, and Valentine use the metaphor of colonialism to describe these dynamics:

> Clients arrive for the therapeutic encounter rich in the "resources" of suffering and complaint. Like an underdeveloped nation, the client is ripe for colonization. This can occur as the therapist selects for attention those features of the client's story which articulate the therapist's predisposition or expert knowledge. From a position of power/certainty—supported by . . . the therapist's own need to adhere to certain theories about the client and therapy—the therapist ventures forth as colonizer. Therapy begins with the therapist having the upper hand.[20]

Pastors often dismiss this crucial point because we simply do not see ourselves as potential colonizers or subjugators of our parishioners. Yet the colonizing power that automatically grants us the upper hand is subtle and tempting. To counter it requires a conscious effort toward mutuality.

Agency

Pastors adopting brief counseling approaches move toward this mutuality of relationship by focusing on parishioners' agency. This includes several steps:

Ensuring that parishioners set the goals. Since we cannot know the meaning of others' experience, we cannot be the experts on their lives. They know what goals for counseling are most appropriate for them. I often begin sessions with questions such as: "What results would you like to accomplish today?" "When our time together is finished, what would you like to be doing differently?" "How will you know that you have defeated this problem?"

If parishioners find their goals for counseling difficult to articulate, therapist Steve de Shazer's miracle question may help. "If a miracle happened tonight while you were asleep and tomorrow morning you awoke to find that this problem were no longer a part of your life, what would be different?" It may be that envisioning a future without the problem is all parishioners need to help them see more clearly what they want.[21]

Complimenting parishioners. Most people who have taught or raised children have witnessed the empowering effect of compliments. It is by no means limited to childhood. Carefully used compliments assure parishioners of their own abilities, affirm and accept, and minimize the frustration of setbacks in progress.[22] To do their work, of course, compliments need to be specific and

concrete. Vague praise ("You did a great job last week!") is less helpful and cred-
ible than detailed feedback ("I am impressed that you were able to come up
with an exception to the problem every day in the very first week"). Usually pastors can offer sincere compliments about the courage it took for parishioners to
come in, the determination they have shown in working to resolve the problem
on their own,[23] ways in which the pastor has benefited and learned from them,
the actions they have already taken to ease the pain, or their refusal to give up.[24]

   Aligning with parishioners against the problem. Pastors adopting brief pastoral counseling assumptions do not see the parishioner as the problem.
Instead, we see the *problem* as the problem, and we align ourselves with the
parishioner against it. How many times have we heard people say that a former
counselor told them they were "codependent" or "angry"? Ministers seeking to
empower others separate the problem from the person; the parishioner is a
human being who happens to be behaving in a way that may be interpreted as
too dependent or angry. I speak to them in language that conveys my understanding that they have agency against the problem.[25] For example: "I'm curious about the strategies you are using against the depression," or "When anger
threatens, how do you typically stand against it?" This frees parishioners to see
their resources, strengths, and special knowledge more easily.

Guests and Hosts

Although a focus on empowering others may be our preferred way of working
with parishioners, the lure to colonize may call our name in seductive ways. To
resist this call, pastors need to develop an abiding sense of Christian hospitality, as God's guests and as hosts to others.

   The biblical story of the fall in the Garden of Eden offers a powerful illustration. In this narrative, the host—God—has graciously prepared for our visit with
the finest of care, attending to our physical needs, our aesthetic needs, and our
need for community. But in a brazen move, we attempt a coup. We turn our backs
on God's hospitality. We insult our host with constant worry about whether our
physical needs will be met. We come to think that we own the beautiful sur-
roundings, and so we rape and plunder them at will. We ignore the delicate balance between community and autonomy, instead seeking power over others and
things. In violating our role as guests of God, we conveniently forget that temporality and finitude limit our stay—that we are pilgrims, not full residents.

   The story of the fall reminds us that we are all guests of God, a role carrying within it a requirement to receive, not take, and in that sense embodying a
certain passivity. For pastors who generally find ourselves in the role of host,
with all its temptations for colonizing power, this is a needed lesson.

   The role of host actually embodies some complex energies,[26] and further
reflection on it might help us invite mutuality. Hosts wait with eager anticipa-

tion for the guests to arrive, aware that others bear the gift of Christ to enrich them in surprising ways. Hosts also reside in their homes, with all the centeredness, abundance, and jurisdiction that implies. These two types of energies imply passivity, yet hosts actively invite guests into their home and create space in which guests may freely do and be. The power implied in this initiative, however, is paradoxical (writes Nouwen) in that

> it wants to create emptiness, not a fearful emptiness, but a friendly emptiness where strangers can enter and discover themselves as created free; free to sing their own songs, speak their own languages . . . free also to leave and follow their own vocations. Hospitality is not a subtle invitation to adopt the lifestyle of the host, but the gift of a chance for the guest to find his own. . . . Hospitality is not to change people, but to offer them space where change can take place.[27]

As understood from an abiding sense of hospitality, God's gift of human freedom may be the ultimate example of the paradox of power in the role of host. God desires an intimate relationship with us, yet eschews outright power over us in favor of our freedom. Here is the role of host, perfectly fulfilled. In a sense, God takes the initiative, the active role as host by creating a home, inviting us in, and giving us freedom. Yet God also takes the host's passive role, patiently waiting as we wander around deciding whether or not to accept the invitation.

As brief pastoral counselors seeking to alleviate the imbalance of power between us and our parishioners, we endeavor to understand the role of host. We learn from the fall that ultimately we are all guests. And we learn from reflecting on the complex energies of the host role that often we must simply wait and reside. Hospitality teaches us that ultimately power is only powerful when it is relinquished.

Offering care from this unity of host and guest, we seek to foster mutuality in relationship with our parishioners. Pastors who understand the role of host from hospitality's perspective more easily make space for people to set their own goals. Aware that we are all guests, we align ourselves with parishioners against the problem, and we offer genuine compliments that acknowledge the inherent value of the other's agency and worldview. When we embody the complex energies of the host in doing brief pastoral counseling, we do not assume an epistemology that says, "I know who this person is or what this person should do." Often we simply wait, curious and open, while parishioners consider our offer of hospitable space. It is there that, with our respectful help, we hope they will begin to see options, move forward, and then leave and follow their own vocations.

Eschatology

As she continued her reflection on their initial meeting, Pastor Taylor wondered to herself how Steve, Karen, and Laura might come to see each other in a
new way. "If they could ease their rigid views, these escalating arguments might
end and they could find a new way. Hospitality offers a doorway into seeing and
acting differently. If only they had heard that in my sermon."

We have seen that the theme of hospitality recurs throughout biblical literature and in many ancient cultures. It also appears as a persistent theme in the
fine arts. Near the end of the film *Babette's Feast,* the sophisticated General
Loewenhielm is a guest at a dinner party in the home of two elderly sisters, prepared by their housekeeper and cook, Babette. Some twelve years earlier,
Babette, a refugee from political unrest in France, had stumbled into their little
village on a stormy night, bedraggled and in shock, requesting refuge in the sisters' meager home. They welcomed her as an act of Christian charity. Although
the letter of introduction she bore only casually mentioned, "Babette can cook,"
she had in fact been the chef at a renowned Parisian restaurant. For all these
years Babette had humbly prepared each meal as the sisters requested, serving
their standard, dreary fare of dried cod and ale-bread soup.

When Babette wins ten thousand francs in the lottery, she decides to spend it
all on a sumptuous dinner for the sisters and their guests who, excepting the general, are all that remains of their late father's congregation and whose bitter arguments have produced intolerance and schisms among them. Only the general is
able to appreciate the magnificence of the feast. As one savory course follows
another, he finds himself suddenly aware of a great truth. He rises and
announces:

> Mercy and truth have met together. Righteousness and bliss shall kiss
> one another . . . We in our weakness believe we must make choices in
> life. We tremble at the risk; we know fear. But, No! Our choice is of no
> importance. There comes a time when our eyes are opened, and we
> come to realize that mercy is infinite. We need only await it with con-
> fidence and receive it in gratitude.[28]

The meaning of hospitality is then made clear when the sisters and their
guests realize that the infinite grace of which General Loewenhielm speaks has
been allotted to them, and they do not even wonder at the fact, for it is but the
fulfillment of an ever-present hope. The vain illusions of this earth have dis-
solved before their eyes like smoke, and they see the universe as it really is. They
have been given one hour of the millennium.[29] Their arguments and intolerance cease. The sisters and their guests are healed.

This story illustrates an eschatological view of reality in which our problems dissolve when we reconstruct our perceptions of them. Remember that brief pastoral counseling borrows from social constructionism the notion that we build our reality as we relate to others and engage them in conversation. We need to keep our eyes open, to see and seek new data, to continually recreate ourselves and our relationships. In our role as pastoral counselors, we work together with parishioners to interpret experience in a way that allows for positive change.[30]

This co-creating of reality helps parishioners reframe their experience and give it new meaning. (See chapters 4 and 7 for a more complete explanation of reframing.) Reframing occurs when we look at a situation from another point of view, see an event in a new light, ascribe different motivations to the actions of another. When people are stuck in their perception of a problem, they often repeat the same unsuccessful behaviors, unable to let go of the belief that these behaviors *should* solve things. I often urge parishioners to do something different. "It doesn't matter so much what you do; just break out of this cycle of more of the same behaviors that aren't helping." Frequently they come back reporting that their whole perception of the situation has changed.

Reframing can occur in simple ways. For example, it is not particularly uncommon for parishioners to tell me something like, "Pastor, I can't seem to find any joy in anything any more; I feel like God has abandoned me." As we talk, I might discover that they spend their free time gardening, or collecting pretty china cups and saucers, or creating wreaths for special occasions. I often respond by sharing my own belief that God inhabits beauty, and I wonder about their sense of God's presence as they go about working with and creating these lovely things. For some, this new way of considering things opens them to a healing experience of God's presence, and they catch a glimpse of the reign of God, an already but not-yet experience.

In Jesus' healing ministry, we find many examples of reframing. The blind beggar Bartimaeus (Mark 10:46-52) hears that Jesus is passing by and shouts for his attention. He won't shut up. When Jesus calls for him he jumps up, throws off his cloak and pleads, "My teacher, let me see again." Jesus reframes Bartimaeus's clamoring demands: "Go; your faith has made you well." The hemorrhaging woman (Mark 5:25-34) covertly touches Jesus' garment, an act others might interpret as desperation, but Jesus reframes it as faith. She too is healed.[31] These New Testament narratives make it clear that Jesus saw what was there all along—the secret abundance built into the heart of reality. What was *not-yet* to Bartimaeus and the hemorrhaging woman was *already* to Jesus.

To move into awareness of God's grace, of that secret abundance that surrounds us, is to enter a new reality where pain can mysteriously change into joy or, to put it more mundanely, where problems dissolve or become opportunities for growth. Yet it is perilous business to think that we can predict such transformations, or that a particular counseling technique can bring them about routinely. Even in the abundance of God's kingdom that surrounded Jesus, there was vulnerability and danger. Koenig notes that in the violent deaths of John the Baptist and Jesus, "the kingdom itself suffers violence. Powerful as it is, it enters into human affairs as a stranger, subject to injury from many of those who are meant to be its guests and hosts."[32]

The parallel danger in brief pastoral counseling's co-creation of solutions and new realities is that the pastor, in a rush to see people healed, may disregard other important tenets of both brief counseling and hospitality. We cannot be certain about others' experiences, the meaning they attribute to them, or what adventures await in our encounters with the unfamiliar. We may disregard the importance of an open and optimistic attitude and turn our desire to see God's healing into an attitude that subtly demands it. Within that demand is a covert play for power that only serves to abuse the delicate workings of the spirit. Hospitality requires that, as guests of God, we let go of our closed and fixed views in favor of an attitude that expects epiphany but does not demand it.

The Case for Hospitality and Brief Pastoral Counseling

In the days between Sunday and Thursday, Mary Taylor's reflections led her to consider her own need to extend hospitality to the Jones family. Her recent attention to hospitality in sermon preparation focused her attention not only on the hospitality issues facing this family, but on ways she could open up a space for them, could come to understand their struggles and guide them toward mutual goals for Laura and for their family life. She did not refer them to a mental health therapist. While fully adopting a not-knowing stance remains an issue calling for more work on her part, Pastor Taylor's reflections imply that she is well on her way toward confident and effective pastoral counseling, not only with the Jones family, but with all of her parishioners.

At the heart of the incorporation of hospitality into brief pastoral counseling lies a profound respect for those who seek our help as well as an expectation that, in some mysterious way, as we experience others we may experience Christ. By highlighting genuine curiosity, optimism, and openness, brief pastoral counseling helps ministers understand that we all share the same human condition, that we are all broken and in need of healing. Host and guest alike share the healing enterprise. Our first act as healers is to create enough space within ourselves so that we can receive our guests and hear their story, so that we can offer them a similarly open space in which they can express their pain and find a new way.[33]

With this understanding of hospitality guiding us, we offer ourselves to others courageously and adventurously as vehicles of God's healing grace.

Notes

1. Frank Thomas and Jack Cockburn, *Competency-Based Counseling: Building on Client Strengths* (Minneapolis: Fortress Press, 1998), 16. The authors cite numerous research studies indicating that that "clergy are as likely as mental health providers to be sought out even for major mental health concerns" and that "a majority of ministers appear assured of being engaged in a certain amount of counseling."

2. Some problems, of course, do require referral. In *Brief Pastoral Counseling: Short-Term Approaches and Strategies* (Minneapolis: Fortress Press, 1994), 163, Howard W. Stone recommends referral for "persons who appear to have a genetic, biological, chemical, or neurological problem, persons who need in-patient care, those who want long-term care and are not willing or able to modify their expectations, people who need to be under the primary care of a physician for medication, and individuals who have considerable difficulty establishing a relationship and are reticent to accept help."

3. Mary P. Koss and Julia Shiang, "Research on Brief Psychotherapy," in S. L. Garfield and A. E. Bergin, *Handbook of Psychotherapy and Behavior Change*, 4th ed. (New York: Wiley, 1994), 664. The authors note that "brief treatment methods have . . . been shown to be effective in treating a wide range of psychological . . . problems" and that brief treatment methods have "generally reported the same success rates as longer treatment programs."

4. Henri J. M. Nouwen, *Reaching Out: The Three Movements of the Spiritual Life* (Garden City, N.Y.: Doubleday, 1975), 46.

5. Although this chapter draws mostly on solution-focused brief therapy arising from the work of secular theorists and practitioners such as Steve de Shazer, Insoo Kim Berg, Scott Miller, Michele Weiner-Davis, and Bill O'Hanlon, other types of brief therapy are available. The reader may be interested in investigating brief therapy from the analytical, cognitive, or behavioral modalities as well.

6. Thomas and Cockburn, *Competency-Based Counseling*, 12. This work is an example of brief counseling from a pastoral perspective. Other brief pastoral counseling theorists and practitioners the reader may wish to investigate include Howard W. Stone, Brian Childs, and Charles Allen Kollar.

7. Nouwen, *Reaching Out*, 46.

8. Ibid., 74.

9. John Koenig, *New Testament Hospitality: Partnership with Strangers as Promise and Mission* (Philadelphia: Fortress Press, 1985), 106.

10. Ibid., chap. 4.

11. John L. Walter and Jane E. Peller, "Rethinking Our Assumptions: Assuming Anew in a Postmodern World," in Scott Miller et al., eds., *Handbook of Solution-Focused Brief Therapy* (San Francisco: Jossey-Bass, 1996), 20.

12. Charles Allen Kollar, *Solution-Focused Pastoral Counseling: An Effective Short-Term Approach for Getting People Back on Track* (Grand Rapids, Mich.: Zondervan, 1997), 69.

13. See Michele Weiner-Davis, *Divorce Busting* (New York: Simon & Schuster, 1992), 137.

14. Thomas and Cockburn, *Competency-Based Counseling*, 32.

15. Moshe Talmon, *Single-Session Therapy: Maximizing the Effect of the First (and Often Only) Therapeutic Encounter* (San Francisco: Jossey-Bass, 1990), 73.

16. Ibid.

17. Nouwen, *Reaching Out, 51*.

18. Daniel S. Wolk, *"And He Ran to Greet Them,"* *Parabola: The Magazine of Myth and Tradition* 15, no. 4 (November 1990): 83.

19. Koenig, *New Testament Hospitality, 130ff.*

20. Jon Amudson, Kenneth Stewart, and LaNae Valentine, "Temptations of Power and Certainty," *Journal of Marital and Family Therapy* 19, no. 2 (April 1993): 112–13.

21. Due to space limitations, I have opted not to draw attention to the future orientation of both brief pastoral counseling and hospitality. Brief pastoral counseling generally spends little time discussing the past, instead opting to focus on helping parishioners move into the future God intends. I hope it is plain to the reader by now that hospitality also beckons us toward adventure, toward movement into an unknown future.

22. Insoo Kim Berg and Scott D. Miller, *Working with the Problem Drinker: A Solution-Focused Approach* (New York: Norton, 1992), 97–102.

23. Howard W. Stone, *Brief Pastoral Counseling: Short-Term Approaches and Strategies* (Minneapolis: Fortress Press, 1994), 31.

24. Talmon, *Single-Session Therapy, 51, 76*.

25. See Amudson et al., "Temptations of Power and Certainty," 120.

26. Paul Jordan-Smith, "The Hostage and the Parasite," *Parabola: The Magazine of Myth and Tradition* 15, no. 4 (November 1990): 26.

27. Nouwen, *Reaching Out, 51*.

28. *Babette's Feast,* a film written and directed by Gabriel Axel, based on a story by Isak Dinesen (Orion Home Video, 1988).

29. R. Baker, "Surprised by Grace," *Parabola: The Magazine of Myth and Tradition* 15, no. 4 (November 1990): 89. Baker quotes from Isak Dinesen, *Babette's Feast and Other Anecdotes of Destiny,* originally titled *Anecdotes of Destiny* (New York: Vintage, 1953), 40.

30. Kollar, *Solution-Focused Pastoral Counseling, 82*.

31. Donald Capps, *Reframing: A New Method in Pastoral Care* (Minneapolis: Fortress Press, 1990), 65. See chap. 3 for further examples of Jesus' reframing.

32. Koenig, *New Testament Hospitality, 42*.

33. Nouwen, *Reaching Out, 65, 68*.

6

Making Brief Pastoral
Counseling Wholistic

Howard Clinebell

I BEGAN MINISTRY more than forty-five years ago as a parish pastor. I served several Methodist churches on Long Island in New York for about a decade. I had not been there long before I sensed an immense need for pastoral care and pastoral counseling. The longer I was there, the more human need I saw and the more people came to me for help. Rarely, though, did individuals, couples, or families give more than two, three, or four sessions to the counseling. In one sense this was fine with me, because so many other tasks of ministry were vying for my time. But it created dissonance because what I had learned about counseling at this point in my ministry had focused on pathology and assumed a long-term counseling relationship.[1]

Eventually, I felt the need to adopt pastoral counseling methods that were more wholeness-oriented and had a short-term focus. Without realizing it, the seeds for my later work and ultimately for *Basic Types of Pastoral Care and Counseling* were germinating in these day-to-day encounters with members of the parishes I served.

After my years in parish ministry, I served as a hospital chaplain and also the minister of pastoral counseling on the staff of a large urban congregation. Following that, I was a seminary teacher for some three decades, during which I also directed the pastoral counseling and growth center where our doctoral candidates received their advanced supervised training. I have traveled throughout the world, lecturing and leading seminars with pastors and pastoral counselors. These experiences have strengthened my early conviction that the need for counseling in the parish is still great—perhaps greater than when I first began—and that most counseling in the congregational context is brief in nature.

Parish clergy face three realities when they do counseling. First, pastors usually need to use a brief counseling approach, because most counseling in church contexts involves individual and (more often) family *crises* or *losses*. This need calls for a focus on wholeness, strength, and growth rather than exclusively on what is wrong; concentrating on pathology and personality reconstruction is rarely effective in such cases. Brief approaches to pastoral counseling draw on the strengths of human beings, affirming the goodness inherent in creation.

Second, most such counseling *must be limited to a few sessions* because a limited number of sessions is what parishioners want, and parish clergy have an abundance of other vital, wholeness-enhancing ministries to perform. Even if pastors have the needed training to provide longer-term pastoral psychotherapy, they cannot afford the time required to do reconstructive psychotherapy with a few individuals and families, while neglecting the others. It is a matter of justice.

Third, *brief pastoral counseling often can be highly effective* in achieving the goals of those who seek our help. Short-term methods are appropriate for giving persons spiritual and emotional support, evaluating their immediate need for either brief pastoral counseling or referral to a psychotherapy specialist, and coaching them as they learn ways to mobilize coping resources by developing and implementing strategies for handling their problem more constructively, one aspect at a time.

It is good news that the modern pastoral care and counseling movement has become increasingly wholistic and systemic. There are strong indications that such approaches will be increasingly normative; the work of many of the authors in this volume is leading the way. So it is appropriate to ask what constitutes a whole-person (whole-family, whole-society, whole-world) approach to brief pastoral counseling and ministry.

My understanding of healing and growth ministries has evolved in wholistic directions over the past four-plus decades. The horizons of healing and circles of caregiving have gradually grown more inclusive in my thinking, teaching, and practice. This wholistic evolution has led to a seven-dimensional model of pastoral care and counseling. This working paradigm has proved to be a valuable cognitive map, not only for myself, but for many others whom I have had the privilege of teaching and counseling. But as this model has become increasingly wholistic and more widely used by congregational ministers, it has confronted users with a serious dilemma: how can those who do the great bulk of such caregiving—congregational ministers—use a wholistic model effectively when their interventions must be relatively brief? This chapter will offer a way to begin to resolve the dilemma.

Overview of the Seven-Dimension Paradigm

Caregiving and counseling (as well as all ministry) should involve cultivating healing and nurturing the wholeness of those who receive our care in seven interdependent areas of their lives. These seven areas constitute what John describes in his Gospel as "life in all its fullness" (John 10:10 LB).

Spirit

Wholistic brief pastoral caregiving can and should enable parishioners to experience enrichment of the spiritual dimension of their lives so that they put down their spiritual roots "deep into the soil of God's marvelous love" (Eph. 3:17 LB). It taps into the movement of God already present in their lives, helping them collaborate with the changes God is making to bring them a fuller life. This is the key and integrating core of all human wholeness and therefore the heart of pastoral caregiving, including brief pastoral counseling. The degree of health in this area has a profound impact on the wholeness of the other six dimensions.

In identifying persons' strengths and resources in brief counseling, it is important to inquire, as a possible door opener for healing dialogue, "How is your faith helping you handle this difficult (sometimes miserable) situation?" Spiritual and ethical problems can lead to the psychological, physiological, and relational difficulties that bring people to counseling. In our society, starved as it is for healthy soul food, there is a crying hunger for healthy spiritual nutrition. The clergy is the only professional group with disciplined training for the nurturing of spiritual and ethical healing and wholeness. Enhancing wellness in this vital area is the ultimate objective of all caregiving that is truly pastoral—certainly of all brief pastoral counseling.

Mind

Wholistic pastoral caregiving of all types, including brief pastoral counseling, can and should enable parishioners to discover and develop more of the rich unused resources of their minds through better mental self-care and mental exercise. Creative thinking and imagination are essential elements in brief pastoral counseling. Growth in mental wholeness involves lifetime learning and the use of this learning to reach out in healing, growth-enabling ways to respond to the needs of individuals, families, institutions, and our wounded earth.

How can we address this responsibility when doing brief pastoral counseling with bored adults who have lost the spark of learning that is so refreshing in young children? One productive way of exploring the intellectual dimension is to ask a door-opening question, such as, "What do you enjoy reading, watching on public television, reflecting on, or creating?" Another way is to tap into the imagination by way of the miracle question: "If a miracle happened tonight while you were sleeping, and your problem were solved, how would you know it in the morning?" As evidence mounts to confirm the many ways in which humans can use their minds to hurt or heal their total well-being and that of others, pastoral caregiving must respond by enabling people to adopt wholeness-enhancing attitudes, images, stories, and mental practices.

Body

Wholistic brief pastoral caregiving can and should enable parishioners to experience physical healing, strengthening and enlivening their bodies through enhanced self-care so they can glorify God in their bodies as temples of the Spirit (1 Cor. 6:19-20). This means regularly giving their bodies the gifts of adequate attention in four areas: eating a healthy diet, exercising vigorously, resting and sleeping enough, and reducing to a minimum the intake of toxins like nicotine, alcohol, and some food additives. In wholistic brief pastoral counseling, it often is productive to ask people about their self-care in these four areas. They can make the small changes that trigger larger change, the "differences that make a difference," in the words of Gregory Bateson.[2] Persons under the heavy stress of painful crises should be urged to give their bodies these gifts, especially when they do not feel like doing so. In this way, they become less vulnerable to stress-related illnesses that proliferate during such difficulties. Because our bodies, minds, and spirits are deeply interrelated in our total organisms, physical and mental self-care are best understood by religious people as spiritual disciplines.

Love

Wholistic brief pastoral caregiving can and should enable parishioners to learn the skills of nurturing wellness-supporting love in themselves and their relationships. Especially in relationship counseling, a focus on exceptions—times when love outweighs problems—can help persons discern the ways God already is at work to increase love in their relationships. Such love equips them to live out the second great commandment of Jesus: to love God by loving others as one loves oneself (Lev. 19:18 and Mark 12:31). In practical terms, this means discovering how parishioners in our care can benefit from the development of interpersonal skills, particularly love-nurturing and conflict-resolving communication skills. Practicing these skills in the setting of the small group in the church community can be another way of triggering larger change through small behavioral changes.

For the people who have a severe deficiency in interpersonal skills, referral to a competent specialist in relationship therapy is appropriate. For those with a less acute relational deficit, often the best approach is short-term relationship counseling by the pastor, followed by involvement in family or creative single-hood enrichment groups or other organizations within the congregation.

Work

Wholistic brief pastoral caregiving can and should enable parishioners to develop increased wellness in their work. This will equip them to commit their work to the Lord, as the wisdom literature of Hebrew scriptures puts it (Prov. 16:3-4), and thus find more purpose, creativity, zest, and a sense of vocation or calling in their occupation. In the chaos of many workplaces today, vocational guidance that focuses on the strengths and resources people bring to their professional lives and that offers life and work planning is extremely valuable. This much-needed but often neglected aspect of wholistic caregiving can occur as part of the educational component of various types of brief counseling and growth ministries, and may include such things as vocational wellness classes and retreats for youth and adults.

Play

Wholistic brief pastoral caregiving can and should enable parishioners to balance and enliven their lives with playfulness, laughter, and joy. By so doing they can experience the biblical truth that "a cheerful heart is a good medicine" (Prov. 17:22 NRSV). The appropriate use of playfulness is an enlivening but under emphasized resource in much pastoral caregiving. Persons struggling with stressful events and circumstances often can reframe their situation and cope more effectively if they are encouraged to find the humorously absurd aspects that almost always are hidden within it. For example, as African American and Jewish humor illustrates, laughing at oneself and one's peers (and at the oppressors) is a constructive way of maintaining perspective and equilibrium in cases of social injustice. Brief pastoral counseling that treats interventions as experiments, trying out tentative and playful ways to make positive changes, taps into people's neglected ability to enjoy life.

The World

Wholistic brief pastoral counseling can and should enable parishioners to heal themselves by helping to heal God's wounded world—that is, the intertwined social and natural milieu in which we live. By encouraging care for the community, social institutions, and the natural world around them, caregivers thus become both more pastoral and more wholistic. Such a focus on the total environment can enable us to live out the prophetic call of Hebrew scriptures in which *shalom*, meaning both peace and wholeness, was understood to include justice in the community.[3] We can learn to become people of the covenant who join hand in hand with others to help heal the injustice, oppression, and poverty that breed individual and family brokenness as well as environmental destruction on a massive scale.

In traditional pastoral counseling, this prophetic, ecological caregiving has been a most under-emphasized dimension. In today's world, hyper-individual-istic, privatized caregiving that ignores the wholesale social and environmental causes of the multiple pandemics of pain and brokenness is a luxury available only to middle-class, relatively affluent persons—certainly a small minority of the human family. Truly wholistic brief pastoral counseling must be prophetic—that is, it must call people back to God's will for their lives, for their human society, and for their world, focusing on the change already underway and enhancing parishioners' sense of agency in cooperating with those changes.

The Challenge

What is the challenge in all this? It is to face the fact that to be whole and effective today, pastoral caregivers must help their parishioners learn to give loving care to the earth so that all the children of all species will inherit a healthy planet on which they have the best possible opportunity to live healthy lives. The crucial eco-therapeutic aspect of prophetic caregiving is the most radical and innovative challenge facing our field today.

Pastoral caregivers and other religious leaders in all faith traditions have unique and crucial roles in helping to heal God's living earth. This is because the deepest cause of the global eco-justice crisis is a spiritual and ethical sickness that pastoral caregivers have some expertise in healing. It is also because, as the astrophysicist Carl Sagan said, only as the environmental movement is infused with the kind of passion and commitment that religious people have had through the ages will it be effective in healing a wounded world.

Exploring this challenging frontier of our field needs to become a passion for wholistic pastoral caregivers, and it is vital that we understand the theory and practice of eco-therapy and education on environmental issues. In caregiving and educative counseling, people become motivated to make their lifestyles more earth-respectful and earth-healing when they discover that doing so is the path to wholistic health for themselves and their children. When they see that the social and natural world around them affects their wellness and sickness, and in fact all dimensions of their lives, it is like turning on a light in a dark room.

Perhaps the reader is wondering, "How can anyone integrate all this in brief pastoral counseling, or even, for that matter, in long-term counseling?" Three guidelines make it possible. First, it is important to understand that this multi-dimensional model is simply a flexible tool, a set of glasses with which to see people and their problems more wholistically. Clergy doing brief pastoral counseling seldom (if ever) deal with all seven dimensions in a particular counseling relationship. The focus in brief pastoral counseling instead should be on spiritual-ethical issues, and on those other dimensions that apply to the healing and growth of the unique individuals, couples, or families involved.

Second, remember that it is inappropriate to initiate exploration of any other dimension until attention has been paid to the dimension(s) clearly involved in the primary problem of those receiving our care. Pastors must first respond to the initial goals of the parishioners and help them move toward what they came to achieve. Brief pastoral counseling accepts the problem as it is presented and does not attempt to intervene in other areas at first. For example, in counseling a couple who are reeling over the suicide of their teenage child, to confront them with issues of mental development, work, or the environment while they attempt to process the enormity of their tragedy would be counseling malpractice (as well as unfeeling and unethical). Effective brief pastoral counseling begins by responsively listening, with a few focusing questions, in order to explore and illuminate the immediate situation and the parishioners' vision of how they want things to be different. Troubled persons are then helped to mobilize their coping resources to address the problem and achieve their goals. This includes guiding them to develop and implement an incremental action plan that will gradually make things better. (Several models are included in this book.)

Even so, while listening and gaining a tentative sense of the nature and dynamics of the problem, it is helpful for pastors to hold the seven-dimensional model in the back of their minds so that they can gain impressions concerning which of the parishioners' seven dimensions seem to be in need of healing, self-care, and growth. Listening for strengths in these areas is one way to begin to build solutions to the problems people bring to counseling. These impressions, along with the wisdom of the persons receiving care, may provide guidelines for deciding which dimensions merit further attention.

The third guideline reminds us that the most helpful perspective in resolving dilemmas is simply to view problems as potential doorways of opportunity. The first steps on a journey of wholeness often are taken in a few sessions of informal or formal brief pastoral counseling, focusing only on one or—at best—two of the seven dimensions. But whatever steps parishioners take, they should be encouraged to give attention to other needy areas of their lives—whether in counseling or in education. It is wise to urge them to become involved in receiving and giving care through the rich array of mutual caregiving opportunities available in the groups and programs of a faith community with an intentional covenant to wholistic corporate ministry. This means that clergy and lay leaders consciously commit their congregation to grow as a center for implementation of "life in all its fullness" throughout the life stages of those they serve. The trust that often grows in brief pastoral counseling relationships can motivate parishioners to follow their pastors' recommendations concerning which growth groups, classes, or outreach task groups to join in their congregation and in the wider community.

An Illustrative Case

Pastor Nancy Jones is feeling as if she is hovering on the brink of burnout. The plethora of conflicting demands from her job and her family has caused her to neglect much-needed self-care.[4] As she looks over her discouragingly long "to do" list, the telephone rings. Bob Carlson, a Christmas-and-Easter parishioner, speaks in an agitated voice. He is a successful insurance agent who on the surface seems to have a functioning marriage with Jean, a primary school teacher. He frantically tells Pastor Jones that his wife "dumped on me out of the blue last night." He says she "clobbered" him with intense anger over what she incorrectly sees as his gross neglect of her and their two children. Jean let him know in no uncertain terms that she had "about had it" with him and their marriage.

Pastor Jones' first thought, as she struggles to listen, is "Oh, no! This is all I need!" But she quickly recovers enough aplomb to recognize that she must do what she can to help. She invites Bob to say more about the situation, thus letting him experience the support of having his agonizing feelings heard. It also lets Pastor Jones gain a tentative sense of the dynamics of the marriage crisis and a preliminary assessment of how urgent it is to see him (and probably both of them) face-to-face. Brief questioning and listening makes it clear that, although Bob seems somewhat depressed, he shows no signs of being a danger to himself or his family. Pastor Jones asks if Jean would be willing to come with him the next day to discuss their situation. He replies that he thinks so but passes the telephone to Jean so she can speak for herself. After a brief conversation, during which the pastor explains why hearing their differing views would be helpful, the Carlsons both agree to come in the next day.

When the Carlsons arrive and are seated in her study, Pastor Jones asks each of them to describe what each hopes to accomplish by coming in to see her. She limits talk about the problem in order to identify the couple's counseling goal and begin building solutions to their marriage problems. It becomes clear that they both want to make their relationship work, but they do not have much hope that it can happen. They agree that their marital problems have increased gradually almost from the beginning of their marriage, just over a decade ago.

Because Bob and Jean are agitated and stuck in "problem talk," Nancy changes her strategy. She listens as they pour out their mutual accusations and pain at some length. When their anger seems lessened, she summarizes what she has heard to let them know that she has been listening carefully.

Then she reframes the dialogue strategically, saying, "Things are painfully messed up in your relationship and you're hurting each other a lot." (They nod in agreement.)

"But I'm curious," she goes on, "what do you still like about your relationship?" They respond with surprise at the question. Here Pastor Jones is looking for exceptions—times when their problems have not ruled their marriage; she is also looking for what they see as strengths in their relationship that they can build upon. They are able to mention several things they still value in their marriage and family life. Bob enjoys Jean's cooking, the way she hums while she is cleaning the house, and her stylish appearance. Jean also likes the way Bob looks, though she is less thrilled with his expanding waistline; she also appreciates that he picks up after himself, earns a good living, and sometimes makes breakfast for both of them in the morning. They tend to agree with each other on most political issues. The pastor uses these points to help them awaken a glimmer of hope. She says, "To me it's hopeful that you still appreciate some things about each other and want to make your marriage work, for yourselves as well as for your two children. You probably have more going for your marriage than you think you have when you're filled with hurt and anger." This approach illustrates how a pastor can intentionally awaken reality-based hope, which is an essential aim of wholeness-oriented brief pastoral counseling.

Toward the end of the interview, Nancy asks a wholistic, door-opening query: "Things are very difficult in your family right now, but how are things going in other areas of your lives?" This question invites Bob and Jean to focus on other dimensions of their lives that may be intertwined with the marital struggles and alienation. They both mention several frustrating physical health problems. When asked about their physical self-care, they say that they have been too busy and burdened to do much self-care. Listening, Pastor Jones makes mental notes to see if they are open to using their marriage problem as a doorway to enhance their wellness in other areas of their lives. Bob and Jean both report feeling burdened by overload in their careers as well as by their pre-adolescent son's behavior in home and at school. As Bob puts it, "My job is going great financially, but it's eating me alive, and this kid frustrates me!"

Obviously, Bob and Jean are caught in mutually reinforcing cycles of stress and neglect of essential love-nurturing, conflict-reducing communication in their deteriorating marriage—the "love" dimension described earlier. They are made more vulnerable to marital burnout by neglecting the cultivation of relationships with their extended family and close friends. All their problems are exacerbated by their neglect of physical, mental, emotional, and spiritual self-care. When asked about their spiritual life, they agree that it is a blank space. They also say that their enjoyment of living, including their sexuality, is "on a scale of ten, minus three." It seems they have forgotten how to play. Remembering the

self-care vacuum in her own life and its consequences, Pastor Jones rightly sus-
pects that their neglect is a key factor contributing not only to their marital difficulties, but also to the health problems they mention.

Pastor Jones next asks the Carlsons if they are willing to spend three or four
sessions to help them strengthen their marriage and achieve some of the hopes
(goals) each has for the marriage. Out of concern for their wellness, she wants to
begin helping them to develop a multifaceted strategy to facilitate that growth by
better self-care and by participating in the congregation's caregiving programs
to complement their work with the pastor.

By the second session, the Carlsons' cold anger has thawed enough to
enable faint positive feelings to reawaken in them. Sensing this, Nancy invites
Bob and Jean to plan to do something together that they would both enjoy during the next week. They recall that before their marital distancing got so
advanced, they had enjoyed taking brisk walks together after supper. Nancy
encourages them to try this again, pointing out that getting more exercise out-
doors together might enhance their physical wellness while it improves their
relationship. In this way Bob and Jean begin to water and fertilize the seeds of
enjoyment and playfulness in the dry desert of their emotional lives.

In the fourth weekly session, knowing that they have begun to relate more
openly and positively, Pastor Jones suggests that the Carlsons meet with her
again after two weeks' time, just to see how things are going. At that session it
becomes clear that their relationship is opening up and growing in several directions. They are feeling at home in the couples' class the pastor recommended.
They also report that they are using the self-care plans that they have developed
with her guidance. Pastor Jones assures them that her pastoral interest in them is
ongoing: "My phone and door are open to you if you decide that you'd like further pastoral conversations." As they end their time in brief pastoral counseling,
the Carlsons know that their pastor is available to them on a continuing basis.

Several months later, when Nancy talks with Bob and Jean by telephone,
they report that they continue to experience growth in their relationship. Sensing that they are ready, the pastor invites them to participate in a marriage
enrichment retreat, with several follow-up sessions, sponsored annually by the
congregation. This can help them enlarge their caring circle of friends and thus
diminish their social isolation as a nuclear family. They will gain the perspective
of knowing that their problems are not uncommon, that other couples struggle
with similar issues and are successful in resolving them positively. They will
have opportunities for relaxation and fun, away from the stresses of jobs and
children. And their activities and conversations in this church-sponsored weekend will occur in a spiritual context, which will encourage them to tend and
nourish this neglected dimension of their individual and shared lives.

The care of Jean and Bob demonstrates how a pastor can help a couple to use their problem as an open doorway to do what is needed to enhance their wholeness in several dimensions of their lives. It is important to point out that many parishioners will not, on their own, raise issues in areas of their lives other than the immediate crisis-inducing problem unless they are guided to do so by their pastor (see chapter 3). Unfortunately, most parishioners miss crisis-generated growth opportunities by ending counseling as soon as the pain of the crisis is reduced (or as soon as they give up hope that counseling will help). Having a wholistic, door-opening, guiding paradigm that includes methods of implementation and a plan of action helps to equip clergy with brief pastoral counseling approaches and methods that enable troubled people to increase their well-being in many areas of their lives and thus to grow in wholeness, to live life in its fullness, including loving God with all of their heart, soul, mind, and strength.

Notes

1.   Exploring seven-dimensional pastoral caregiving (relevant resources by Howard Clinebell):

Anchoring Your Well Being: Christian Wholeness in a Fractured World (Nashville: Upper Room Books, 1997). A do-it-yourself manual for use by individuals, families, and church wellness classes and other growth groups.

Ecotherapy: Healing Ourselves, Healing the Earth (Minneapolis: Fortress Press, 1996). A guide to ecologically grounded personality theory, counseling, therapy, education, and spirituality for therapists, teachers, clergy, and parents.

Well Being: Exploring and Enriching the Seven Dimensions of Life—Mind, Body, Spirit, Love, Work, Play, the World (San Francisco: HarperSanFrancisco, 1992; reprint, Kadena Books, 1995); available from the Upper Room Healing and Spiritual Development Program, Nashville. A do-it-yourself guide to self-care for spiritually centered wholeness, written in "crossover" language for people who are hungry for spirituality and wholeness but do not read religious publications.

2.   Gregory Bateson, *Mind and Nature: A Necessary Unity* (New York: Bantam, 1979), 105.

3.   See Hosea 2:18 and 4:3; Isaiah 11:6-9 and 24:4-5; and Luke 4:18-19.

4.   This is a composite case based on several short-term crisis counseling relationships.

Part II

Brief Pastoral Counseling Strategies

7

Elements of
Brief Pastoral Counseling

Howard W. Stone

WHO ARE THESE PERSONS who come for counsel? What do they really want from their pastoral caregiver? What beliefs do they bring into the relationship? What hopes do they hold out for its outcome? Do they actually want to change—regardless of what they say?[1]

Over the past three decades I have become increasingly interested in knowing more about the people we help and not just the pastor-counselee relationship, the intervention methods used in counseling, or theological reflection on the pastoral counseling process. One way to find out what people want in counseling is to look at what they actually do. Several authors in this book have noted that most people do not return for many sessions after the first one, and therefore that (besides relief from their distress or solutions to their difficulties) what they appear to want from counseling is that it be brief. Brief pastoral counseling addresses people's own view of their needs, their own goals for the counseling relationship, their own vision for a better life.

Brief pastoral counseling is not just a series of methods—it is a total orientation to the pastoral helping process that subsequently forms what we do, a particular vision of helping that influences all aspects of the care enterprise. This chapter will summarize what I believe to be the major elements of brief pastoral counseling: brief orientation, an empathic relationship, a solvable focal problem, assessment, exceptions to the problem, limited goals, a plan of action, active counseling, achievable homework, and building on strengths. It acknowledges that even brief counseling sometimes fails, yet advocates its methods as the best choice for pastoral caregivers in the congregational context.

Although brief counseling as a field encompasses a wide variety of approaches, therapeutic models, and techniques, these elements are likely to be shared by most theorists and practitioners of short-term pastoral counseling.

91

Brief Orientation

The case has already been made that the majority of all counseling is, de facto, brief. Consequently, short-term counseling cannot be defined only by number of sessions. Instead, it is the orientation of the minister toward the care being offered that distinguishes it from other approaches. Brief pastoral counseling has as much to do with the caregiver's attitude toward the helping process and the specific interventions employed, as it does with an actual number of sessions. After all, a helper may well plan on seeing counselees for twenty, thirty, or an indefinite number of sessions and proceed accordingly. The fact that some of them fail to return after the first or second visit does not alter the nature of the long-term approach; it only truncates it. True brief pastoral counseling utilizes the least extreme, least invasive, simplest method in every situation, on the premise that it makes no sense to start out with an elaborate approach before we know whether or not a counselee will come back for a second session.

Brief pastoral counseling also does not attempt to fix all or even most of people's difficulties. It does, however, predict that a change initiated in one area of an individual's life will expand to other areas. As Milton Erickson puts it, "That little hole in the dike [does not seem like it will] flood the land, except that it will, because once you break through an altered pattern of behavior in some way, the cracks keep traveling."[2] Change is contagious.

The brief orientation, partly due to the small number of counseling sessions, also deters the formation of dependency in the helping relationship and stimulates counselees to get back to the real world and continue addressing their problems. The important thing is to start the process so that successful changes in one area will spread to others.

Finally, the short-term orientation takes our finitude into account. It assumes that we are part of a world caught up in individual and corporate sin, conflicts, losses, doubts, and anxieties too many to mention. Evil is pervasive. Pastoral counseling aims not to eradicate all of these maladies, but rather to guide those whom we serve to begin addressing their problems and to be faithful to God's call.

Empathic Relationship

The crucial first step in counseling, doubly important in brief pastoral counseling, is to establish a solid base of rapport and acceptance rapidly with the troubled individual. From the onset of the first session, the minister encourages parishioners to become motivated and cooperate with change. This involves accurate physical attending, careful listening, temporarily suspending judgment, and offering appropriate warmth and respect. Sometimes pastors already have a good relationship with a person who comes in with a problem, in which case they need only to strengthen an already existing bond.

In pastoral counseling relationships, we must earn the right to say certain things or use certain interventions. Most troubled individuals do not take helpers seriously unless they respect them. Respect is not automatically attendant upon one's vocation; it is earned primarily through skillfully establishing relationships with parishioners. (These skills have been detailed extensively in the pastoral care and psychotherapeutic literature and in Part I of this book.)

Empathy is expressed in brief pastoral counseling by an attitude sometimes called the "not-knowing" position. As pastoral caregivers we recognize that those who come to us for help are the authorities on their own problems and solutions, and we counsel within that frame. We are unendingly curious—especially about parishioners' strengths and what is going well for them. There is a quality of relationship in which pastoral caregivers structure and focus conversation while encouraging the full participation of the counselees in the process. (For a discussion of empathy, the not-knowing position, and the collaborative counseling relationship, see chapters 3 and 9.)

Solvable Focal Problem

"If therapy is to end properly," observes Jay Haley, "it must begin properly—by negotiating a solvable problem."[3] An initial task in brief pastoral counseling, therefore, is to identify the focal problem clearly and in specific, concrete terms that make it seem solvable. Describing someone as having low self-esteem, for example, would not serve as a specific definition of a problem because it is too vague; how will you (or the parishioner) know when the self-esteem is successfully elevated? A more precise definition might be: "I am depressed because I wanted to leave my home back East but now I miss the activities and friends I had there. I have been too passive about finding new things to do or making new friends—I have made my family here my only friends. I will start developing new friends." The more concrete and specific the definition of the problem, the more readily it will lend itself to a solution. Therefore it is essential from the opening moments of brief pastoral counseling to guide parishioners to a clear focus on the key problem(s). Personality change is not a primary goal; instead, it will come naturally as a by-product of problem management.

Assessment

The medical model of diagnosis followed by treatment is not necessarily the pastoral model. Diagnosis and treatment—assessment and change-oriented activities—occur simultaneously throughout the whole enterprise. The process of bringing about change to peoples' difficulties can begin within minutes after the beginning of the first interview. Because assessment is an ongoing process, much is learned after parishioners begin to act. Assessment in brief pastoral counseling focuses upon cues (or stimuli) that trigger the onset of the problem and upon reinforcers (or rewards) that maintain it.

Pastors and parishioners cooperate in the task of assessment (see chapter 3). In pastoral counseling for the short term, assessment as a separate task is not lengthy, although the process of assessment never actually stops from the first session until termination. We do not need to explore parishioners' history extensively or discern the underlying causes of their problem behavior. Parishioners do not need insight in order to begin acting. Weakland suggests that no matter what appears to be the cause of complaints (if a cause can even be reliably discerned), those complaints "persist only if they are maintained by ongoing current behavior of the (person) and others with whom he interacts. Correspondingly, if such problem-maintaining behavior is appropriately changed or eliminated, the problem will be resolved or vanish, regardless of its nature, origin, or duration."[4]

Ministers must ask counselees the vital question: "Why now? With all of the problems, stresses, and strains you find yourself under each day, what has led you to counseling at this very moment?" The question may elicit a prompt answer. Many parishioners, however, have to be asked more than once and in several different ways. Sometimes mental health professionals and ministers alike, in the absence of a quick answer to the "why now" question, tend to begin addressing obvious character flaws in the counselees. To do so is to move automatically into long-term counseling in which the helpers set the goals for counseling; it can lead to what Budman and Gurman describe as "total overhaul therapy."[5] It almost automatically screens out the strengths of counselees and their existing networks of support, and zeroes in on their liabilities. To omit or shelve the "why now" question is to put aside peoples' needs and concerns.

"How fast do you want counseling to go?" is another useful assessment question to ask of eager individuals who want the counseling to be over quickly. It is important to communicate that very brief counseling will be just as competent and effective as long-term therapy, but that it will be a rigorous experience: "You will have to work extremely hard and you should only consider doing it if you are desperate enough to go through it." Sometimes it is a good idea to let people consider it for a few days before they make a decision.

During the assessment process it is important to discern what previous attempts at change have been made by parishioners so that the helper does not try to lead them down these same paths again. W. C. Fields's admonition applies:

"If at first you don't succeed, try, try, again. Then give up. There's no use being a damn fool about it." If it hasn't worked, don't do more of it. Try something unrelated to all previous attempts at solutions—perhaps even the opposite.

Exceptions

Many authors in this book refer to exceptions, a vital element of brief pastoral counseling. People who seek counseling tend to think that their problem exists all of the time, twenty-four hours a day, seven days a week. When it does not, they do not notice it or pass it off as an accident. Good assessment pays attention not only to cues or reinforcers of problem behaviors but also to what de Shazer calls exceptions—"whatever is happening when the complaint is not."[6] Parents may think their son "is beating up on his sisters all of the time." But of course, he is not. De Shazer suggests that

> problems are seen to maintain themselves simply because they maintain themselves and because clients depict the problem as always happening. Therefore, times when the complaint is absent are dismissed as trivial by the client or even remain completely unseen, hidden from the client's view . . . the problem is seen as primary (and the exceptions, if seen at all, are seen as secondary).[7]

In brief pastoral counseling, exceptions to the problem are of primary importance and may even serve as the central focus of the counseling.

Looking for exceptions requires different questions from those customarily raised in counseling. Instead of asking about a couple's anger toward one another or their troubled marital history, we may inquire: "How are periods when you are not fighting with your wife different?" "How did you achieve that?" "What is it like?" "Did your family or friends notice when you were not fighting?" "How could you tell that they noticed?" "How did you stop the fighting?"[8]

Another approach to discovering exceptions is to offer a compliment to one or both spouses: "I am impressed you did not get into a fight last weekend when your son took the car without permission." In this way you call attention to the time that they did not get into a fight—thus emphasizing a strength rather than focusing on their discord. State the compliment in the present tense even if their positive behaviors occurred a long time ago, under the assumption that they have the ability to achieve it again.

Homework tasks may encourage parishioners to find exceptions to their problems: "This coming week, observe whatever happens in your relationship with your wife that you want to happen more." When they report exceptions, urge them to repeat whatever they were doing at the time of the exception.

Doing more of something they already have done certainly seems more possible—and less threatening—than embarking on new territory. The exceptions themselves can even become the goal of counseling.

Limited Goals

Defining a specific, concrete problem and discovering exceptions to the problem readily lead to the establishment of limited target goals that clearly set out the sought-for change or solution. Pastor and parishioner mutually consider the goals for counseling, collaborating to identify realistic and reachable targets that can be achieved in a short period of time. It is critical that parishioners not attempt to cover too much ground or change too quickly. (They can always set new goals, once they have attained the present ones.)

Communication theorist Robert Norton has suggested that while "much of psychiatry spends time trying to unravel the correct, clear cause of the problem with a crystalline analysis devoid of inconsistencies and pure in its structural flow, the brief therapist will settle for a dirty solution that works. The flow of the structure can be marred, illogical, and inconsistent as long as the solution works."[9] O'Hanlon and Weiner-Davis note that helpers "often get stuck because they have too much information rather than too little, or too much information about the problem and too little about the solution."[10] I have noticed that many pastoral counseling trainees tend to spend more time developing an analysis of the problem than helping counselees seek a goal or solution.

In the first session, the minister's task is to help parishioners claim a vision for the future, for what life will be like when the complaint is resolved. From the first moments of their time together they should be defining that goal and determining how they will go about getting there. Two methods have helped me steer people from obsessing on problems to forming a vision of the future; both can be discussed in the session or given as written homework. In the first, *the future question,* I say, "Tell me how you want your life to be different a month (or three, six, twelve months) from now. Be realistic, recognizing work, family, and financial constraints. Also, be very specific." I offer examples, such as: "I will register for an accounting class so I can get a better job in the comptrollers office"; "I will join Alanon and learn how to live with an alcoholic spouse"; "I will join the choir at church to help me get out and interact more with people, instead of staying at home feeling sorry for myself." (See chapter 4 for a fuller discussion of the future question.)

A second approach has been influenced by de Shazer.[11] In a variation of his *miracle question* I ask: "Suppose that you awakened tomorrow morning and your problem was magically gone, how would you know? If by magic the problem was no longer there, what would be different in your life? How would your family or friends know? How would they say that you had changed? How would I recognize the change?" After two or three sessions I may ask additional questions: "Are there days when a little bit of the magic has occurred?" "How are these days different from before?" The purpose of these secondary questions is to help parishioners to see that change is not only possible but is already happening. (The miracle question is also discussed in greater detail in chapters 4, 8, and 12.)

Not only the questions you ask, but how you phrase them can influence parishioners to develop workable counseling goals. Most individuals in counseling tend to speak of their problems in the present tense. A subtle way to reframe their difficulties is to switch to the past tense. At the same time it is good to use "when" rather than "if" in reference to counseling goals: "What do you think will happen *when* you start to come home earlier from work?"

Married couples coming to the minister for counseling tend to describe their spouses in rather sweeping characterizations. The statement "he is totally inconsiderate" does not give the spouse much to work with; it needs restating in words such as, "he doesn't pay attention when you want to discuss something." Thus, the counseling goal shifts from revamping a personality construct to making specific changes in a person's behaviors.

Some people in counseling only want to talk about problems and deflect every initiative to discuss solutions for their difficulties. With such persons, the miracle question or a question such as "What is the difference between the times when the problem is better and the times when it is worse?" is appropriate. Or you might ask, "What will be the very first sign that change is on the way?" Most parishioners have a tendency to focus on the ultimate answer, when everything will be completely as they wish, and do not want to notice the first subtle signs of transition and growth. Such questions help sensitize them to the first nuances of change.

Other individuals think that the problem resides only in someone or something outside of themselves. Their inevitable answer to every suggestion is "Yes, but. . . . " Sometimes it helps to compliment these people for their suffering, tell them you recognize that they still must have some sense of hope or they would not be there in front of you. Commend them for being good historians of the causes of their problems.[12] The objective is to change their view of themselves and their thinking about the problem to see that they have some part in the solution.

Berg suggests the use of scaling or coping questions with especially challenging counselees. A scaling question might be: "If ten means that you will do anything whatsoever to solve the problem of fighting with your wife, and one means that you will just sit there and do nothing, where are you on a scale of one to ten? How about your wife—where would she say you are? Your neighbor? Your best friend? What will it take for you to go from (for example) five to six on the scale? What will it take for your wife to say that you have gone from five to six?"[13]

In situations that seem completely hopeless to parishioners, coping questions may be useful: "How do you cope?" "How do you get through the day?" "Why are things not worse?" "With what you have told me about your background, how is it that you are coping as well as you are?" Such questions focus not on the problem, but on the strengths that reside within the person that allow him or her to deal with it.

The sudden flood of unrelated problems that sometimes occurs when parishioners are discussing their problems is not necessarily a time for referral to long-term therapy, but is the very time when strict adherence to target goals is essential—no matter how significant the newly introduced problem or problems may seem. Simply suggest, "That sounds like something important. After we have achieved (the target goal), we can take up that issue if you would like." Wells puts it this way: "Implicit in the short-term helping process is the belief that change is most likely to ensue from a concentrated focus on a single but significant problem in living (and, conversely, the belief that much natural problem solving is weakened by attempting to deal with too many difficulties simultaneously)."[14] Therefore, pastors must help parishioners facing an assortment of problems to choose one or two of them as the highest priority. Since time is limited, goals also must be limited. Narrowing the focus to one or two objectives increases the likelihood that actual change will occur.

I have encountered many counselees whose previous experience in counseling was disappointing. In any number of cases they had gone in for one problem but were treated for another that the therapist deemed to be more important. For example, one overweight man who wanted help in controlling his weight spent most of his therapy sessions reconstructing his relationship with his parents, especially his mother; the therapist thought that these family relationships were key to his losing weight, but the man dropped out after more than twenty sessions with little attention given to his overeating. He did not begin to shed pounds until he entered brief pastoral counseling and focused directly on his goal: weight loss. Successful brief pastoral counseling absolutely requires a target goal that is directly related to the parishioners' own objectives. If for whatever reason you and the parishioner are unable to agree upon such a goal, do not accept the person for counseling.

A Plan

My wife and I occasionally travel with our dear friends of nearly thirty years, Bob and Jon-Lea. Every morning, whether we are in Mexico or Guatemala, England or Arizona, the morning begins with a nice breakfast, and then Bob (a school superintendent and educational leader) announces: "We gotta have a plan." Dutifully, we plan. Of course we stay flexible, seize the happy surprises, turn even near-disasters into adventures. Sometimes, when things go wrong or opportunities arise, we stop and make a new plan. Never have we wasted so much as a morning in indecision; even a "down" day is the result of choice, not inertia. The success of our trips rests not only on interesting destinations and good company, but on having a flexible plan for the day ahead.

Many times all that pastoral caregivers need to send parishioners on the journey toward resolution—no matter how complex or intractable the problem—is a plan that calls for one small change, one tiny alteration in the way they go about doing things. The corollary is that when people face a vast or all-encompassing task and lack a specific plan for change, they are likely to fail. A vital task of brief pastoral counseling, therefore, is to develop a working strategy that gets people moving, doing, making changes right away. Like a good travel plan, it is flexible, subject to course corrections and new inspirations; without it counselees may dither away their chances for positive change.

The pastoral caregiver bears the primary responsibility for helping parishioners to develop a plan of action. To work, the scheme must be understandable and attainable. Your parishioners must be able to comprehend the specific actions they will take to address their difficulties; there can be no fuzzy definitions or unresolved decisions. Equally important, the steps they take must be achievable within a short time. The tasks should be small—things they can do successfully within hours and days of the session. Parishioners need to recognize and believe that the tasks facing them are within their scope and ability.

If the plan consists of more than a single step, put it in writing. Make sure there are no areas for misinterpretation; every item on the plan needs to be spelled out in concrete detail. Ideally, the parishioners do the writing; sometimes I ask them to sign the plan, as a contract, in order to focus their attention on it and as a sign of their commitment to the task. With a clear and attainable plan, and a commitment to acting upon it, even their difficulties can become opportunities for change, growth, and adventure.

Active Counseling

Ministers need to take a proactive stance as they help parishioners with their problems of living. In 1974, Wayne Oates noted that "early emphases upon listening and later emphases upon non-directive methodology in counseling have habituated several seminary generations of pastoral counselors to a passive approach to counseling."[15] Unfortunately, the congregational context does not afford the luxury of such passivity. Although the skills of nondirective counseling are useful for the establishment of a relationship, we have seen that parish pastors simply do not have time to unhurriedly develop rapport, listen passively, and take extensive history—all of which tend to fit into a long-term counseling model and which parishioners many times see as irrelevant to solving their problems.

Although it is primarily the task of parishioners to select counseling goals for counseling, it is the minister's job—collaborating with them—to design interventions that will be used to achieve these goals.[16] A proactive stance means that the pastor selects the specific techniques and procedures to be used. To quote Wells, "The change methods employed are structured, in the sense of comprising a series of steps (or phases) that break the process of change into component parts and guide the activities of both helper and counselee."[17] Such methods are well described in the literature of pastoral counseling as well as psychotherapy.

Achievable Homework

O. Hobart Mowrer once stated, "It is easier to act your way into a new way of feeling than to feel your way into a new way of acting."[18] One of the quickest ways to bring about change is to address and act on specific issues in real life using outside-of-sessions tasks. It is important that ministers and parishioners agree on these tasks, though the selection of appropriate homework assignments will tend to rely on the minister's expertise. I have already mentioned homework tasks in connection with other elements of brief pastoral counseling. Frequently ideas for homework arise as a natural part of the conversation, and pastors translate those ideas into actual tasks that parishioners can perform out in the real world. Virtually every activity and discussion that takes place within the counseling session (even in an informal counseling encounter) can generate a homework task. Doing homework emphasizes parishioners' agency; it places the responsibility for change squarely on their shoulders and ensures that changes occur not only in the rarefied environment of a counseling session, but in the person's day-to-day life.

Building on Strengths

"The human soul at its best experiences invading spiritual forces which can transform, illumine, direct, and empower life."[19] These words of Harry Emerson Fosdick express in poetic language a sense of the strengths that reside within all humans. "I have become convinced, at times amazed," writes Charles Kemp, "at the power of the human spirit to transcend pain and difficulty and to attain higher levels of courage and faith. This is true not only in the biographies of the saints, but it is true of a lot of common people in every congregation in America."[20]

It has been my experience that people who are going through difficult times tend to underestimate their own strengths and resources. The focus of brief pastoral counseling is to build upon parishioners' own coping resources and strengths, latent though they may be. One of the quickest ways to help people begin feeling better about themselves, thus enhancing self-esteem, is to get them to use some of those latent strengths. Budman and Gurman point out that short-term counselors need to adopt a health rather than an illness orientation, seeking to help persons "build on their existing strengths, skills, and capacities."[21] Exposing defense mechanisms or gaining insight into one's protective armor generally is not necessary for the management of a problem; it is usually quicker to help people develop their own resident strengths than it is to break down their defenses. It is also more humane.

Brief pastoral counseling, therefore, strives for specific changes in people's environment or in their particular activities toward handling a problem. It views changes in emotions or insights as secondary—not unimportant, certainly, but not the primary target for change. As Franz Alexander writes, "No insight, no emotional discharge, no recollection can be as reassuring as accomplishment in the actual life situation in which the individual failed."[22] Both emotional release and insight are natural results of a short-term pastoral counseling process that builds upon individuals' own latent strengths.

In short: the what, not the why, of human problems is the goal. Brief pastoral counselors seek to discern specific behavioral changes that will be beneficial and aim for their achievement. Building upon existing skills is the best (perhaps the only) way to reach this goal. When people make specific changes in and for themselves, they experience relief from the painful stress and demoralization that accompany their problems.

A principal way to build upon peoples' strengths is to show them hospitality (see chapter 5). The counseling session needs to be a place where parishioners are welcomed, encouraged, and complimented for what they are doing well, not where their past wrongs or present pathologies are dredged up. Near the end of the initial (perhaps only) session and before discussing homework tasks, it is good to give parishioners appropriate compliments in order to create what de Shazer calls a "yes set" that puts them in a frame of mind to accept new tasks and behaviors[23]—compliments such as, "I'm impressed with how hard you have been working to improve your eating problem; even though you have not achieved what you wanted, it is obvious you have given considerable effort to it" or "I would like to compliment the two of you on the extensive and detailed information you have given me regarding your son's behavior."

If people do not seem to want to work on a problem, welcome them and compliment them for coming: "It must have been difficult for you to come to my office today. I want to compliment you on your courage to be here and talk about these things." You cannot coerce people to work on their problems, but you can offer them hospitality and respect. Sometimes that is all they really need.

When Best Efforts Fail

You can't help everyone. It is a popular belief among highly successful individuals that people can do or be anything, that no goal is too high if they are motivated and persistent—in short, if they only "try hard enough." You may have heard famous overachievers express this view on late-night television talk shows. It is jolly to think that if you have "made it," you did so by dint of your own efforts.

That sentiment is not only patently untrue, it is a cruel joke on people whose dreams far outstrip their abilities and resources to achieve them. A person of limited intelligence who cannot grasp basic mathematical functions has no hope of becoming an astrophysicist. The young girl whose birth defects left her legs twisted and misshapen—or who is merely clumsy—hasn't a prayer of dancing for the Bolshoi Ballet. In pastoral counseling, even the most effective therapeutic techniques, used by the most skilled pastoral caregiver, cannot achieve results in people who are unable (or unwilling) to change.[24]

Brief pastoral caregivers must avoid viewing their parishioners through rose-colored glasses. They cannot force their methods and terminology (and certainly not their own goals) upon people in need. There is no ironclad guarantee that the methods of brief pastoral counseling will lead to the changes parishioners desire in their lives. People have limitations. They may be so filled with fear, anger, resentment, or pride that they cannot bring themselves to do what is needed to resolve their difficulties and move into the future. The hurdles in their path may be illness, mental or physical disability, or plain stubbornness.

Based on research findings to date as well as our own experience, proponents of brief pastoral counseling believe that short-term, solution-focused approaches work as well or better than longer-term, more invasive approaches. However, they are not a panacea for every problem or ill that befalls the members of our congregations. When certain parishioners do not respond to our best methods and efforts, we face the prospect of referral—but we cannot force parishioners into that, either. Ultimately we may need to let go and turn them over to God.

The Method of Choice

An analogy from the medical world that aptly summarizes the different gestalt of long-term psychotherapy versus brief pastoral counseling was suggested by one of my students. She compared long-term therapy to major exploratory surgery in which doctors cut the heavily sedated patient "from stem to stern" in an attempt to discover, and hopefully to remove, whatever is amiss. The procedure is invasive and dangerous, and recovery is slow. Brief counseling is more like a laparoscopic procedure; the tiny incision is made under a local anesthetic, bleeding is minimal, the problem is repaired, and the patient goes home (perhaps even back to work) within hours.[25]

Few people have the time, the perseverance, the financial resources, or even the need to undergo extended periods of invasive, exploratory psychotherapeutic treatment for their problems of living. The elements of brief pastoral counseling provide a methodology that can shorten the process of counseling while preserving and even enhancing the quality of care that ministers offer to those who come to them for counsel. These methods are doable, well within the ability of most parish pastors who learn and use them. They are flexible, lending themselves to modifications and creative variations (as evidenced by other chapters of this book) that suit the personalities and circumstances of pastors and parishioners alike. Like laparoscopic surgery, they cannot cure every ill. But they are ethical, because they honor the needs, strengths, and goals of the people we serve . . . and because, more often than not, they benefit them.

Notes

1. For a fuller discussion of the elements of brief counseling, see H. W. Stone, *Brief Pastoral Counseling: Short-Term Approaches and Strategies* (Minneapolis: Fortress Press, 1994) where these ideas were first discussed.

2. J. Haley, *Conversations with Milton H. Erickson, M.D.*, vol. 1 (New York: Triangle, 1985), 102.

3. J. Haley, *Problem-Solving Therapy: New Strategies for Effective Family Therapy* (San Francisco: Jossey-Bass, 1976), 9.

4. J. Weakland, R. Fisch, P. Watzlawick, and A. Bodin, "Brief Therapy: Focused Problem Resolution," *Family Therapy Networker* 13 (1974): 145.

5. S. Budman and A. Gurman, *Theory and Practice of Brief Therapy* (New York: Guilford, 1988).

6. S. de Shazer, *Clues: Investigating Solutions in Brief Therapy* (New York: Norton, 1988), 53.

7. S. de Shazer, *Putting Difference to Work* (New York: Norton, 1991), 58.

8. W. O'Hanlon and M. Weiner-Davis, *In Search of Solutions* (New York: Norton, 1989).

9. Quoted in S. de Shazer, *Putting Difference to Work*, 53.

10. O'Hanlon and Weiner-Davis, *In Search of Solutions*, 58.

11. S. de Shazer, *Clues*, 5.

12. I. Berg, "Working with the Problem Drinker: A Solution-Focused Approach" (lecture presented at American Association of Marriage and Family Therapists National Convention, Dallas, Tex., 1991).

13. Ibid.

14. Wells, *Planned Short-Term Treatment* (New York: Free Press, 1982), 12.

15. W. E. Oates, *Pastoral Counseling* (Philadelphia: Westminster, 1974), 121–22.

16. H. W. Stone, *Brief Pastoral Counseling* (Minneapolis: Fortress Press, 1994). See especially chaps. 4–11.

17. Wells, *Planned Short-Term Treatment*, 43.

18. Quoted in H. Clinebell, *Basic Types of Pastoral Counseling* (Nashville, Tenn.: Abingdon, 1977), 171.

19. H. E. Fosdick, *A Faith for Tough Times* (New York: Harper, 1952), 96.

20. C. Kemp, *The Caring Pastor* (Nashville: Abingdon, 1985), 174.

21. Budman and Gurman, *Theory and Practice of Brief Therapy*, 14.

22. Quoted in Wells, *Planned Short-Term Treatment*, 44.

23. S. de Shazer, *Keys to Solution in Brief Therapy* (New York: Norton, 1985), 91.

24. For further discussion of when brief pastoral counseling does and does not work, see my *Brief Pastoral Counseling*, 155–66.

25. D. DeLuca, "Pastoral Counseling" (student paper, Brite Divinity School, Texas Christian University, 1999).

8

Staying Solution-Focused in
Brief Pastoral Counseling

Charles Allen Kollar

TRADITIONALLY, PASTORAL CAREGIVERS in congregations have been skilled empathic listeners to the problems of their parishioners. Their grasp of various nuances of those problems has guided countless pastoral counseling sessions. People come for counseling in the first place because they are so focused on their problems and hardships that they find it difficult to visualize options for change. They are, in a word, stuck.[1]

Why is it, then, that pastoral caregivers have so long maintained their focus on their parishioners' problems when those parishioners already are focusing too much on their problems—indeed, are oppressed by their problems?

The approach to mental health caregiving that has come to be called brief counseling challenges this problem orientation. The underlying concepts of brief counseling constitute a paradigm shift that, once made, affects the entire pastoral care and counseling process. Concentrating on solutions rather than problems opens up a world of options previously unseen by counselees. Brief pastoral counseling is brief only in that it swiftly encourages individuals to get unstuck and back on track. As such, it is a highly effective counseling approach. It is also supportive in nature; that is, it undergirds and sustains the work that the Spirit is already doing in people's lives.

A Solution-Focused Conceptual Schema

If a method is difficult to remember, we probably will not use it. The diagram on page 106 is user-friendly and will help the pastoral caregiver stay focused throughout the counseling session.[2] Its purpose is to present a biblical, joyful, creative, hopeful, expectant, and common-sense way to stay on track in counseling. It can give structure to a pastoral caregiver's own personal style and gifts. It is a means of staying focused in the counseling interview and opening various doors to solution-oriented conversations. I offer it as a way to address a familiar conundrum in pastoral counseling: what to do and say next. (Note that this discussion focuses on the initial counseling session, but the schema can be used as well in subsequent sessions, if any.)

Hear, Fit, Watch, Wait

Without a plan, counseling becomes a frustrating experience; the diagram below places the plan in a visible format. At the top of the solution-focused pastoral counseling circular diagram (12 o'clock position) are the words, *hear, fit, watch,* and *wait.* They represent the first part of the process of giving help. Each word opens up a thought or concept, and together they reveal the first responsibility of the pastoral caregiver doing brief pastoral counseling: to listen.

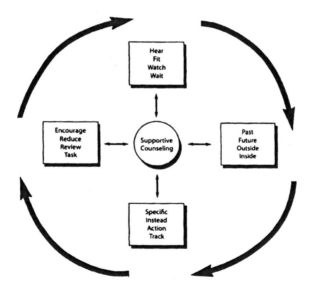

Hear. Some counseling approaches concentrate on the cognitive side of counseling, while others center on the affective. These approaches differ in the extent of importance each attaches to the acknowledgment and expression of emotions in the counseling process. To what degree is the cathartic expression of feelings beneficial to the process of change? The question is beyond the scope of this chapter. I would suggest that the driving force of change is primarily in the revision of constructs, or in how we make sense of things. Shifting to a focus on solutions rather than problems represents one such revision. As pastoral caregivers, we walk a fine line between hearing feelings of anger or frustration and concentrating overmuch on the problem that these feelings represent.

Most pastoral counseling interviews begin with questions. "What brings you in to see me today?" Or more simply, "How can I help?" Any opening that encourages counselees to tell their story is fine. Caregivers could even encourage a more outcome-oriented story by asking: "What is your goal in coming to see me today?"

The purpose of listening to parishioners as they tell their stories is to establish a collaborative relationship with them (see chapter 3). Most of what we try to accomplish in counseling will be fruitless if those coming for help do not feel that their experience of the situation has been heard. At the beginning of the brief pastoral counseling process, caregivers need to be quick to listen and slow to speak (James 1:19), so counselees feel that their emotions are respected, that they are accepted and heard (see chapter 2).

So we listen carefully, opening the door for others to express a part of their experience to us. These troubled persons represent God's most priceless creative effort; when we hear their stories we are listening to the unfolding of God's intention—even if that intention has been damaged or injured.

Fit. When we seek to help others, we have the unique opportunity to enter into their world. In doing so, it is important to show that we understand their concerns. This is what I mean by *fit.* The prophet Amos wrote, "Do two walk together unless they have agreed to do so?" (Amos 3:3 NIV). In hearing, and now in fitting, we simply want to walk together with individuals as they move forward with God. We "rejoice with those who rejoice, and mourn with those who mourn" (Rom. 12:15 NIV). In this way we show them that we are with them in their light emotions (rejoicing) and in their intense or heavy emotions (mourning).

Our response needs to fit theirs. We want to pay attention to both verbal and nonverbal responses—our words as well as our tone of voice and even posture—when responding to them. If parishioners are sitting back, relaxed, with their legs crossed, eventually we can take a similar position. When they lean forward anxiously, we can join in that position—not becoming anxious, of course, but being with them in their concerns.

Watch. Look for God's activity in parishioners' lives. Watch for any indication of exceptions to their problems, any times that they have successfully dealt with similar problems, moments when God has been active in their personal story but they have not noticed or appreciated it.

Not all church caregivers are comfortable with note taking, but I find it helpful. I inform people that I am jotting down bits of information that are significant in a positive sense. I am not writing down problems beyond a basic description, nor am I developing a social history. Rather, I am looking for any evidence of exceptions and for strengths—personal, family, or social strengths that parishioners have employed in the past but are not utilizing now.

Wait. At some point, after a time of attentive listening, you will notice that people begin to shift from the retelling of past concerns to a present request for support. This shift, in essence, issues an invitation to the pastoral caregiver to join in the conversation. It may also come in the form of simple silence. Or perhaps they will look down, shake their head, wonder if there is any hope. It is wise to pay attention to—but also wait for—such an invitation. Enter too soon, and your parishioners may assume they have not been understood. Wait too long, and you may miss an important opportunity to help them bring change to their lives. What we say at this point sets the tone for the rest of the conversation.

Past, Future, Outside, Inside

Think about how you gather information. Often it is by asking questions. Questions can lead us to view a situation in a new way. In brief pastoral counseling the questions are not especially critical in and of themselves; rather, they are a particular type of question with a particular end in mind. Each question helps to move counselees through a doorway into a more solution-oriented approach to living.

For those we are counseling, questions offer access to a vision of life where they are not dominated by their problems. What will that life look like? How will this make a difference? What will be happening when they are on track toward this kind of life? What will this track look like? Can it be described? What will the first step look like? How about the second and third steps? What will they need to do to stay on track? What part of this is happening already?

Most people, no matter how troubled, possess the ability to imagine a future when the problem is resolved. This incredible resource is often under-utilized in problem-oriented pastoral counseling. Even though the problem is still a dominant factor in their lives, a solution begins to emerge. The task of pastoral caregivers is to support an increasingly clear picture of the solution.

Let us look at four doorways to a life where the problem no longer dominates and solutions emerge, and at questions we can ask to lead troubled people through those portals (see the 3 o'clock position in the diagram on page 106).

Past. Passing through the first doorway assumes possible change in the past. Since God is always active, we should not be surprised that God already has placed clues for possible change or improvement in the lives of troubled people. We discover something that has already been going on—something that reveals at least a small improvement in the problem. Typically, parishioners have not viewed this as meaningful, or have overlooked it altogether. Pastoral caregivers need to help parishioners to recognize the significance of even slight murmurs of change in their past.

One man expressed to me that he felt depressed all of the time. After hearing his story, I asked him, "What has been slightly better in the last few days?" Here I assumed past change. After a pause, he recalled that he had gotten out of his apartment more often. He was not merely going to work and staying at home each evening. I asked him how he had been able to get himself to do that.

My first question had opened a door to a small exception to his depression. I was simply curious, but I assumed the possibility of the exception. In response to my second question he informed me that he had spontaneously decided to drive past his usual freeway exit on his way home and go bowling instead. There he met some members of his church and had "a pretty good time." At this point, I used several clarifying questions to highlight this change from being depressed "all the time." I said, "Is it different for you to do these things? How do you account for this change in your attitude? What will you have to do to continue to feel better? How will you do that?"

These clarifying questions keep us peeking through the door at exceptions, at what life looks like when (not if) the exceptions happen more often. I am not suggesting that pastoral caregivers ask one question after another in a shotgun approach—but do ask them, in a matter-of-fact way, because you care and because you are interested.

If this first doorway (exceptions from the past) has opened up new possibilities, I skip forward to *Specific, Instead, Action, On Track*, elements of the third component of the counseling diagram (see the 6 o'clock position in the diagram on page 106). However, the first doorway will not always bring about the hoped-for response. The exceptions probably are there, but counselees cannot see far enough beyond the problem to recognize them. When this happens I resort to future-oriented questions.

Future. The second door shifts counselees' perspectives to a future focus. (See chapter 4.) In Romans 8:28-30, Paul urges us to view our future in God as already achieved. Anxiety is an extension of present or past fears onto the future. It represents a conviction that the near or distant future will consist of nothing more than a continuation of the present or past experience of unease.

This fear has a relational as well as a theological basis. It was born in the garden when Adam and Eve first hid from God (Gen. 3:10). Fear has bound the entire human race; in a very real sense, all people are hiding from God. Fear culminates in a hopelessness that makes our hearts sick (2 Tim. 1:7). Many individuals who have experienced sorrow, frustration, or fear in the past have an increasingly hopeless expectation for the future. This hopeless stance can be a self-fulfilling prophecy; as Job put it, "What I feared has come upon me" (Job 3:25 NIV).

Solomon wrote: "Hope deferred makes the heart sick, but a longing fulfilled is a tree of life" (Prov. 13:12 NIV). Hope is an antidote to depression. The future doorway helps counselees to project their faith onto the future, thus creating a more hopeful expectation. Solution-oriented brief pastoral counseling makes them more sensitive to God's view of the future; this new vision produces hope. The past takes on new meaning as counselees begin to view it as part of life's learning process. It is instructive rather than shameful, educational rather than traumatic.

Various hypothetical questions can be used to open up the future: "If coming to see me turns out to be helpful, what will you be doing differently?" "Let's step out on faith and say that our time together has been helpful to you; how will you know it has been helpful?" To clarify we might ask further questions such as: "Can you tell me more about that?" "What will you be doing differently when you are not (doing the problem)?" "What will your (family, spouse, child, etc.) notice that is different about you when . . . ?" For children, a *pretend question* can be helpful: "Let's pretend the problem is solved and you are getting along better with (family, school children)."

In every case, the emphasis is on doing: what *will* be happening, not what *would* be happening. Again, the question itself is less significant than the hypothetical possibilities it opens up. Asking what will be different helps to build upon this alternate possibility. By encouraging a future focus, we support actions that can lead to new feelings, rather than seeking to alter feelings in an attempt to change actions.

Scripture offers abundant opportunity for creating a future focus. "Set your minds on things above," writes Paul, "not on earthly things. For you died, and your life is now hidden with Christ in God" (Col. 3:2-3 NIV). This passage refers to our death and new life in Christ, which already exists. In that spirit we might ask counselees: "If you die and live again in Christ, and the problems that we have been discussing today no longer trouble you, what will you observe that will demonstrate to you that this new life has already begun?"

Scripture focuses on solutions as well. "Rejoice in the Lord always. I will say it again: Rejoice! . . . Do not be anxious about anything, but in everything, by prayer and petition, with thanksgiving, present your requests to God. And the peace of God, which transcends all understanding, will guard your hearts and your minds in Christ Jesus" (Phil. 4:4-7 NIV). After mentioning this passage to parishioners, pastoral caregivers might ask: "If a miracle happened this afternoon and you were no longer being controlled by anxieties, but rather experienced this peace of God, what would you notice that is different? This miracle transcends our ability to understand it. What is the first thing you will notice that is different? What else? What will you be doing differently?"

Again Paul writes: "No temptation has seized you except what is common to man. And God is faithful; he will not let you be tempted beyond what you can bear. But when you are tempted, he will also provide a way out so that you can stand up under it" (1 Cor. 10:13 NIV). Again, this Scripture could be followed by a question: "What will be the first sign that God is providing a way out from this problem? What will you be doing differently?"

As before, questions focusing on the future will not always bring the hoped-for response. Parishioners who are not able to see any possible hope for change remain stuck in their present perceptions. After you have tried the past and the future, try looking outside (the third doorway), deliberately viewing the problem as the problem, that is, as something outside of us.

Outside. Sometimes when people tell me their problems I am reminded of a story about a boxer. Bruised and bleeding, he leans over to his trainer and pleads, "Please throw in the towel! This guy is killing me!" The trainer responds, "Oh, no, he's not. He's not even hitting you. He hasn't laid a glove on you!" The boxer replies, "Well then, I wish you'd watch that referee, because somebody is sure hitting me!"

Sometimes people are simply being pummeled by their problems. To them we might ask, "How long have you been getting beaten up by this problem?" "How long are you going to let it get the best of you?" "When was the last time your problem tried to get the best of you, but you didn't let it?" "How did you do that?"

The problem can be anything from blaming in a marriage relationship to a child's fear of the dark. In any case, we help people to visualize the problem as something outside of them, to externalize it by viewing the problem as the problem. Counselees need to stop seeing themselves and others—spouses, children, family members, neighbors, coworkers, or strangers—as the enemy or the problem. We have Paul's words that "our struggle is not against flesh and blood, but against the rulers, against the authorities, against the powers of this dark world and against the spiritual forces of evil in the heavenly realms" (Eph. 6:12 NIV). There is an outside force to contend with. Even sin is something external to us: "For sin, seizing the opportunity afforded by the commandment, deceived me, and through the commandment put me to death. . . . I do not understand what I do. For what I want to do I do not do, but what I hate I do. And if I do what I do not want to do, I agree that the law is good. As it is, it is no longer I myself who do it, but it is sin living in me. Now if I do what I do not want to do, it is no longer I who do it, but it is sin living in me that does it" (Rom. 7:11, 15-17, 20 NIV). Pastoral caregivers assist parishioners to become partners in defeating this outside influence. We encourage them to cooperate in a battle against the problem, to break out from its grip on their lives.

Some questions that assist people to externalize their problems might include: "If (the problem) represents an attack by the enemy, what will you be doing differently when you are defeating this attack?" "When you are winning, what are you doing (or what will you be doing) differently?" "When was the last time you were under attack but you didn't let this (problem) win?" "How did you do that?"

Sometimes, however, parishioners are so focused on the present difficulties that they cannot externalize them or see other possibilities. If that is the case, we want to maintain our fit with their sense of hopelessness (to be with them in their discouragement, not to buy into it). The fourth door helps us to do just this.

Inside. When those we counsel are unable to discover any exceptions in the past, or to envision life without the problem in the future, or even to imagine the problem as outside of them, we can resort to taking the conversation inside. These are times to mourn with those who mourn. We agree momentarily with their hopeless feelings. We can ask questions about how they have kept things from getting worse. For example: "From what you say, it seems the problem is serious; how is it that things are not worse?" "What are you (and spouse, family, etc.) doing to keep this situation from getting worse?" "It's amazing that you have been able to put up with this; how have you been able to manage?"

Such questions ask counselees to go inside themselves and evaluate how they have been able to keep things from deteriorating further. When asked what they are doing to manage when things are so bad, counselees may be able to identify some reasons—even if they are just getting by. In this fashion, they discover potential exceptions to the problem. Once they respond with an example of how they have managed, or why things are not worse, pastoral caregivers can follow up with clarifying questions: "How has that been helpful to you?" "What will it take to make that happen more often?"

Continue by asking questions such as: "When more of this happens, and things start to get better, what do you imagine yourself doing?" "How did you come up with that idea?" "How did you do that?" "It seems to me that God is active in your life; what are some of the signs that it is happening right now?" Again, the questions naturally flow out of a common-sense approach to helping people see their situation from a new perspective. This change in perspective will in turn offer a change in the meaning of a situation. Any change in meaning can truly make a difference.

When Every Door Is Blocked. The purpose of brief pastoral counseling is to offer support that helps persons get back on track with their lives, and then to get out of the way. Sometimes nothing you try will help your parishioners to see other possibilities. Before referring them to another professional, you may ask them to consider what their future would be like without their desired change. For example: "What if your (spouse, boss, teenage son) does not change; what will you do?" Such questions help them define what they will do, what is within their control, even if the external situation does not change for the better.

When nothing helps, and people remain caught in despair or frustration, caregivers often are tempted to offer advice. If God has given you wisdom in a counselee's trouble area, by all means offer it—keeping in mind the uniqueness of each person's journey. If not, refrain from giving advice.

What remains is the pastoral caregiver's hospitality and sympathetic ear. Simplistic statements of encouragement, however, might have the opposite of their intended result. The experience of persons in the midst of great personal travail is unique, and familiar words of comfort may seem more like bromides than real encouragement. Even the Bible can have this effect when it is utilized as a quick fix. What we offer best to those who despair is our non-anxious presence and an abiding trust in the Holy Spirit.

Specific, Instead, Action, On Track

When a shift in focus from the problem to the solution begins to take place, it is time to proceed to the third part of the solution-focused helping circle (see the 6 o'clock position in the diagram on page 106). This step has one purpose: to further clarify the new vision of the future, the solution. Considerable time already has been spent in seeking to understand the problem. We have listened. We have begun to glimpse the counselee's life without the problem. Now we want to give an equal or greater effort to understanding the solution.

Specific. Have you ever watched a mystery movie in which a crime has been committed and the detective is gathering information by asking questions of a witness? These questions help to sharpen the memory of the one who is being questioned. After asking a few fact-gathering questions, the detective begins to get a picture of what was seen. As the process continues, a clearer description of the event develops. In this way the detective's questions focus the memory of the witness, enabling a recall of the events with greater clarity than was initially possible.

Like a detective seeking to clarify a witness's memory of a crime, pastoral caregivers try to clarify the initial memory of a solution—past, future, outside, or inside. In this way the solution is developed one piece at a time: "Can you tell me more specifically how you and your husband will be communicating when you are doing this?" "How exactly will you be doing this?" "What will he be doing specifically when the problem is absent?" "What will she be saying?" "What will he be thinking?" "What will others be doing and saying?"

Through this kind of discussion, a clearer picture can emerge in parishioners' imaginations; the caregivers' questions only facilitate it. From this growing picture of the solution, a new direction will arise. Later, the initial steps toward reaching that solution will be supported.

Instead. It is best to focus on the presence of something rather than the absence of something. Usually counselees start out by telling us what they do not want (their problems). Now we have opened up a doorway to what they do want. For example, the wife who says she does not want to argue with her husband anymore finds it impossible to envision not arguing. The only picture that she can imagine is of the two of them fighting. Brief pastoral counseling helps her use her imagination to discover what she will be doing instead of arguing.

When people describe their problems in terms of what they do not want, they state a negative goal. Negative goals actually tend to reinforce the problem. Whenever a goal is stated in the negative, ask counselees what they will be doing differently when they are not having the problem. The presence of something gives them a goal to envision.

Action. I have never watched the making of a Hollywood film, but I think when the shooting is about to begin, the director shouts something like, "Ready, places, action." The motion picture being created will be a description of action. In solution-focused brief pastoral counseling we want a moving picture, not a snapshot, to form in the minds of those we are counseling. We want to encourage responses that describe their own actions or the actions of others.

To form a moving picture in parishioners' minds, pastoral caregivers ask questions that begin with the word *how*. For example, a husband who is willing to help his marriage get back on track, but who has been angry and unresponsive, could be asked, "How will you be showing your wife that you love her in a way that she will feel loved?" He might respond: "I will be hugging her and looking into her eyes more," or "I will be having dates with her more often." This husband describes what he will be doing and therefore creates a clearer picture of the goal for the couple. Again, it is the how question ("How will you be doing this?") that elicits a picture of action.

On track. Pastoral caregivers help people clarify their initial description of the counseling goal by asking them to describe more specifically and concretely what they will be doing. They can also help parishioners discover what they actually want by clarifying what they will do instead of the problem. It is important that counselees do not imagine the action as something they will do eventually.

To couples who want to strengthen their marriages, for example, pastoral caregivers might ask: "When you are on track to strengthening your marriage, what will you be doing differently?" This type of question helps persons to see what they can do immediately. They create a more immediate track to that future hope: "What will be the first sign that you are on track to getting a little better?" "As you continue to do these things, will you see yourself as being on track to getting what you hoped for?"

Helping parishioners to organize and visualize a picture of the solution, and clarifying the direction they are to go, can be facilitated using scales or scaling questions. The answers to a scale are based entirely on the individual's view of the situation. The basic form of a scale question is: "On a scale from one to ten, where ten means the way you want things to be and one means the worst that things have ever been, where would you say you are right now?" Scaling questions can help counselees assess their level of commitment to a relationship, organize specific goals, appraise self-concept and self-esteem, clarify communication, measure hopefulness, and determine their willingness to work toward solutions. The following are some examples of scaling questions.

- To judge a couple's commitment to their relationship: On a scale from one to ten, where ten is "I will do anything to improve this relationship" and one is "I have given up on this relationship," where would you put yourself at this moment?
- To clarify specific goals: On a scale from one to ten, with one meaning "I don't feel like I can get any of this work done" and ten meaning "I feel like I've got it all together with my work," where would you say you are today? What will have to happen to move you to the next higher number?
- To encourage a greater communication of commitment in marriage: On a scale from one to ten, with ten meaning you are totally committed to your marriage and one meaning you are not committed at all, where would you say you are today? On the same scale, where would you put your spouse? What will your spouse have to notice that is different about you in order to say that you are moving up to the next higher number?
- To create a clearer vision of the future without the problem, take their response to any of the above scales and ask them what the next number will look like. For example: Since you are a four on the scale of wanting your marriage to succeed, imagine that over the next

two weeks you have moved to a six on the scale. What will be happening differently then? What will you have done to move yourself from a four to a six? What else will be different then?

So far we have listened, maintained fit, watched for clues, waited for an invitation, walked through a doorway, and (once in) helped counselees to clarify a new vision of a potential solution. Now we will want to have a clear plan for finishing the conversation on a positive note that encourages parishioners, reduces their fears, reviews what they have envisioned, and gives them a clear and uncomplicated way of continuing this process of change on their own.

Encourage, Reduce, Review, Task

The final step in this solution-focused pastoral counseling model is to offer supportive feedback (9 o'clock position in the diagram on page 106). Pastoral caregivers want to develop an environment that continues to offer hope. Instead of feeling embarrassed or overwhelmed for having openly discussed their problems, people should feel positive and expectant of change. "For I know the plans I have for you," declares the LORD, "plans to prosper you and not to harm you, plans to give you hope and a future" (Jer. 29:11 NIV). This hope creates a sense of expectancy, a belief that the future can be better than the past.

Encourage. When parishioners sense that they have been heard, when they have developed a clearer picture of a potential solution, it is time to move toward a closing. In my practice, I take a break for a couple of minutes to form my thoughts and then return with specific comments and suggestions. This draws a clear line between the counseling session and my feedback so that counselees know it is now time to listen.

In some church-related settings, an actual break may seem too awkward. If that is the case, you can draw the line by saying something like, "Why don't we pause now for a moment so I can give you some feedback?" This is not a complete break, but shifts the flow of the discussion.

These closing thoughts should begin with whatever legitimate compliments or praise you can offer. Often parishioners do not view their initial efforts as meaningful, and even the smallest amount of effort needs to be encouraged. For example, to a parent who had expressed deep concern to me regarding her daughter, and who in counseling envisioned a possible new course of action, I said, "I am very impressed by the love and support you obviously have for your daughter. It is clear that you deeply love her. Just wanting some help demonstrates how much you want to encourage her, and I congratulate you on your persistence." This may seem like I was "pouring it on," but persons who have just opened up their lives frequently feel vulnerable. I want them to know that I appreciate their openness and honesty.

In fact, praising this mother also accomplished two other purposes. First, it helped to normalize the problem. There are times when she may feel quite alone with her frustrations. She even wonders if there could be something wrong with her. She may think, "Perhaps I am the only one who has a problem like this." By offering praise and encouragement, I reminded her that, in Paul's words, nothing has taken hold of her except what is common to us all (1 Cor. 10:13).

Second, my encouragement reinforced her personal responsibility, her agency. I wanted to point out what good she had done. Most parishioners who come to us for help desperately need to realize their agency, to recognize that whatever good has happened is due to their efforts. More important, they need to realize that God wants them to succeed. Honest praise and compliments not only allow people to enjoy their efforts, but also encourage them to continue taking responsibility for the changes in their lives.

Reduce. Everyone wrestles with fears. These include, most commonly, fear of change and fear of rejection. Pastoral caregivers must make an effort to help reduce these fears. The fear of change can be made manageable. Even though change is inevitable, the unknown is scary. You can mitigate people's dread of the unknown by meeting each small step forward with genuine reassurance and praise.

The fear of rejection may be the most difficult for Christians to overcome. It is important to rehearse in your mind how you will respond when counselees confide something that shocks or disappoints you. What will they say about admitted sin? My response to a Christian man who confessed adultery to me was, "You knew I would be up front with you about the sin of adultery when you came to see me. Yet I am impressed by your openness and honesty. I can see that you are struggling with a difficult transition in your life, whether to go forward with God and rebuild your marriage, or to continue living with lies and possibly lose your marriage." I added, "I also think it took a great deal of courage to come and talk to me in the first place. It shows that this is an issue that you are very serious about. You clearly have the determination to follow through once you make a decision. The question before you is, which direction is your life going to go? This is a question only you can answer."

I believe as pastoral caregivers we have liberty to normalize the experience of sin; after all, we also have sinned. None of us is in a position to cast the first stone.

Review. Instead of reinforcing the problem, which your parishioners in counseling have been doing quite thoroughly by themselves, take a moment to reinforce the initial image of a solution. This is a brief process. Simply review what they will be doing instead of the problem, how they will do it, and how they will know they are on track.

For example, while counseling parents who were trying to help their son feel more loved, I helped them summarize and rehearse their goal in this way: "You said that you usually showed your love for your son by providing for his physical needs, and you both felt that this should be enough, but now you have discovered that it hasn't been enough after all. Since what you were doing has not been working, you have decided to try doing something different. You mentioned that you would no longer assume that he knows you love him. Instead, you will specifically go out of your way to tell him, and you will find the time to go out alone with him. You also said you will now seek to make loving eye contact as often as possible, to touch and hug him often each day." The beginning of a solution was clearly described and acknowledged one more time before the conversation ended.

Of course this does not "fix" any deep-rooted issues. That is not the intention of brief pastoral counseling. Helping counselees to get unstuck and back on track is a way in which God's Spirit begins to heal. Positive changes that arise out of parishioners' own lives and experiences are the goal. They occur as you concentrate on solutions, as you work together with parishioners to clarify that focus, and finally as they do a small part of what has been imagined and then observe what happens. This last part is called *presenting a task*.

Task. Will Rogers once quipped, "Even if you are on the right track, you'll get run over if you just sit there." After offering encouragement for every effort, seeking to reduce fears, and reviewing the potential solution, it is time to draw the conversation to a close and move to action. Your final words of the session will be to offer a specific suggestion or task. Unlike advice that seems good to the giver, this suggestion will reinforce the parishioners' imagined solution, not yours.

The task will invite the deliberate performance of one part of the solution. Its purpose is to encourage a kind of ripple effect, like radiating waves on the surface of a pond when a pebble is tossed in. What one person does affects the next person, who then reacts differently, which affects the next, and so forth. Our hope is that those we help will experience positive changes long after they have left counseling. Again, they are doing the real work, a sign of the work of the Holy Spirit within them.

The counselees' task usually includes the following components: doing a small piece of their envisioned solution, carefully looking for what works, deliberately doing more of what works, and observing what takes place as they do so. (For example, a couple whose commitment to the relationship was at three on a scale of one to ten is able to describe what will be different when they are at a four or a five.) A task may be offered in the following fashion:

> *What I would like you to try this week is to deliberately do whatever it takes to move from three to a four or five. It will probably be a part of what you have already described. When you do this, I want you to notice what is helping. You don't need to write anything down, just make a mental note. Whatever you do that is helping, I would like you to do more of it. Again, please take note of what happens that is different when you do this. Ask yourselves what is different within you and what is different with your spouse or your family. I think it would also be helpful to continue to let each other know what is working so you can work together and do more of it on purpose. Okay? Great!*

Future Sessions

The solution-focused pastoral counseling diagram (page 106) is a continuing circle. Counseling conversations in future sessions (if there are future sessions) will follow the same basic processes. First, we hear about the parishioners' experience with doing the task and, once invited in, proceed to an appropriate doorway in response to their present condition. Life for them will have shown some improvement, remained the same, or gotten worse. Each of those positions should be respected and utilized as the initial entrance back into solution-oriented conversation. It is important not to slip into deficiency- or problem-focused language when a second or subsequent session is required. Pastoral caregivers can avoid that trap by starting the conversation with questions such as: "What is better since the last time we got together?" "Since we last met, what changes have happened that have been helpful?" These questions assume positive change. They encourage people to search for it, find it, and consider its implications.

The pastoral caregiver wants to assume that positive changes have occurred, highlight any changes by asking for details, support all change as meaningful, consolidate these changes by encouraging greater specificity, and ask what additional changes have been helpful in order to expand the breadth of the solution. If parishioners report positive change concerning a described goal, you need to highlight, support, and consolidate this change. Highlighting asks for more detail: "What is different when you do that?" "What would your friends and family say is better?" "That is an interesting idea; what made you think of it?" "How did you do that?" "When did this happen?" "What happened that helped?" "How did you know that was the right thing to do?"

To *support* these changes, that is, to help people see them as meaningful, encourage them to describe the changes. Any mention of change can be highlighted by a raised tone of voice, by enthusiastic expressions (Super! That's great! Wow!), and by nonverbal positive gestures such as raising eyebrows or leaning forward. Along with these gestures, pastoral caregivers can interrupt, when positive change is mentioned, with questions such as: "What was that you just said?" "Now, hold on a second—you did what?" "Did you know this was something you would be able to do?"

To *consolidate* these positive changes, ask questions such as: "What will you have to keep on doing to get that to happen more often?" "If you could see a couple of months into the future, what other changes would you notice?" We must always be ready to discover more change. After developing, supporting, and consolidating any and every positive change, repeat the cycle of change by asking: "What other changes have been helpful?" Or, "What else is better since the last time we met?"

If parishioners do not recognize anything as having changed for the better, it could be that no positive change stands out in their memory. Assume that change has occurred anyway. Go into detective mode, looking for clues. Before you can highlight, support, and consolidate change, you need to unearth an incidence of strength or an exception. Proceed to the past doorway, asking questions that will help discover any recent exceptions: Was there at least one good day since we last met? What was your best day? What was the best part of that day? If any exceptions at all can be unearthed, highlight them; support and consolidate that change. If not, move to a variation of the future doorway.

When people are unable to picture their lives without the problem, the questions for the outside doorway can be employed; if those are unproductive, use the inside doorway. If they report that things have gotten worse, you may want to proceed directly to the inside doorway; for example: "How have you managed to get through the week?" "What are you doing in order to get by as well as you do when things are so bad?" Again, always assume God's activity. Highlight any changes by asking for details. Support all change as meaningful. Consolidate these changes, and ask about other changes they have noticed in the process. Each doorway leads back to clarifying the envisioned solution, consolidating gains, and encouraging feedback.

～

It is my hope that this model of solution-focused brief pastoral counseling will offer some added structure to enhance your counseling ministry. As ministers of grace and servants of Christ, we offer to others a counseling environment that is expectant and hopeful. We provide for them a non-anxious presence while encouraging creative imagination and solution construction. The traditional pastoral counseling model that concentrates on problems rather than on goals often hinders such an environment. Before we can assist counselees to envision life beyond their problem-focused paradigm, however, we will need to see beyond it for ourselves.

Notes

1.   Portions of this chapter in modified form are included in my article "Staying Solution-Focused in Brief Pastoral Counseling: A Conceptual Schema" in the *Journal of Pastoral Care* 53, no. 1 (Spring 1999): 57–70.

2.   For a more detailed explanation of the conceptual schema presented in this article, see my book *Solution-Focused Pastoral Counseling: An Effective Short-Term Approach for Getting People Back on Track* (Grand Rapids, Mich.: Zondervan, 1997).

9

Collaborating with the Spirit: Brief Spiritual Direction in Congregational Ministry

Duane R. Bidwell

THE FIRST TIME someone asked me to be her spiritual director, I froze. Bette, a professional colleague I had known briefly, invited me to lunch at a busy diner to "discuss something important."[1] When she made her request, I did not know what to say. I stammered something about being unqualified and lacking the time needed to commit to a relationship that could last for years. While I could recommend some reading, I told her, serving as a director was beyond my abilities. I never saw her again.

Today I cringe to think of that wasted opportunity. Had I felt equipped to deal with spiritual issues, had I thought of spiritual direction as a type of conversation rather than as a lifelong relationship, our time together might have been a catalyst for significant change in day-to-day experience of God. Blocked by my preconceived notions of what spiritual direction ought to be, however, I did not even ask what Bette wanted from direction or what she expected of a director. Had I engaged her request, we might have addressed her questions in a single conversation.

Few parishioners in a typical Protestant congregation ask for formal spiritual direction. But every congregational pastor and community minister receives requests for help with spiritual issues, and sometimes those issues go beyond momentary crises or questions about ethics and theodicy to address the core of a person's relationship with God and how God works in the world. Consider the following situations:

- A forty-year-old man, healing the wounds of incest, sees the happiness of an ex-girlfriend who hurt him considerably and wonders why God has favored her over his own needs for intimacy, believing that God has abandoned him and is no longer active in his life.
- A successful community leader confesses that her life is out of balance and spiritually bankrupt, and she cannot imagine how to

repair her relationship with her family, let alone with God. She feels that her packed schedule forces her to choose between her love for her children and her need for God—either family or church, worship or a morning with her husband.

- A man in his thirties, recovered from a brutal depression that cost him his job, family, and nearly his life, tells you that nothing he believed about God is true and that he cannot pray, worship, or read Scripture anymore. Understanding God's role in the depression has become a preoccupation even as he doubts that God exists.

- A student wonders if his decisions about graduate school are in line with his vocation and asks for helping in discerning God's will for his life.

All of these situations were requests for spiritual direction, and all of them could be (and were) addressed in a few sessions using the assumptions and methods of brief pastoral counseling. This is not to say that long-term spiritual direction is unnecessary or has no value; I have worked with my own directors for years and have consulted with several directees over a period of years as well. But the majority of my spiritual direction relationships last only a few sessions.

Most Spiritual Direction Is Brief

An informal survey of colleagues in Spiritual Directors International revealed that it is not unusual for direction to take fewer than six sessions. While most directors see people over an extended time, as many as half of their spiritual direction relationships are short-term either in duration or in number of sessions. They may see people frequently over a brief period of time, or infrequently—as few as four or five times—over a period of years. This is not the intense, monthly, long-term relationship most directors are trained to expect. One colleague, a spiritual director for ten years, wrote:

> Most of my spiritual direction relationships last from two to five sessions. This has left me with some ambivalence and confusion, as my training . . . provided the model and the belief that spiritual direction relationships were long-term, slow, and quiet . . . I have never shared this with another until your query came. But I'm aware I have had numerous questions as to whether this seemed to be others' experience or whether I had inadvertently ended up practicing a bogus variant of spiritual direction.[2]

Other spiritual directors describe relationships that last a few sessions—or even just one—and then resurface months or years later. "A few weeks ago I received a letter from a woman I met with for less than an hour . . . ten years ago," another director wrote. "She wrote to tell me how important that time was for her. So—we never know how the Spirit may use us."[3] Another colleague said she has begun to think of some of her work as "Christ kinship moments," single brief encounters that have an impact on the person's spiritual life. Such moments arise frequently when one is open to them.

These experiences are not recent developments rising out of our mobile, high-tech society. On the contrary: they have always been the norm for spiritual direction. For example, during the era of the desert mothers and fathers, pilgrims would endure days of rough travel for a single meeting or a few days with a gifted ascetic. The Russian Orthodox Church has always recognized the *staretz*, a holy person who shapes lives across vast distances, often with no more than a single meeting or a letter. Luther and others provided brief spiritual direction in the form of infrequent letters to those seeking advice. In the medieval era, clergy and laypeople alike sought the advice of *anchorites*, holy men and women who provided wisdom to seekers, often without an ongoing pastoral relationship. In fact, outside of monastic settings, most spiritual direction in history was brief in nature until the advent of modern psychology and its bias toward long-term therapy.

Parish pastors already provide spiritual direction, whether they are trained in it or not, and they certainly can provide effective spiritual direction in brief encounters. This chapter will help pastoral caregivers apply the insights of brief counseling theory to the task of spiritual direction in the parish, the home, and the coffee shop. It will begin with a look at the person of the director and the purpose of direction, followed by the hallmarks of brief counseling, the initial session of spiritual direction, the guidance provided by brief counseling, and specific interventions. The chapter will close with the case for brief spiritual direction in history and in the twenty-first century.

An Acknowledgment . . . and an Invitation

Not every practicing pastoral counselor or secular therapist embraces brief counseling theory. Some will complain that applying its ideas to spiritual direction cheapens the direction relationship. Others will think that it overly "psychologizes" the direction process. Still others might say that congregational pastors lack the training to do effective spiritual direction or to make effective use of brief therapy ideas and techniques.

I acknowledge these criticisms, but I do not believe they are accurate. Research and anecdotal evidence supporting brief therapy suggest that dialogue between the disciplines could be helpful to pastors, just as spiritual directors turned to (and often embraced) the ideas of psychoanalytic theory, Jungian psychology, and developmental psychology earlier in the twentieth century.

My conviction that spiritual direction and brief counseling can work well together rests in the belief that God is a God of possibilities, a belief that is affirmed and confirmed by the assumptions of brief therapy. In identifying exceptions or unique outcomes—times when difficulties do not dominate one's life—brief counseling opens the parishioner's eyes to new possibilities and the experience of a different sort of life. From a pastoral perspective, this approach affirms that God is always present, working for abundant life, even when we fail to recognize it.

Likewise, God works at the intersection of brief counseling and spiritual direction, and we could be surprised at the results. I invite skeptics and opponents, therefore, to consider the possibilities that might be borne of the conversation between spiritual direction and brief counseling theory before rejecting these ideas out of hand.

The Pastor as Spiritual Director

Spiritual direction is not a mystical process requiring arcane knowledge or esoteric spiritual formation. The director does, however, need experience and maturity in spiritual life. "Hard-headed realism," writes Josef Sudbrack, "not misty-eyed enthusiasm, is the key feature of spiritual guidance."[4] These qualities do not relate to chronological age or academic degrees. Rather, you must be able to sustain relationships and to listen, and you must be a person of prayer. While spiritual life can be confusing and enigmatic, the director may take comfort in knowing that common sense is the most reliable guide, when coupled with an attitude of acute awareness and openness to others' experiences and meanings.

A spiritual director does not make decisions or tell people what to do, but helps them (in the words of Thomas Merton) "to recognize and to follow the inspirations of grace" in their own lives.[5] In a way, the title "spiritual director" is a misnomer. The true director is the Holy Spirit; the human director is merely a guide who helps track the Spirit through the landscape of the directees' lives.

The pastor as spiritual director works with the stuff of everyday experience, but in a different way from a therapist or counselor. Therapists strive to resolve people's problems, or at least to help them respond to difficulties in a healthier way, whereas spiritual directors focus on helping people discern God's hand in

their lives, to engage in a dialogue with God, and to determine the most appropriate response to God's action. Simply put, spiritual directors offer assistance
to persons in their growing relationship with God.

In spite of the differences between spiritual direction and therapy, brief
pastoral counseling approaches have much to offer the pastor doing spiritual
direction in the congregation, with its attendant limitations of time. A look at
the characteristics of short-term therapy will reveal the many areas where the
two practices may intersect.

Hallmarks of Brief Counseling Theory

There is no single understanding of brief therapy. Orientations range from psychoanalytic to behavioral therapy. While most brief counseling concludes in
fewer than ten sessions, the actual amount of time spent is less important than
a commitment to intervene as little as possible in a person's life.

This chapter focuses on narrative, solution-focused, and competency-based
approaches to brief therapy. Several of these models have been adapted for pastoral care and counseling.[6] They share a theoretical base in social constructionism, the idea that we form our hopes, problems, beliefs, relationships, and the
meanings we give to our experiences out of our interactions with others.

A number of hallmarks and assumptions characterize brief counseling.
Among them, the counselor:

Avoids diagnostic labels and pathologies. The problem, not the person, is the
problem, and the problem is separate from the person. This statement is consistent with classical spiritual direction, which avoids diagnostic or clinical
labels. Thus we do not speak of people as depressed, but we note that depression is running their lives. The difference is subtle but important.

Emphasizes people's existing strengths and resources. We assume that all persons,
no matter how problematic their lives have become, have at least some resident
abilities and strengths that can contribute to a solution. Such an emphasis is
wholly consistent with classical spiritual direction. William J. Connolly has written: "there is an approach to 'direction' that concentrates primarily on a person's
strengths and another that concentrates primarily on [the person's] weaknesses,
and the choice between these approaches is a crucial one."[7]

Finds exceptions to the problem. Exceptions, or times when the problem is
absent or less troubling, always exist. The trick is to identify those exceptions,
amplify and expand them to establish the foundation for a new experience of
life without the problem.

Negotiates goals and solutions. The pastor and the person seeking help "co-create" a new reality. They share power in a mutual and collaborative counseling relationship that respects the self-determinacy of the person seeking help.

Affirms that people are the experts on their own lives. Pastors assume no expertise about how others should live their lives or resolve their problems. Their expertise lies in the process of counseling, not in the content of the problem and solution.

Focuses on the present and future. The past is of secondary importance, and too much emphasis on times gone by can even impede growth and change.

Knows that small changes can trigger big changes. In fact, people who find a major life change too daunting to attempt can achieve tremendous positive growth one tiny, nonthreatening step at a time.

Tailors counseling to the individual. Brief therapy is not a cookie-cutter approach. Because people are the experts about their own lives, brief counseling pays close attention to their own meanings and needs.

Establishes clear goals. Change is always happening, but people do not always notice it. Part of successful brief counseling is helping people to identify the change already occurring and to find ways to cooperate with it.

Underlying all of these assumptions is the pastor's *not-knowing* attitude. Because parishioners are experts about their own lives, we adopt an attitude of genuine and far-ranging curiosity. We assume nothing about them. We become like anthropologists seeking clues to a unique culture. For example, Pastor Smith does not automatically assume that a parishioner's crucifix represents the sacrifice of Christ. Rather, she asks what meaning the parishioner gives to the crucifix, where it came from, why it is hanging in the dining room, how it impacts dinner guests, and so forth. Only by asking these questions can she understand the importance of that particular crucifix to this particular person in this particular time and place.

The not-knowing attitude of brief pastoral counseling is similar to the *docta ignorantia*, "knowing unknowing," of spiritual direction.[8] Directors have knowledge about God and the spiritual journey but cannot guess how to create spiritual growth or healing or even know for certain what parishioners experience in a particular situation. Francis Vanderwall describes the director as a paradox, "a competent incompetent—competent in having the expertise, but quite incompetent in effecting the healing or the growth that people seek in spirituality," who despite this awareness can take heart in God's competence to enable great changes to take place.[9] Once again, the Holy Spirit is the true director. Through an attitude of not-knowing, the human spiritual director honors the presence of God by refusing to assume power, expertise, and knowledge that belong to God alone.

The First Meeting

The first step in providing brief spiritual direction is to clarify what sort of help your parishioners want. What do they hope to accomplish? The best way to find out is to ask. Remember that you cannot assume what others want or expect. A good opening question might be, "What did you hope would be different after our conversation today?" If they need help in identifying community resources, solving a behavioral problem, or grieving a death, other sorts of pastoral care and counseling would be more appropriate than spiritual direction. If, however, people ask for help in learning to pray, clarifying God's role in their lives, or exploring the meaning of an event, dream, or relationship, spiritual direction may be the most appropriate form of care. Again, remember that you have expertise to help people, but you must rely on them to tell you what they need and what meanings they assign to the people, places, and events in their lives. This is the essence of the not-knowing position.

Once you have heard enough to determine that spiritual direction is the most appropriate form of care, the next step is to learn about people's spiritual lives and what specific needs brought them to spiritual direction. Barry and Connolly suggest two diagnostic questions: "Do you listen to the Lord when you pray?" and "Are you telling [God] how listening . . . makes you feel?"[10] (These two questions are good brief spiritual direction in and of themselves.) Other helpful introductory questions might include: "Are you aware of and committed to God?" "What are your habits in prayer?" and "What event in your life awakened your desire to become closer to God?"[11]

Parishioners' answers to these questions will help you understand why they are seeking spiritual direction. Phil Marshall Negley identifies five areas of concern that bring people to spiritual direction: union with God, imitation of Christ, ways of prayer and forgiveness, making sense of foundational experiences, and searching for meaning in life.[12] Specific needs within these areas of concern include guidance in spiritual reading, detecting mediocrity or inner weakness, handling dry and difficult prayer, doing penance, discerning vocation, assessing progress, and receiving support and accountability.[13]

After identifying needs, we turn our attention to God's presence in parishioners' lives. Negley stresses that, in the first three to five sessions, spiritual directors strive to sustain believers in God's love and encourage their unity with God and others by focusing on emotions, thoughts, and behaviors. We do not have to lure God into this relationship. Just as brief counseling recognizes that exceptions to the problem always exist, so at this stage brief spiritual direction looks for the movement of the Spirit already present in parishioners' lives. The issue is not to resolve spiritual difficulties but to identify God's work already taking place and to find ways to collaborate with it.

Clarifying parishioners' needs and discerning God's presence in their lives are the primary tasks of the first (and sometimes only) session of brief spiritual direction. In fact, helping them notice God present and at work in their lives can be enough to resolve the difficulty that brought them to spiritual direction in the first place. When more action is required, the practice of brief counseling can provide the pastor with guidance for proceeding.

Taking Action: Guidance from Brief Counseling

The underlying concepts of brief counseling, set forth below, apply as well to brief spiritual direction. They include: working with everyday life, focusing on possibilities in the present and the future, tailoring care to the individual, and persevering in the face of boredom or frustration. They help pastors take action. If you think of spiritual direction as a specific type of pastoral conversation, you can view these concepts as parameters to shape that conversation.

Working with Everyday Life

Sometimes parishioners receiving spiritual direction want to talk about sublime experiences or describe their life with God in sweeping generalities. Like brief pastoral counseling, however, brief spiritual direction acknowledges that growth comes in everyday thoughts and behaviors, and that progress is best measured by changes in daily experience. Failing to do so may allow parishioners to detach their faith from the reality of their lives. Alan Jones, in fact, has called for a kind of "non-spiritual non-direction" in recognition that God reaches out to us in the everyday events of our lives.[14]

The "raw material for spiritual growth comes from the grit of our life and human experience," writes Howard Baker; God's Spirit "calls us through our families of origin, our personalities, our choices, and all of the conditions of soul we encounter."[15] It is essential for brief spiritual direction to return again and again to parishioners' daily life experiences, especially their relationships with others. The quality of those relationships can be a good measure of their spiritual lives; our relationship with God, one another, and indeed the whole created order is bound together. The Orthodox tradition of spiritual direction, for example, focuses simultaneously on inner movements—the workings of one's own heart—and on the words and deeds that pass among us, God, and our neighbor.

Ask parishioners to reflect critically and prayerfully on their daily life, looking for indications of God's presence and direction, and to articulate what they discover. Little growth will occur in the absence of such reflection. It may be helpful to organize the questions into three areas of concentration, as suggested by Morneau: *disposition* (what parishioners expect of life and how they approach the givens of life); *experience* (events as well as perceptions and feelings about those events); and *process* (reflection on experience and its relationship to disposition).[16] These three strands are, in fact, the underlying structure of all spiritual growth.

Simple questions may be the most effective intervention in spiritual direction—as in brief pastoral counseling—especially when they spark reflection on the experiences of daily life. For example: "How do you hear God speaking to you in this situation?" "What makes it difficult to hear God now?" "What would healing or growth look like here?" "What difference will this make in your life? In the way you know God? In the way you pray?" "How will you be changed by what you find?"

Focusing on Possibilities

Brief counseling looks at what is possible in the present and in the future, devoting little energy to what has happened in the past. It guides parishioners toward discovering and taking the first, small steps to a transformed life. Likewise, brief spiritual direction focuses on the present and future. It constantly redirects parishioners' attention away from the problems of the past and toward the many ways God is creating possibilities for their lives in the present moment.

This is not sugarcoating. It is more than an attitude adjustment. It requires a change in one's entire being. To be successful in brief spiritual direction, pastors must communicate trust in God's presence and the assurance that their parishioners can grow closer to God. Above all, they need to believe without a doubt that the people in their care possess resources and capacities to address their own difficulties and spiritual struggles.

Tailoring Care to the Individual

Counselees determine the goals and content of brief pastoral counseling. They are the acknowledged experts on their own lives. Likewise, in brief spiritual direction the directees are the experts and the work centers upon their own agenda, not yours—no matter how much knowledge and skill you bring to the table. This results directly from the not-knowing attitude discussed above and from attending to parishioners as individual persons. We cannot come with the same set of questions for each individual. Quoting scripture or using arcane theological language that has a particular meaning for you has the effect of imposing your template upon their experience. Never forget that the Spirit of God is the real director, and your role is to help people discern the Spirit's way for their lives.

Perseverance

Brief therapy takes the position that change is always happening and that dramatic change can happen quickly. Nonetheless, God sometimes chooses to act slowly. It can take time to discern God's action in our lives. For that reason, brief spiritual direction requires patience and perseverance.

Some parishioners will feel bored and frustrated when God seems to move very slowly. Others may begin to doubt God's presence and agency in their lives. At such times, the minister doing spiritual direction needs to model constancy, emphasizing the possibilities inherent in the present and in the future, and focusing on the stuff of everyday life. This requires attention to the meaning and significance that bogged-down parishioners place upon God's seeming inactivity. It also means helping them devise an honest and faithful response to the situation. If they are bored or frustrated, use their ennui as the focus of spiritual direction. How do boredom and frustration influence the way they perceive God? Have they shared their feelings with God? In what way is God calling them to wholeness through this time of stillness? Your persistence in attending to their experiences can help them not only to survive but also to benefit from the doldrums until they catch the wind of the Spirit moving them once again—sometimes with astonishing speed.

Interventions for Brief Spiritual Direction

I must admit that I feel resistant to talk of "interventions" in spiritual direction. It seems to reflect a mechanistic, problem-solving approach to spiritual growth, and I do not think successful spiritual direction is about technique or interventions in that sense. The most important tool for spiritual direction of any type is careful and active listening from a not-knowing position. Pastors who lack well-developed listening skills and an ability to draw people into their own stories will find it difficult to provide effective spiritual care. That said, I have found that a number of tools from brief therapy as well as from the ancient tradition of spiritual direction lend themselves to brief spiritual direction in the congregational context of the dawning millennium.

Opening Contemplative Space

Many people, frustrated by efforts to "connect" with God or deepen their prayer lives, lack space in their lives for quiet reflection in the presence of God. The speed, volume, pressures, and superficiality of modern life present significant hurdles to growing closer to God.[17] The overall effect is a loss of reverence. Therefore, the first task of brief spiritual direction is to open contemplative space in the parishioner's life.

The easiest way to do this is to identify opportunities in daily life for centering on God. At each stoplight, commuters can breathe deeply three times and recall that they are in the presence of God. Busy parents might repeat a chosen *monologia* (one-word prayer, such as Jesus, Love, or Peace) as a way to center themselves while preparing lunch or playing with their children. Even the morning shower can be a contemplative space when the bather focuses on being cleansed to face the day as a child of the Lord. Short prayers from the Celtic tradition also suit our need for brief moments of spiritual contemplation—for example, workers could silently pray, "The same One that made thee, made me likewise," each time they encounter a colleague in the hall. The Jesus Prayer, repeated in rhythm with one's breathing, is a classic spiritual discipline that can be taught and practiced in a few minutes: "Lord Jesus Christ, Son of God, have mercy on me, a sinner."

In the beginning, pastors should aim to create five to ten minutes of contemplative space in a busy life. Longer periods are desirable in a deepening relationship with God, but striving for longer periods of silence and reflection can frustrate people who are trying these disciplines for the first time. Even a few minutes of reflection and centering can have an enormous positive effect.

Identifying Exceptions

For parishioners who claim that something "never" or "always" happens, pastors might want to draw on the brief counseling practice of identifying exceptions to locate those times when the person's life is free from the difficulty. For example, I had the following exchange with a man who claimed God was never active in his life:

> PASTOR: How would you know God was being active in your life?
>
> ROB: I would just have a sense of being protected. I would see good things happening to me—I would feel hope.
>
> PASTOR: When was the last time you felt protected or hopeful? What was the last good thing that happened to you?

Rob: Well, I had a job interview. And the poem I'm working on is going really well. I don't worry so much about my bills right now.

Pastor: So good things have happened, but God hasn't been active in your life?

Rob: Well, I guess he has been present in my life. I just hadn't thought of those things being a part of God acting in my life.

Pastor: I wonder what kept you from noticing them as a part of God's presence.

The focus of this spiritual direction conversation thus moved from an unsolvable difficulty—God's inactivity, over which Rob had no control—to something he could control—learning new ways to listen for the presence of God.

Deconstruction

The brief therapy technique of deconstruction looks at the underlying assumptions in parishioners' thoughts and behaviors to discover where they came from and how they shape experience, and then examines ways in which different assumptions might lead to different experiences. It is a useful tool in brief spiritual direction as well. For example, one woman talked at length about what she wished for her relationships with her family but said she did not know how to ask God to help bring those changes about.

Pastor: One way is to ask in prayer. And what you just said was a beautiful prayer about the things you want for your family.

Mary: Really? (She begins to cry.)

Pastor: What are those tears about?

Mary: I was always taught that you only pray for other people. I guess I always thought it was wrong to pray for yourself.

Pastor: I wonder where that idea came from?

Mary: I don't know if anyone ever told me that. I just never heard my mother or my grandmother pray for themselves.

Pastor: How does it feel to think you just prayed for yourself? (She nods, smiling.) What would your life have been like if you had known as a child you could pray for yourself?

Mary: (Silence.) I guess it would have felt less alone. I would have known there was someone other than my family that I could rely on.

Pastor: Now that you know that, how will your adult life be different?

Rule of Life

A "rule of life"—a formal way of attending to the different aspects of one's spiritual and religious life and relationships—is a classic tool from the ancient practice of spiritual direction. Borrowed from the monastic tradition, it consists of a list of activities that nourish our spirit and tend our relationships with God and creation. Parishioners in spiritual direction commit to their own personal rule of life, making those acts a priority in their daily routine. For example, my rule of life includes daily prayer and scripture reading, service in ministry, weekly worship in community, monthly communion, and an annual contemplative retreat.

Helping parishioners to identify the rhythms of their spiritual life and build them into a routine will take one or two meetings. Some people find it transforming to examine how they spend their time and identify what is important to them spiritually. Margaret Guenther suggests that we structure a rule of life around four relationship patterns: our relationship to God, to others, to creation, and to our "own deepest selves."[18] Surely those four relationship patterns can serve as a useful guide to pastors as they help their parishioners develop rules of life suited to their own lives and spiritual needs.

Confession

Sometimes people who seek me out for spiritual direction wish to confess some act or omission that is blocking their relationship with God and others. They do not seek easy forgiveness but rather someone to listen, to recognize the guilt or doubt they feel, and to affirm that God will accept them despite what they have said or done. At times a ritual or act of penance negotiated between the pastor and the parishioner—offering a gift to someone they harmed or burning a letter in which they have listed their offenses, for example—can help. The Episcopal *Book of Common Prayer*, the Presbyterian *Book of Common Worship*, and the *Lutheran Book of Worship* all offer liturgies for individual confession that can be heard by laity or clergy.

In spiritual direction, confession provides both accountability and the experience of forgiveness. Guenther writes of the "overlapping of spiritual direction and sacramental confession. In both it is essential that the story be told candidly, that sins and shortcomings be named, that the directee see himself clearly."[19]

Letters

Letters of spiritual guidance have a long tradition in the church. Brief counseling, especially narrative therapy, also makes use of letters. For example, in pastoral counseling, I sometimes send letters that sum up a particular session and then encourage counselees to identify people who have noticed the changes they are making and to initiate conversations with those people. I may even suggest new areas for reflection. In brief spiritual direction, letters can summarize a meaningful conversation between pastors and parishioners, raise questions for directees to ponder at leisure, or affirm the progress people are making while providing suggestions for the future. Letters also help to create contemplative space. Invite people to write to you (or to themselves, or God, in journals). As Hinson points out, "Exchange of letters allows for, indeed almost forces, extended reflection. By its very nature spiritual guidance needs fallowing time, as the great spiritual masters repeatedly underline."[20]

Visualization

Guiding parishioners through a visualization exercise is helpful for those who feel "stuck" in their relationship with God or seek direction in their lives. For example, I used the following guided visualization as the centerpiece for six weeks of group spiritual direction. Months afterward, members reported they were still wrestling with its implications.

After the parishioner is relaxed and focused, the pastor slowly reads the following narrative, pausing for a time between paragraphs:

> You are standing outside a door. Notice its material and shape. Inside is a statue made to commemorate your life. Feel your emotions as you reach for the door and step inside.

> Stand at the doorway and look at the statue in the center of the room. Notice its shape, its material. Notice the colors, the mood, the size. Now walk closer. Walk all around the statue, noticing its detail. Touch it. Feel the texture, the temperature, the materials it is made of.

> Now you become aware of another presence in the room. Jesus has entered and is watching you from the doorway. You step back and watch him walk all around the statue of your life, noticing it. Watch Jesus interact with the statue. What emotions does it raise in you as you watch him?

> Now Jesus reaches out to touch the statue. He changes it in some way, makes an adjustment to this record of your life. Then he leaves.

> Approach the statue again. Walk around it as before and take note of the change that Jesus made. Notice your thoughts and feelings as you walk around this new statue.

> Now you will take leave of the statue. Walk back through the door and open your eyes.

The directee's reaction to the change Jesus makes to the statue can provide rich material for spiritual reflection and a way to move out of the "stuck" position.

Brief Spiritual Direction in Action

By now it should be evident that the principles and methods of brief therapy and brief pastoral counseling can contribute to successful brief spiritual direction. Indeed, I have made the point that much ancient spiritual direction would qualify as brief direction. Historical examples of such brief encounters abound. Saint John Chrysostom, for example, provided direction to Olympias, a deaconess, in a series of four letters.[21] In the monastic community at Thavata, near Gaza, two famous directors provided care to hundreds of people by letter without ever seeing their directees face-to-face.[22] People often traveled for miles through wilderness for a single encounter with a spiritual master, whose word influenced them for the rest of their lives.[23] The story of Jesus and the rich young man is a masterful illustration of single-session spiritual direction (Matt. 19:16-22).

I believe that spiritual direction outside the monastic community adopted its long-term focus, for the most part, only when it began to incorporate reflective, Rogerian, and Jungian schools of psychology into its theories and methods. These schools influenced twentieth-century spiritual direction in important and essential ways. But it will be equally important, in the twenty-first century, that spiritual direction and the pastors who practice it reclaim this ministry's original, brief orientation.

A better model of spiritual direction for the coming century may come directly from the language of brief therapy—that is, intermittent spiritual direction over a person's life span. This approach reflects the reality encountered by pastors and spiritual directors of our day. (Gone are the times when Kevin G. Culligan could recommend ten sessions to evaluate whether or not people were fitting subjects for spiritual direction and hear their story.)[24] The idea of intermittent spiritual direction over the lifespan is not new, however. We have seen examples of this approach from the ancient discipline. In 1938, Hubert S. Box recommended that "occasional interviews at long intervals" were sufficient for most spiritual direction,[25] and in 1989, Kenneth Leech wrote that "spiritual direction involves a number of temporary, though important, relationships during the course of one life."[26]

There is no brevity in our burgeoning, ever-changing, cradle-to-grave relationship with God. History and experience, however, do not reveal a need for a lifelong (or even long-term) relationship with a single spiritual director to tend that spiritual journey. Instead, assistance from a spiritual guide may be required at various crossroads along the way. Pastors offering spiritual counsel to their parishioners have much to gain from the underlying assumptions and even the methods of brief pastoral counseling as their ministry intersects with their parishioners' growth in grace.

The lifelong journey of faith, not the long-term guidance of a spiritual director, is the one true thing.

Notes

1. Names of individuals and facts about their lives have been changed to preserve confidentiality.

2. Personal communication, 6 April 1999.

3. Personal communication, 8 April 1999.

4. Josef Sudbrack, *Spiritual Guidance,* trans. Peter Heinegg (New York: Paulist, 1983), 22.

5. Thomas Merton, *Spiritual Direction and Meditation* (Collegeville, Minn.: Liturgical Press, 1960), 17.

6. See, for example, Charles Allen Kollar, *Solution-Focused Pastoral Counseling: An Effective Short-Term Approach for Getting People Back on Track* (Grand Rapids, Mich.: Zondervan, 1997); Gary J. Oliver, Monte Hasz, and Matthew Richburg, *Promoting Change through Brief Therapy in Christian Counseling* (Wheaton, Ill.: Tyndale, 1997); and Frank Thomas and Jack Cockburn, *Competency-Based Counseling: Building on Client Strengths,* in the Creative Pastoral Care and Counseling Series, ed. Howard W. Stone (Minneapolis: Fortress Press, 1998).

7. In Jerome M. Neufelder and Mary C. Coelho, eds., *Writings on Spiritual Direction by Great Christian Masters* (New York: Seabury, 1982), 97.

8. Richard Woods, *Mysticism and Prophecy: The Dominican Tradition,* Traditions of Christian Spirituality Series, ed. Philip Sheldrake (Maryknoll, N.Y.: Orbis, 1998), 14.

9. Francis W. Vanderwall, *Spiritual Direction: An Invitation to Abundant Life* (New York: Paulist, 1981), 87, 98.

10. William A. Barry and William J. Connolly, *The Practice of Spiritual Direction* (San Francisco: HarperSanFrancisco, 1982), 6–7.

11. For more questions that can be helpful in the first session of spiritual direction, see Gordon Jeff, *Spiritual Direction for Every Christian* (London: SPCK, 1987), 30–31.

12. Phil Marshall Negley, "The First Steps of the Journey: The Historical-Theological Metaphor of Pilgrimage and the Charism and Ministry of Initial Spiritual Direction" (diss., Andover Newton Theological School, 1996), 107.

13. Thomas Dubay, *Seeking Spiritual Direction: How to Grow the Divine Life Within* (Ann Arbor, Mich.: Servant, 1993), 55–62.

14. Alan Jones, cited in Margaret Guenther, *Holy Listening: The Art of Spiritual Direction* (Cambridge, Mass.: Cowley, 1992), ix.

15. Howard Baker, *Soul Keeping: Ancient Paths of Spiritual Direction* (Colorado Springs: Nav Press, 1998), 29.

16. Robert F. Morneau, *Spiritual Direction: Principles and Practices* (New York: Crossroad, 1992), 29, 83.

17. See Morneau, *Spiritual Direction*, 101–2.

18. Margaret Guenther, *Toward Holy Ground: Spiritual Direction for the Second Half of Life* (Cambridge, Mass.: Cowley, 1995), 66.

19. Margaret Guenther, *Holy Listening*, ix.

20. E. Glenn Hinson, "Letters for Spiritual Guidance," in *Spirituality in Ecumenical Perspective*, ed. E. Glenn Hinson (Louisville, Ky.: Westminster/John Knox, 1993), 162.

21. Joseph J. Allen, *Inner Way: Toward a Rebirth of Eastern Spiritual Direction* (Grand Rapids, Mich.: Eerdmans, 1994), 133.

22. Muriel Heppell, "The Role of Spiritual Father in Orthodox Monasticism," in *Monastic Studies: The Continuity of Tradition*, vol. 2, ed. Judith Loades (Bangor, Gwynedd, Wales: Headstart History, 1991), 23–24.

23. Merton, *Spiritual Direction*, 13.

24. Kevin G. Culligan, "The Counseling Ministry and Spiritual Direction," in *Pastoral Counseling*, ed. Barry K. Estadt, Melvin Blanchette, and John R. Compton (Englewood Cliffs, N.J.: Prenctice-Hall, 1983), 41.

25. Hubert S. Box, *Spiritual Direction: A Short Introduction to the Ars Artium Regimen Animarum* (London: SPCK, 1938), 50.

26. Kenneth Leech, *Spirituality and Pastoral Care* (Cambridge, Mass.: Cowley, 1989), 48–49.

10

Competency-Based Relationship Counseling: The Necessity of Goal Setting and Counselor Flexibility in Efficient and Effective Couples Counseling

Frank Thomas

PARISH PROFESSIONALS are torn in many directions. They work with committees, administer the business of the congregation, prepare sermons, attend functions, marry, bury, and celebrate, participate in community activities, study, pray, and meditate. Above all, they care for their parishioners: they call, attend, advise, and counsel. Allow me to outline a couple of assumptions that probably will resonate with your own experience as a parish professional:

- Both you and your church consider the counseling of parishioners as an ongoing expectation.
- You want to be an effective counselor, attending to the whole person (individual, couple, family, or extended family) in context.
- Couples counseling is one of the most challenging and yet rewarding tasks you encounter.
- You cannot work sixty to eighty hours a week and remain a viable helper.
- In order to attend to the needs of the whole congregation as well as to individuals, you must be time-efficient as well as effective.

In this chapter I will address the last assumption, concerning the need for careful time management in the parish, because I am convinced that without efficient methods of counseling, a pastor's time will become dominated by counseling to the detriment of other vital areas of ministry.

Let us consider a nuts-and-bolts illustration of how difficult parish work can be if it is not both efficient and effective. You are the busy pastor of a 250-family church. During your first year with the congregation, you have come to see them as pretty normal folks with a broad range of resources and needs. Based on this conclusion, you begin to project your foreseeable time commitments for the coming year. You need time for sermon preparation, reading and reflection, prayer, hospital and shut-in visitation, membership growth, staff supervision, continuing education, denominational commitments, and . . . oh, yes, counseling.

You can budget a maximum of ten hours per week (twenty percent of a fifty-hour work week) for this important commitment—any more and you will neglect other important functions of your position (more than likely, your family and your health as well). Currently you average one wedding a month (members only, for now); if you require four premarital sessions per couple, you now have nine hours a week remaining for other counseling. This congregation has, on average, one funeral per month; responding to surviving family members should take about one hour a week of pastoral care/counseling, as you figure it. You are now down to eight hours a week. Currently you have four individuals and two couples engaged in weekly counseling sessions, all of whom express both need and motivation, and you know every counselee values this time with you. If you add just one individual or couple every other week and fail to end any of your current counselee relationships, you will hit the ceiling of ten hours a week in only one month!

If this scenario corresponds to your experience in some small (or significant) way, you may already be seeking ways to make your counseling time more efficient without sacrificing effectiveness. This chapter aims to provide ideas that can help you to do so.

Believing and Acting

"One's premises determine one's therapeutic approach."
—M. Durrant

I believe that most parish professionals can be productive and time-efficient with couples in counseling by adopting a few basic premises. One is that people have within their experience a wealth of skills and resources, both known and unknown to them. They have competence in at least some areas, though their problems often blind them to their strengths and capabilities and to the solution-oriented behaviors they already perform.

To ground a counseling approach upon people's competence is not wishful thinking. To the contrary—it is realistic and even a bit pragmatic. Competency-based counseling[1] places its emphasis on empowering couples and increasing agency, focusing more on what is useful in their situation than on speculation about past causes. Well-known marital researcher and author John Gottman has come to assume that "in the field of marital therapy . . . a psychotherapy of marriage had been constructed by extending methods of psychotherapy to the design of marital interventions, instead of building a marital therapy from the way people normally go about the process of staying happily married."[2]

Change Is Inevitable

"Change is so much part of living that [people] cannot prevent themselves from changing," write Berg and Miller.[3] This approach to pastoral caregiving posits that, more often than not, it is more important to call attention to experiences that differ from people's static descriptions of their problems by increasing or amplifying those differences, than it is to solidify a problem's place in the couple's lives. Most people enter counseling because they are "stuck" and seek relief from their discomfort or dilemma. Without some relief, and without the generation of realistic hope, insight into contributing factors and causes may not be enough to keep a couple engaged in the counseling process.

Small, Early Steps

It is important to take a small step in a positive, useful direction as soon as possible. Knowing where you are going as a couple and getting a positive, affirming start down that path is empowering. Pastoral caregivers do not necessarily know what will work best for their counselees. Counselees themselves should define the goals of counseling, for they are (or can be) the experts on their experiences. Their motivation is apt to be higher when intervention heads in the direction they wish to go.

Focus on Present and Future

In pastoral care and counseling, carefully timed meetings that focus on what is changeable in the present and future are more effective than long-term, continuous counseling focused on the intractable past. The past offers a picture dominated by the facts of the problem, and, to quote Wittgenstein, "the facts belong only to the problem, not to its solution."[4] Concentrating on past events may even make the situation seem more overwhelming. The future offers the possibility of hope and resolution. Counselees and helpers together construct this future picture of the solution (see chapter 4). Efficient pastoral intervention seizes the moment of motivation, engages the couple's resources, and establishes momentum. Granted, the door is always open and the ongoing pastor-parishioner relationship is important, but the counseling relationship does not need to exist in a fifty-two-weeks-a-year meeting schedule.

Why adopt a solution orientation? Therapies focusing on counselee strengths—such as solution-focused,[5] solution-oriented, possibility, narrative, and competency-based—have stormed onto the counseling scene over the past fifteen years. Once considered "therapy lite" by some, what I have come to call competency-based counseling or CBC models have shown effectiveness in a broad range of settings. Brief by design, these therapies could not have come at a better time for the pastoral caregiver.

Competency-based therapies originated from the work of psychiatrist Milton Erickson and the brief therapies generated by Paul Watzlawick, John Weakland, and Gregory Bateson. Although there are many competency-based traditions and models, much of what has been written both clinically and theoretically has focused on the individual counselee; little has been written to apply these ideas to couple or relationship counseling.[6] In this chapter I apply some of the critical ideas from competency-based therapies to the pastoral counseling of couples. These include: being brief (not any longer than necessary); the art of setting goals; and the need for counselor flexibility.

Why (Not) Brief?

For most caregivers, the struggle is in the philosophical realm, not between long- and short-term counseling. Shorter does not seem appropriate, and more time in counseling somehow means better outcome. A quick review of research might serve as a comparison between what should be and what is.

Cooperating with What Is Realistic

It is an old and well-substantiated claim that, whatever the theoretical orientation or methods of the helper, counseling usually is short-term in actual practice. The average duration of counseling by psychotherapists, whether in a private or a community-based setting, is from four to eight one-hour sessions.[7] The typical duration of counseling in parish ministry is two or three sessions.[8]

The majority of people who come for help do not expect to do continuous counseling for months or years. Generally, they expect to remain in counseling for fewer than ten sessions over the course of less than three months. In one study, 65 percent of counselors preferred to continue the counseling relationship over fifteen sessions, while only 12 percent of counselees expected counseling to take that long. Overall, the picture seems to be this: large numbers of people will terminate counseling before the counselor and the counselee mutually agree upon completion. People rarely stay in counseling until the counselor declares that the process is finished.

Research Supporting Brief Counseling

A definitive body of research supports the idea that doing counseling briefly is both efficient and effective.[9] Self-studies, external outcome audits, and independent research, both quantitative and qualitative, overwhelmingly support brief counseling as an effective approach to problem resolution, with the added benefit that people tend to report a continuation of positive change over time. Research on solution-focused therapy at the Milwaukee Brief Family Therapy Center reveals that 77 percent of counselees who completed counseling felt they had met their treatment goal and an additional 14 percent thought they had made progress toward their treatment goal. At eighteen months (164 cases), 85 percent thought they had experienced long-term improvements.[10] Koss and Butcher write that "Brief treatment methods have generally the same success rates as longer term treatment programs."[11] They only take less time.

Caregivers who are prejudiced against providing short-term counseling should examine their assumptions about change, redemption, and restoration to see if some space could be made for a brief approach that could be deemed successful. Both clinical outcome research and counselee-based, descriptive research support the idea of efficient and effective intervention that is time limited. One study is of particular interest to those who fail to see their own participation in outcome expectancy.[12] Therapists who were given a twelve-hour training program in brief therapy obtained lower rates of attrition (unplanned/non-mutual treatment termination) and recidivism (return for treatment), and higher success rates than did untrained or self-trained therapists. Participants in the study ranged from beginners to experienced therapists, and the results held up among all skill levels. Once therapists accepted the value of brief therapy, their effectiveness in therapy increased. As the famous constructivist Heinz von Foerster once said, "If you wish to see, learn how to act."[13]

The Joy of Goal Setting

Helping counselees to set goals needs to be near the top of any solution-oriented brief counselor's must-do list. Research supports the idea that setting goals with couples results in more efficient and effective counseling; several fine chapters and examples on goal-setting can be found in the CBC literature.[14] I would like to borrow from one of the best lists of goal qualities, found in Berg and Miller, and apply some of their definitions to couples counseling.[15]

1. *Goals must be important to the counselees.* Counselees are more likely to cooperate in the counseling process when they have controlling interest in the

direction and preferred outcome. Where you head with couples should not be a compromise that eliminates the passion for change that brought one or both of them into counseling.

For example: Joe and Mary argue almost constantly. They fight about a wide range of topics, from the substantive (child-rearing philosophies) to the mundane (who drank the last soda). They even fight about fighting![16] As with most severely conflicted couples, each is firmly entrenched in her/his own experience of right and wrong ("I'm right; you're wrong"). To find a midpoint or compromise on child rearing, each person would have to abandon cherished ideas, thus admitting error or even fault before any goodwill has been established. To ask people to cede hard-won ground without any tangible personal gain is, most likely, to fail. The CBC approach would ask them to speak about their experiences (arguing) and what they would like to change (to fight differently, less frequently, with less emotion or reactivity, out of the presence of their children, and so on). For the sake of their marriage, their personal well-being, and their children, both Joe and Mary are willing to talk about arguing less frequently. If the pastoral caregiver can create a mutually beneficial beginning that the counselees feel is meaningful, motivation increases and the parties are more likely to cooperate.

2. Goals should result in the presence rather than in the absence of something. Imagining a future is difficult enough for many counselees. Thinking of life with something often is easier than envisioning experience without something. For example, a future of "maintaining sobriety" has more possibilities than "not drinking," because achieving a state of not drinking requires one to focus on drinking.

Let us continue with Joe and Mary. Both have identified "fighting less" as a starting point in their discussion. As a pastoral caregiver, it is important that you seek their ideas about what might replace the arguments. One question to propose in this direction might be: "If you were fighting less, what would you be doing?" or "When you're not arguing, what are you doing instead?"

3. Goals need to be small and focused on the beginning rather than on the end. Counselees' goals should fall within the realm of possibility in the thoughts of everyone involved. They should be realistic and achievable within the scope of counselees' resources. In this same vein, goals set with couples should be important yet modest, and step-by-step success toward each goal should be easy for all parties to recognize. The surest way to continue a couple's pattern of failure is to set a lofty standard for success that cannot be achieved incrementally.

For example, "never arguing again" is a poor goal for several reasons, mostly because it is unrealistic to expect two cohabiting adults to refrain from arguing over the course of their relationship. Instead, "handling our disagreements more positively" could be a starting point of constructive change for both spouses. In fact, they may achieve some immediate changes during the counseling session that the helper can point out as a successful beginning to a longer-term goal. ("You're not in agreement on everything, but you seem to be handling it differently than you do at home.")

4. *Goals need to be concrete, specific, and behavioral.* It is paramount to establish goals that are observable to both members of the couple as well as to the pastoral caregiver. In competency-based counseling, all facets of people's experiences—affective, cognitive, interactional, behavioral, and spiritual—are important. However, CBC stresses observable behaviors and interactions because it is easier for counselees as well as for pastoral caregivers to validate change toward goals when they can cite specific, concrete examples.

With Joe and Mary, movement toward their goal of handling disagreements more positively can be expressed in affective terms ("I feel closer to Joe") or cognitive terms ("I think differently about our marriage now"), both of which are important to the counseling process. However, the pastoral caregiver does best to encourage behavioral changes that have interactional consequences, particularly through homework tasks, because behaviors are more within counselees' control than are feelings and thoughts. While it would be unfair to ask Joe to increase his positive feelings toward Mary in the coming week, it is reasonable to ask him to continue certain behaviors that he already has tried (such as continuing to give Mary a hug every morning and evening, since she has indicated this is a very meaningful change for her).

While setting goals, the ability of the caregiver to mesh with counselees' expectations has a great impact on the counseling experience. It requires openness, flexibility, and a thorough knowledge of counselees' needs and resources. It is critical to the success of the endeavor.

Counselor Flexibility

The research discussed above is not an argument for the demise of longer-term counseling or a paean to brevity in counseling. However, it demonstrates clearly that clergy need to be prepared to meet the needs of their parishioners with a variety of responses, thus avoiding the Procrustean bed of extended counseling for each and every presenting problem. It is the soul of wisdom to resist enshrining any single model or approach to counseling.

In fact, having the ability to relate to, empathize with, and positively value those seeking counsel appears to be much more important than any particular strategy to the success of the therapeutic process, and the emphasis of this article is on particular caregiver attitudes and activities. Fitting with counselees' expectations requires that caregivers adapt to their contexts, beliefs, and needs. Therefore, caregivers must take a flexible, non-normative approach in their work with couples in order to fit closely with each counselee couple. This approach precludes the use of any particular intervention template, communication norm, or diagnosis schema. Instead, as you will see below, the counselor, assuming a non-normative or idiosyncratic stance, seeks to relate to couples one member at a time, with respect and curiosity.

Assuming a non-normative position leads to flexibility in several areas. First, it allows counselees to have their own experiences. Any good clinician or researcher knows that there is no "normal" (fiftieth percentile) counselee; as Gregory Bateson once said, "The generic we can know, but the specific eludes us."[17] Therefore, adjusting one's approach to fit with the counselee's experience of grief, depression, or marital conflict is the road of least resistance and highest success.

Next, to be non-normative means to use counselees' lived experience as the primary source of information. This moves the caregiver away from a preconceived image of what should or might be, and requires the full participation of the couple in the process. Instead of diagnostic tools that standardize (and can dehumanize), competency-based counseling attempts to connect with the people who are living their trials and problems. The actual exchanges in the counseling context provide the necessary information for change, rather than reference books, assessment tools, or philosophy of treatment.

Finally, accepting the counselees' experiences as the primary data source allows every outcome to be unique. Counselor flexibility is often strained at this point, as many professionals believe that a final solution must be reached in order for counseling to terminate. If the pastoral counselor is flexible, however, counselees themselves decide when they have achieved enough and whether or not they will return for additional sessions. Since no one has an error- or problem-free relationship, CBC urges the professional to adapt to counselees' ideas of "good enough"—and to respect their decisions.

Two Case Examples of
Goal Setting and Counselor Flexibility

While most books on the subject of solution-focused brief therapy illustrate goal setting with a single counselee, I would like to discuss the implementation of goals when the "client" is a couple. In the following case, the problem was indeed the problem, both for me and for the couple. The puzzle was: how does one carry out goal-oriented brief pastoral counseling when defining the goal becomes the therapeutic problem?

Donnie and Suzanne: Working without a Goal

Donnie and Suzanne were referred to me by one of their friends. They had a deep love for each other and wanted to make their relationship better. Each had been married before. When they came together six years before, they were certain that this marriage was to be a lifetime commitment. Donnie had two children from his previous marriage, both of whom lived with his ex-wife. Suzanne had no children. They had agreed to have no more children, and Donnie had undergone a vasectomy.

In our initial interview, both Donnie and Suzanne reported that they needed "sex therapy." Both had consulted physicians and ruled out any physical dysfunction or abnormalities. Neither had any medical complaints that might interfere with sexual activity, nor did they report any performance problems. Intercourse was physically pleasurable to both of them.

I began to explore their common and individual experiences of sexual problems, since this was their agreed-upon reason for seeking help. Unfortunately, that was their last point of agreement. They told me that they disagreed on current sexual frequency, desire, needs, conversation—everything. He was a planner; she was spontaneous. He was a self-described loner whose intimacy needs were met almost entirely by his wife; she was very social and had many friends and outside interests. As Suzanne said, "We couldn't be more opposite!" Donnie playfully responded, "Now see here! I beg to disagree!" and they broke into laughter. He agreed with Suzanne that they were "as different as night and day." When it came to sexuality, Suzanne talked in terms of rhythms, music, presence, and caring, and her side of the conversation was filled with colorful metaphors. Donnie chose his words carefully and focused on facts rather than feelings or stories. Although not devoid of metaphorical description, Donnie was hard-pressed to think abstractly or move away from concrete descriptions about their sexual relationship. They politely disagreed on what constituted good sex, on current sexual issues in their relationship, and on appropriate private and public sexuality. In short, they stood with expertise, firmness, and clear articulation on opposite sides of every possible area of discussion.

We were stuck. Donnie and Suzanne could not come up with any common exceptions (à la de Shazer) or unique outcomes (à la White and Epston) in this problem area. I felt that forcing the adoption of a particular goal at this point in the process could only elevate one person's sexual experience over the other's and possibly make things worse. For example, she wanted sex more often, while he was satisfied with the frequency. She wanted spontaneous, passionate sex and he liked planned, choreographed seduction. Around the house he was rarely naked, while she liked to shed her clothing whenever possible. He did not think talking about sex was productive, helpful, or proper; she spoke openly of her sexuality, both with him and with friends. They both identified exceptions

to their sexual disagreements, but their exceptions did not match. To end the
first session I decided to play it safe and by the book. I gave them the "noticing
task,"[18] asking them to carefully observe, and report back to me, times when the
problem was different in any way.

The second session repeated the pattern of the first; both noticed exceptions, but they contradicted each other from start to finish. At the end of the
second session, I offered a time-tested idea—the removal of all face-to-face discussion concerning sex. A week later, they returned to tell me that the intervention had not worked for them; they ended up fighting over sex more than ever.
Suzanne stated that she was not able to function normally in the relationship
because of a recurring illness, so the task did not have a chance of success for
her. According to Suzanne, things had moved from bad to worse, because now
she was constantly saying to herself, "I am a failure" whenever she entertained
sexual thoughts. Donnie's attitude toward altering the course of their sexual
problems matched Suzanne's.

I remembered the maxim from Berg and Miller: "If it doesn't work, then
don't do it again, *do something different!*"[19] In a Solomon-like (and cowardly)
fashion, I chose not to proceed to the goal-setting stage, but to utilize a principle borrowed not from an eminent psychotherapist but from former California governor Jerry Brown: "Inaction may be the highest form of action."[20] I
promoted the idea of actively not-doing. Often, when one is lost, the best
direction to take is down; that is, to sit still until a correct or useful direction
can be discerned. The only thing worse than being lost is to strike out in a
direction that will get you more lost. So, instead of moving forward, I asked
Donnie and Suzanne to make separate and secret lists of "great little moments"
in their relationship over the next two weeks so I could get a better feel for how
each one viewed the relationship when it was pleasant. Instead of prescribing
or forbidding sex, I simply asked that they have sexual intercourse only if they
both agreed on every aspect of it from the first interaction on the subject to the
last. The latter task would allow sexual relations without either capitulating to
the other's position. The former encouraged them to produce their own exceptions without requiring agreement between them or relying on my efforts to
elicit them.

The fourth and last session took place two weeks later. They still had no
exceptions in common. Suzanne confronted Donnie at the beginning of the
session, asking if he would "totally commit" himself to her sexually. Donnie
responded, "I have my limitations." To break this impasse, I stayed with the do-
nothing theme and offered a metaphor from the sport of track and field. I suggested that in the future they attempt to "clear the high jump" by making sure
the bar is set low enough so that success is easy and fun for both. I continued
the active non-doing approach, asking them to consider two behaviors: first, to

restrict their talk around sex to successful experiences, and secondly to offer ideas to each other only if they believed the idea could not fail. I communicated my view that their repeated attempts to convert each other had only led to greater conflict, and that a period of deliberately doing nothing to solve the problem was worthy of consideration. I remembered a quote from columnist and fellow Texan Molly Ivins: "The first rule of holes: When you are in one, stop digging."[21] Both Suzanne and Donnie committed to stop whatever they had been doing to address the problem up to this point, and we all agreed to take a month off and then check back to see how their experience of the problem might have changed.

I followed up by telephone one, two, and six months later because Donnie and Suzanne decided not to return for counseling. Not only had they lowered the bar; they had occasionally "dug a trench and put it below ground," in Donnie's words, in order to insure mutual success. Over the course of the month following the last session, they coauthored a metaphor that fit their mutual sexual experience. Donnie described their new view during a follow-up phone conversation: "We see sex as an exciting trip down a foggy road. Suzanne used to think she could see over the horizon, and I used to believe the most important thing to do was analyze and measure the road. Now, we simply hold hands and venture forth. We can't see far, but we are both shining our flashlights ahead and enjoying the trip together." Donnie and Suzanne had reinstituted old practices with great success, and they no longer required counseling for problems in their sexual relationship.

Shalandra and Tony:
When Push Comes to Shove and Neither One Works

Shalandra and Tony had been married for fourteen years and had one daughter, Bobbie, age seven. In their ninth year of marriage, Tony had an affair that lasted six months. He also made some terrible business decisions without consulting Shalandra, which had an adverse affect on their family. When Shalandra found out Tony had been unfaithful, she filed for divorce. Ninety days later, it was final. Tony and Shalandra shared custody of Bobbie; as parents they were in regular, positive contact with each other.

Shalandra and Tony came to see me as a couple after Tony called and set up an appointment "so we can put our marriage back together." During the first few minutes, I learned that they were divorced and living in separate residences. Tony stated that he wanted this relationship to succeed, knowing that "it could be better than ever before" if Shalandra would simply give him a chance. During our first hour together, I set a short-term goal: to assess the direction and motivation of "putting the marriage back together" for one additional session, after which we could decide on the future direction of counseling.

During the second session, Shalandra talked a great deal about the emotional pain she had experienced due to Tony's betrayal, while Tony spoke about his undying love and newly realized devotion to Shalandra and their "marriage." For the last fifteen minutes, I asked Tony if he would mind stepping into the waiting area so I could ask Shalandra a few questions in private. Tony said he would do whatever it took to move things forward and left the room. I then asked Shalandra the following scaling question: [22] "If zero means you have no intention of getting back together with Tony and ten means you are highly motivated to mend your relationship, where would you put your motivation right now?"

The tears began to flow as she thought about this question. Finally she responded, "I'm about a three right now. . . . Is that so wrong?" For the next few minutes, Shalandra and I talked over the differences between Tony's expressed desires and her current preferences, and she concluded that now was not the time to attempt reconciliation. I asked her if Tony should know the content of what we had just discussed. Shalandra decided that she would like to have me present when she expressed to Tony the pressure she was feeling from him, rather than hide it or discuss it with him in the car when he drove her home.

I asked Tony to join us once again. Shalandra told him that "I'm not where you are yet" concerning a possible reconciliation. Tony said this was the first he had heard of a difference from her. They both related corresponding experiences of their long-term pattern: Tony pushing hard and Shalandra caving in to his demands. I told them that I would be happy to meet with them if they decided it would be beneficial, but only if their motivations to reconcile were close together. Shalandra stated that she would like to see me alone for a few sessions in order to sort out some of her pain and to envision a future without pain dominating her decisions. Tony heartily seconded this, and so I agreed to the arrangement.

Over the next two weeks, Shalandra and I met twice with the goal of examining her motivation to reconcile, identifying those parts of her experience that she could control and those that she could not. We discussed her need for time away from Tony's incessant questions and pressure, and she came to some important decisions about her part in creating this space. Even though she missed "being a family" (with all three of them together), she did not want to return to a relationship in which she felt limited freedom to think and act. Also, she had come to discover that she could function, pay her bills, be a parent, even thrive without him. Finally, she came to the conclusion that she would have to make significant movement toward forgiving Tony for his infidelity before she could even entertain the idea of remarriage. At the end of our second session together, Shalandra decided that several changes had to take place before she and Tony could return to counseling together, and she made concrete plans to create space between them while continuing their co-parenting plan. She was frightened but also exhilarated by the possibility of a future in which she had a voice in the direction of her life—with or without Tony. At this point, Shalandra said she would talk with Tony and get back to me if they desired future sessions.

Two weeks later, when I didn't hear from Shalandra, I followed up. She told me that she and Tony had been discussing their differences "like equals, for the first time ever." Shalandra felt Tony was respecting her space. She was working full time and "finding out I can live with or without him." She related that their talks were meaningful, filled with both tears and laughter, and she felt they would like to continue talking on their own for the time being "now that the pressure is off."

Her final comment to me related to an episode of the television program *Frasier* that she had viewed that past week. "Frasier's dad told him, 'Stop analyzing everything. Some things, you just can't change.' I heard you talking to me in that episode! You know how you kept saying we should look at what we can change and spend less time looking at things we couldn't change? Well, I think I've come to see that I can only change me—not my past, not Tony, not even what happened between us. I can only try to get the space I need, keep talking with Tony, and see what happens. The pressure's off—if we're going to have our family together again, this is our best chance."

Shalandra told me that both she and Tony felt positive about the time spent in counseling and would call in the future "if we need your input on changing."

My sense of this couple near the end of their second conjoint session was that their goals were very different. Tony was openly seeking an immediate reconciliation, while Shalandra was still speaking about her uncertainty and the unresolved pain of Tony's disloyalty. Because we did not have an agreed-upon direction, let alone a collective purpose, I changed the context to assess whether or not a common goal could be formed. That common goal turned out to be an assessment of the direction rather than a movement forward; however, their best chance for change that was satisfying to both of them was found not in compromise, but in delaying decisions until (and if) they could head in the same direction. Setting a clear short-term goal with Shalandra involved careful examination of ideas around space, commitment, and forgiveness. We did just that—and she felt that counseling had taken her as far as she could go for the moment, knowing that she would have to live out her discoveries and work on changes in her relationship with Tony, not in her relationship with me. I acknowledged and affirmed her wisdom, as we had achieved our confirmed counseling goal.

Some Final Thoughts

Once, when my daughter Allison was little, she presented me with a riddle:

> *Dad, what do you do when you come to a fork in the road?*
> *I don't know—go straight ahead? Flip a coin?*
> *Don't be silly, Dad—you pick it up!*

In both of the cases presented above, a fork in the road presented a problem. In the two cases discussed, instead of assuming that I possessed the wisdom to choose, I stood by the tenets of competency-based counseling and honored the idea that the decision must be left up to the counselees. The strategy and the ideas accompanying it are not necessarily new. Mental health approaches of restraining or forbidding attempts to change have been around much longer than I have been practicing,[23] and concepts such as goal setting and counselor flexibility are well established in the counseling literature. However, applying such ideas to relationship counseling may require patience when it becomes difficult to identify a common beneficial direction. Much of the brief therapy literature stresses the solution-focused model to the point of rigidity. I have found that my application of competency-based ideas must honor the very real predicament of people who can find no commonly agreed-upon exceptions to their problems, who have not arrived at a mutually beneficial goal, in order to help them find ways of getting unstuck.

Setting goals while remaining flexible are valuable standards for parish professionals, indeed, for all caregivers, in their practice of couples counseling. If all parties agree that the direction of counseling is possible and positive, then the process usually will be briefer and mutually satisfying.

Wherever you find the forks in the road . . . happy trails!

Notes

1.   See F. N. Thomas and J. Cockburn, *Competency-Based Counseling: Building on Client Strengths* (Minneapolis: Fortress Press, 1998).

2.   J. M. Gottman, J. Coan, S. Carrere, and C. Swanson, "Predicting Marital Happiness and Stability from Newlywed Interactions," *Journal of Marriage and the Family* 60 (1998): 5–22 (emphasis added).

3.   I. K. Berg and S. D. Miller, *Working with the Problem Drinker: A Solution-Focused Approach* (New York: Norton, 1992), 11; see B. P. Keeney and F. N. Thomas, "Cybernetic Foundations in Family Therapy," in F. Piercy and D. Sprenkle, eds., *Family Therapy Sourcebook* (New York: Guilford, 1986), 262–87.

4. L. Wittgenstein, *Lectures and Conversations on Aesthetics, Psychology, and Religious Belief* (Berkeley: University of California Press, 1972), no. 6.4321.

5. See S. de Shazer, "Brief Therapy: Focused Solution Development," *Family Process* 25 (1986): 207–19; *Keys to Solutions in Brief Therapy* (New York: Norton, 1985).

6. See M. Weiner-Davis, *Divorce Busting* (New York: Summit, 1991).

7. S. L. Garfield, "Research on Counselee Variables in Psychotherapy," in S. L. Garfield and A. E. Bergin, eds., *Handbook of Psychotherapy and Behavior Change*, 4th ed. (New York: Wiley, 1994), 190–228.

8. H. W. Stone, *Brief Pastoral Counseling: Short-Term Approaches and Strategies* (Minneapolis: Fortress, 1994).

9. A. E. Bergin and S. L. Garfield, "Overview, Trends, and Future Issues," in A. E. Bergin and S. L. Garfield, eds., *Handbook of Psychotherapy and Behavior Change*, 4th ed. (New York: Wiley, 1994), 821–30; Koss and J. Shiang, "Research on Brief Psychotherapy," in A. E. Bergin and S. L. Garfield, eds., *Handbook of Psychotherapy and Behavior Change*, 4th ed. (New York: Wiley, 1994), 664–70.

10. S. de Shazer, "Brief Therapy." For an excellent review of research on short-term and time-limited counseling, see Stone, *Brief Pastoral Counseling*.

11. M. P. Koss and J. N. Butcher, "Research on Brief Psychotherapy," in *Handbook of Psychotherapy and Behavior Change*, 3rd ed., ed. S. L. Garfield and A. E. Bergin (New York: Wiley, 1986), 627–70.

12. G. M. Burlingame, A. Fuhriman, S. Paul, and B. M. Ogles, "Implementing a Time-Limited Therapy Program: Differential Effects of Training and Experience," *Psychotherapy* 26 (1989): 303–13.

13. H. von Foerster, *Observing Systems* (Seaside, Calif.: Intersystems), 309.

14. M. Beyebach, A. R. Morejon, D. L. Palenzuela, and J. L. Rodriguez-Arias, "Research on the Process of Solution-Focused Therapy," in Miller, Hubble, and Duncan, eds., *Handbook of Solution-Focused Brief Therapy* (San Francisco: Jossey-Bass, 1996), 299–334; Miller, Duncan, and Hubble, *Escape from Babel: Toward a Unifying Language for Psychotherapy Practice* (New York: Norton, 1997); see also Berg and Miller, *Working with the Problem Drinker*.

15. Berg and Miller, *Working with the Problem Drinker*.

16. Here, "fight" is used to describe their verbal exchanges. As always, client safety should be one's top priority.

17. G. Bateson, *Mind and Nature: A Necessary Unity* (New York: Bantam), 43.

18. "Between now and the next time we meet, I want you to observe, so that you can tell me next time, what happens in your (life, marriage, family, or relationship) that you want to continue to have happen" (see de Shazer and A. Molnar, "Four Useful Interventions in Brief Family Therapy," *Journal of Marital and Family Therapy* 10 [1984]: 297–304).

19. Berg and Miller, *Working with the Problem Drinker*, 17.

20. Cited in J. Winokur, *Zen to Go* (New York: New American Library, 1989), 31.

21. Cited in W. H. O'Hanlon and P. Hudson, *Stop Blaming, Start Loving! A Solution-Oriented Approach to Improving Your Relationship* (New York: Norton, 1995), 67.

22. For the creation and use of scaling questions, see Berg and Miller, *Working with the Problem Drinker.*

23. See P. Watzlawick, J. H. Weakland, and R. Fisch, *Change: Principles of Problem Formation and Problem Resolution* (New York: Norton, 1974).

11

Time-Limited Counseling
for Pastors

Brian H. Childs

TIME IS THE UNDERLYING STRUCTURE of human existence. As finite creatures, we only have so much of it. As fallible creatures, we attempt to flee from the responsibility attendant upon the daily—and ultimate—limitation of our time. As hopeful creatures, we long for the end of troubling times. Our use and understanding of time tells us much about ourselves. Our understanding of time may give us some sense of how God intends us to act and to be in light of our limitations and freedom.[1]

Finite time is a defining feature of parish ministry. Pastors are more than preachers and organizers; they also are teachers, counselors, caregivers, and theologians. The context of their counseling ministry, their pastoral initiative, and indeed their pastoral identity, necessitates time limitations (sometimes severe) upon their every task. It is within this context that pastors need to fulfill their ministry, reflect theologically, and be responsible to their calling.

Critics of Pastoral Counseling

I have often been perplexed by the marginalization of pastoral counseling training within theological education. Many academics in the classical disciplines (such as scripture, systematic theology, and church history) see pastoral counseling education as threateningly enigmatic, socially quietistic, or theologically and spiritually thin. Ironically, some full-time professors of pastoral theology and pastoral care are themselves ambivalent about the practice of counseling, preferring to examine general theoretical issues that are several places removed from the particulars of the parish and of real persons or families in need of counsel (see chapter 13).

Counseling training, as with all theological education in the practical fields (pastoral care, administration, preaching, and education), comes under criticism for having too-readily adopted the professional paradigm of clergy education.[2] Critics argue that the professional model over-stresses the minister's technical ability at the expense of what has been called the distinctive theological and sacramental dimensions of ministry. In pastoral care and pastoral counseling, they argue, the professional model separates ministers from parishioners and therefore truncates what should be an intensely personal encounter.

Serious problems arise when clergy identify their caring and counseling with the office model (fee for service) that typifies psychotherapy. Pastoral counselors who imitate the passive psychoanalyst set themselves apart from counselees' moral and theological struggles. The model of the expert pastoral specialist and the inexpert, needy counselee precludes mutuality—it also contradicts Christian relatedness and the doctrine of the priesthood of all believers.[3]

There is no question that office-bound pastors who avoid being involved in the day-to-day lives of their parishioners sacrifice a valuable part of ministry. However, that does not obviate the place of personal and private counseling in the pastoral study. Often people respond to a minister's sermons, social activity, and pastoral presence with a desire for personal counseling concerning their inner and relational problems. To deny this aspect of ministry, or to deal with it solely by referral to professional mental health providers, is to limit a traditionally important part of the shepherding function.

What is more, many critics of the professional counseling model in ministry are naïve about what goes on in counseling. They entertain a stereotype, the so-called classical long-term psychoanalytic process, as their image of all pastoral counseling. This image could hardly be farther from the truth. I do not know of any congregational pastors—or even full-time pastoral counseling specialists—who put their clients on a couch, avoid eye contact with them, and limit their verbal interactions during the first of what could be four or five years of thrice-weekly sessions.

In fact, pastoral counseling is active and interactive. The relationship between the pastor and parishioner is important from the beginning. Contact between them in normal social and ecclesiastical settings is the rule, not the exception. They know each other. They talk to each other.

Finally, pastoral counseling has been called into question for turning its back on a tradition that predates, by at least two millennia, the advent of modern psychotherapy. While there is much to be learned from the tradition and its interpreters, this argument strikes me as antiquarian at worst and naïve at best. To say that pastoral care before the advent of modern psychology was devoid of a psychological understanding of humankind is arrogant and plainly false.[4] Particularly from a Protestant point of view, Christian life cannot be lived outside of culture. Our vocation as Christians is to live in the world and care for all of creation, not just the world that we attempt to create for ourselves. There is no inherent danger in Christian faith and action availing itself of the human sciences. Counseling theory and method are necessary and appropriate tools for every practicing minister.

The Problem of Time

Pastors in congregational ministry are busy people with many duties to perform. Even for pastors who are called to a specialized ministry of pastoral care and counseling, time often runs short. If they have earned a reputation for counseling work, they may face mounting requests for guidance and therefore shrinking time to give to those in need. It is a difficult spot to be in, particularly for those who enjoy doing counseling.

One way to take care of demand for help that exceeds available time is to develop adequate referral sources. Another solution, when appropriate, is to offer group sessions that focus on certain themes (such as concerns of single persons, single parenting, and marriage). Group work, however, demands its own set of skills, and many individuals will still request—and need—private counseling as well.

The solution I propose in this chapter is called time-limited counseling. Time-limited counseling is *problem-centered counseling focused on a single circumscribed presenting problem (called the focal relational problem or FRP), carried out between a counselor and counselee over a prescribed number of sessions predetermined in a counseling contract.* At the first meeting, the maximum number of sessions is contractually set and irrevocable. I prefer ten sessions as the maximum; many parish pastors, because of time demands, will use a considerably smaller maximum. (A counselee and counselor may use fewer sessions than contracted if they wish.)

Time-limited counseling has been practiced and taught for at least three decades. Surprisingly, few of its major theorists have shown any interest in what time *means* for both caregivers and counselees, except for its effect on scheduling. I believe that time, with its inherent limitations, has a more profound meaning for all humans.

In his work *Time-Limited Psychotherapy,* James Mann writes that "all short forms of psychotherapy, whether their practitioners know it or not, revive the horror of time."[5] We are forced to face the conflict between infantile timelessness and the reality of inevitable loss, the distressing recognition that our days are numbered.

Other thinkers, such as Paul Tillich, Karl Barth, and the Niebuhrs, have pointed to some theological implications of our time-bound existence. Time and relationships (the milieu of most human emotional problems) give us a life of unsettling givenness. As Barth put it, a "human self-understanding genuinely oriented by a general picture of man will be halted by the riddle of human temporality and will have to be content to assert that we must live our life in the absolute uncertainty given with this riddle because we are not asked whether we would prefer a different possibility."[6] Barth goes on to say that a person "without an awareness of history, without definite pictures of what was and the patience to learn from them, would be an escapist, running away from reality and God, and quite unreliable" in dealings with other people.[7]

Time-limited counseling acknowledges the native human anxiety about relationships and about the givenness of time. It uses that anxiety as a prod for problem solving, thus working this basic psychological and theological insight to parishioners' advantage.

Principles of Time-Limited Counseling

Gregory Bauer and Joseph Kobos identify seven basic principles unique to time-limited counseling.[8] I outline them below, with some additional clarifying material borrowed from other theorists. These seven principles can serve as a map for clergy who want to increase the efficiency and efficacy of their pastoral caregiving. They are best applied in congregational ministry for individuals who meet the following criteria:

- Clearly articulated presenting problem usually dealing with here and now relationship issues
- A give and take in the care/counseling relationship and evidence of the ability to relate to others, particularly significant persons in their own lives
- A clear presenting problem (focal relational problem)
- Curiosity about self and relationships (What makes me tick?)
- A motivation to change the focal relational problem.[9]

Some problems by their nature rule out further counseling with the pastor. Significant or repeated suicide gestures and/or ideation warrant immediate referral. Time-limited counseling also is not effective in dealing with chronic alcoholism or other substance abuse. Addiction often requires medical supervision as well as the care of support groups such as Alcoholics Anonymous. In addition, persons who have had chronic psychiatric problems, including psychiatric hospitalizations, are typically not good candidates for time-limited pastoral counseling in the parish.

The following general principles are useful for time-limited pastoral counseling:

Principle One

Pastoral caregivers *act*. They are not passive interpreters of behavior but rather active participants in the counseling, sometimes confronting parishioners but at all times allowing their own emotions, knowledge, and experience to come into play. Pastoral caregivers doing time-limited counseling will have as much to say as their parishioners. (Walter Flegenheimer noted the striking difference between written verbatim records of long-term therapy and transcripts of brief therapy. The former featured long monologues by the patient, interrupted occasionally with brief comments by the therapist. Brief therapy showed approximately equal and fairly short contributions by both patient and therapist.)[10]

This active stance seems to fly in the face of what many pastors learned in seminary pastoral care classes. Indeed, there is a major difference. Many of them were taught to respond passively to whatever their parishioners have to say, to "mirror back" their words no matter where the material might lead. In time-limited pastoral counseling there is no time for free association, regression, or digression to whatever material comes to mind. The counseling focuses on a particular problem and prescribes a specific amount of time within which to find a resolution.

Principle Two

The agreed-upon focal relational problem is the only subject of discussion in each counseling session. In an evaluation session held prior to the beginning of time-limited counseling, pastoral caregivers and parishioners clearly describe a circumscribed problem (FRP). All subsequent discussion and each counseling intervention relate directly to the FRP. This requires that clergy help parishioners keep the counseling focused and solve the problem. Enhanced self-esteem inevitably follows (as Bauer and Kobos have noted), because the small successes in their specific problem-solving work generalize to other areas of counselees' lives and thus increase their positive self-worth.[11] What is more, in this way pastoral caregivers communicate that the situation is manageable and that they are truly interested in the problem and in the parishioner.

This interest, coupled with the strict limits on duration, assures parishioners that optimism is justified for accomplishing the goal and that it can be done in a short time period. "At the same time," Bauer and Lobos add, "the therapist indicates that it is up to the patient to do most of the work. The therapist frequently makes comments that highlight the patient's responsibilities and is quick to intervene when the patient tries to sit back and let the therapist do the work."[12] It bears repeating that brief pastoral counseling is truly an interactive process. Here is no passive expert listening to a struggling nonexpert. Both have something at stake in the process, though ultimate responsibility for change rests with the parishioner.

Principle Three

From the very first interview, pastoral caregivers must communicate to parishioners that this is a collaborative endeavor, that they are allies addressing a particular problem together. They do so by focusing on the FRP and on parishioners' strengths. (According to this principle, concentrating on weakness is a flight into infantile timelessness.) The decision to enter into counseling in the first place is a positive act, the beginning of a continuous movement toward growth. My own image of this therapeutic alliance is of caregiver and parishioner rolling up their sleeves at the beginning of the first counseling session and exclaiming, "Let's get to work!"

Principle Four

The pastoral caregiver firmly points out any resistance in parishioners to solving the FRP whenever it arises. One of the ironies of human behavior is that people often choose to live with uncomfortable and even painful, but familiar, circumstances rather than face the anxiety and uncertainty of the new. The chronically uncomfortable is at least known; the uncharted territory is frightening. Ministers must resolutely confront parishioners whenever they resist taking some needed step to change, particularly if the resistance relates to the FRP. Pointing out each instance of resistance encourages deepening of the therapeutic alliance, focuses the counseling session around the FRP, and keeps hope alive by presuming that the problem can be solved.

Principle Five

In time-limited pastoral counseling, the parishioners' focal relational problem will be enacted and reenacted not only in their past and daily lives as reported in counseling, but also in relationship with the caregiver.[13] Pastors doing counseling must be attentive to indications of feelings that parishioners may have about them—signs such as silence, anxiety, and the changing of subject. When such feelings arise, particularly as they relate to the FRP, they should be discussed openly. Likewise, it is appropriate for pastoral caregivers to express feelings they may have about parishioners, particularly those centering upon resistance to solving the problem. Caregivers' frustrations may echo the frustrations of other people in the parishioners' lives. The important thing is to check these feelings out, not in an accusatory way but in the spirit of collaboration and curiosity.

Principle Six

Pastoral caregivers remind those receiving help that problem solving is the primary task of each counseling session. The goal of brief pastoral counseling is to solve the single presenting problem. Pastors act as role models, communicating the assurance that interpersonal conflict is understandable, solvable, and manageable, and need not be seen as hopeless.

Principle Seven

Strict adherence to the time limitation of the counseling process is vital. Parishioners are not given an opportunity to suppose that counseling may continue beyond the prescribed duration agreed upon at the first session. This is not to say that the relationship with the pastor will end. All of the other ministries of the church continue after the formal counseling ceases.

Although it may not exceed the agreed-upon duration, counseling may (and often does) end before the contracted number of sessions. In this case, the parishioner should understand that the remaining number of sessions are "in the bank" and can be used for follow-up as needed. However, in pastoral counseling based on time-limited principles, the total agreed upon number of sessions is an absolute limit. If parishioners are in need of further counseling, referral may be indicated—but not until parishioners have an opportunity to try out what they have learned. (Of course if they are experiencing a severe crisis or a dangerous state of mind, such as suicidal or homicidal inclinations, referral should be immediate.)

In congregational ministry, time-limited pastoral counseling augments the other ministries of the church. Clergy work in collaboration with parishioners to solve a focal relational problem through mutual give-and-take over a circumscribed period of time.

Time-Limited Counseling Methods

Setting specific limits on the duration of counseling is more effective than merely guessing about the amount of time that will be needed. Many researchers have demonstrated that limiting the amount of time that can be given to counseling has great therapeutic power in and of itself, apart from its convenience to clients and caregivers alike. A key to its effectiveness is the *anxiety* created by the setting of an unalterable and definite termination date. While critics might question the benefits of anxiety—and the ethics of artificially encouraging it—anxiety actually serves a useful function in the day-to-day life of all people. It alerts us of a potential problem or challenge. Animal studies describe it as a "fight or flight" signal. In humans, it is that and more: it also signals that we have a problem we need to address. Theologically and existentially, anxiety serves as a warning that our freedom, responsibility, and place in human relationships may be in jeopardy. It calls us to pay attention to threats or potential threats to our functioning or well-being.

Anxiety, when used positively, can call forth new ways of looking at a situation and new approaches to handling it. By limiting the duration of the counseling and focusing on a specific focal relational problem, pastors use anxiety creatively to help parishioners address a dilemma, a difficulty, or a struggle, and then move on with their lives.

Time-Limited Pastoral Counseling in Action

Edgar came to see Pastor Marcia Weiss with some reluctance. He complained to her about being "sorta down" and was not interested in his usual hobbies—coin collecting, golf with his wife, and fishing with his buddies. A supervisor with the electric company, he was five or six years from retirement. Two of his daughters were already on their own—one a broadcast journalist for a local television station, the other married and living across the country with her husband and newborn son. His youngest daughter was planning to go away to college in the fall.

Edgar was the son of a career Naval officer. Consequently, he had moved every two or three years over his childhood, and on two long occasions his father went to sea without the family. Edgar attended college for a while but felt more comfortable laboring with his hands. He and his wife, Madge, met in college. Their marriage was satisfying.

Edgar's "sorta down" mood started around the occasion of his twenty-fifth year with the power company and the beginning of his youngest daughter's senior year of high school. Around the same time, the previous pastor of the church (who was Edgar's close friend) left for another parish after fifteen years in the community.

Together Pastor Weiss and Edgar catalogued the above background information in order to find a common theme that could be related to his down-in-the-dumps feeling. Clearly, Edgar had experienced a number of close relationships threatened by parting. Having moved frequently during his youth and having been separated from his father for long periods, he devoted his adult years to working and raising a family that would be stable over time. Now he was learning that life is not stable: children grow up, pastors and friends move on, our bodies grow older and we face physical diminishment, and retirement changes our time-tested patterns of daily living. For Edgar the challenge was to adapt, knowing full well that life is lived in the context of change.

Edgar and Marcia agreed that his focal relational problem was the difficulty of facing the changes in his life and the anxiety of saying good-bye to what he must leave behind. Edgar did not want to feel bad. He wanted to enjoy his marriage and children even though the family was in flux; he wanted to enjoy his friends and forge new relationships, including one with his new pastor.

Edgar began a brief course of counseling that used his anxiety as a prod for new ways of living. He contracted with Pastor Weiss to make small, specific changes in his life and to face squarely a few of the changes that loomed ahead of him. He agreed to do homework tasks that would help him adapt gradually to these changes. In Edgar's case, reading Gail Sheehy's book *Passages* was a helpful assignment. He and Pastor Weiss together created other assignments, such as planning his own retirement party, to help him face his anxiety and beat it. His counseling, because it was time-limited, would itself serve as a laboratory for dealing with anxiety as he faced his uncertain but hopeful future.[14]

Ending Time-Limited Counseling

The termination of counseling can be another time of apprehension for parishioners. Will their hard-earned gains evaporate? Will the focal relational problem come back to trouble them? Will they need further contact with the pastoral caregiver?

Some individuals, in their anxiety, may request an extension of the counseling contract at this time.[15] We need to remind parishioners in our care that addressing the focal relational problem during counseling is but a rehearsal for addressing it in real life—including (and especially) when the counseling relationship ends. It is unrealistic to expect that all their problems will be solved in the brief time allotted—much less that the focal relational problem will disappear completely. No one's life is problem free. Counseling prepares people to play the role of caregiver for themselves. They and their close friends and family continue to respond to challenges in their lives. This is one manifestation of the general goal of pastoral counseling: helping people to help (and rally help for) themselves.

The end of counseling can be difficult for pastoral caregivers and for those whom they serve. Pleas from parishioners to extend counseling beyond the original contract need to be handled firmly but tenderly. Knowing that contact between ministers and parishioners will continue in the life of the congregation can soften the blow. Pastors do not abdicate the ministry of pastoral care just because a pastoral counseling contract has been completed. The teaching, organizing, and shepherding ministries (to use Seward Hiltner's categories) go on. Pastors and their counselees/parishioners may even, from time to time, briefly discuss and recall the counseling process in some other setting. This kind of contact not only signals the ongoing relationship between pastor and parishioner, it also reinforces the importance of the intimacy of the counseling process. It was important, and still is.

Those who suffer and seek counseling need not face the time limit with dread. Time-limited pastoral counseling builds upon a theological anthropology and eschatology;[16] the end of the present time—and its troubles—is the beginning of liberation from the bonds of oppression. Civil rights leaders intone this attitude in the exclamation "How long? Not long." The motivation for the realistic end of the present time can, therefore, offer hope for the future.

～

Parish pastoral counseling occurs within a particular context. While some believe that persons who come to a pastor for counseling for all but the most minor problems should be referred to professionals, I have pointed to the legitimacy and necessity for parish pastoral counseling.[17] Pastoral counseling in congregational ministry helps people help themselves while remaining or becoming a part of the faith community. The achievement of counseling goals is enhanced by the significance of time—in a pragmatic as well as a theological sense. Time is limited for everyone; it is part of being human. Time-limited pastoral counseling places this reality in bold relief and builds upon it as a way to help the many who seek our care.

Notes

1.   The ideas in this chapter are based on my book *Short-Term Pastoral Counseling* (New York: Haworth, 2000).
2.   Jackson W. Carroll, "The Professional Model of Ministry—Is It Worth Saving?" *Theological Education* 21, no. 2 (Spring 1985): 7–48.
3.   Alastair V. Campbell, *Professional and Pastoral Care* (Philadelphia: Fortress Press, 1985), 43ff.
4.   For a discussion of the concepts of mind both in modern and pre-modern thought, including that of several theologians, see Charles Hampden-Turner, *Maps of the Mind* (New York: Collier Books, 1982).
5.   Ibid., 9.
6.   Karl Barth, *Church Dogmatics*, ed. G. W. Bromiley and T. F. Torrance, vol. 3, pt. 2, *The Doctrine of Creation*, trans. Bromiley et al. (Edinburgh: T. & T. Clark, 1960), 514.
7.   Ibid., 539.
8.   Gregory P. Bauer and Joseph C. Kobos, *Brief Therapy: Short-Term Psychodynamic Intervention* (Northvale, N.J.: Jason Aronson, 1987), 6–9.
9.   For a further and more complete discussion of the assessment process and the basic criteria for counselee selection, see Childs, *Short-Term Pastoral Counseling*, especially chap. 3.
10.   Walter V. Flegenheimer, *Techniques of Brief Psychotherapy* (New York: Jason Aronson, 1982), 7.
11.   Bauer and Kobos, *Brief Therapy*, 7.

12. Flegenheimer, *Techniques of Brief Psychotherapy,* 8.

13. Lester Luborsky, *Principles of Psychoanalytic Psychotherapy, A Manual for Supportive-Expressive Treatment* (New York: Basic, 1984), 110ff.

14. See Childs, chap. 5 for a full outline of the process of time-limited counseling.

15. For a detailed discussion of this issue as well as other issues in termination, see Luborsky, *Principles of Psychoanalytic* (New York: Basic, 1989), chap. 9.

16. For a fuller account of the relationship of suffering and hope from a biblical theological perspective, see J. Christiaan Beker, *Suffering and Hope* (Philadelphia: Fortress Press, 1987).

17. Counseling should not be attempted without supervision. No counselee should go undiscussed, at least while he or she is in counseling. Most ministers who do extensive counseling have had supervision and training in clinical pastoral education, or have received an advanced degree in counseling, or have had training in an American Association of Pastoral Counseling center. Such supervision should be continued, no matter how experienced the pastor may be, after the training is completed.

There are several ways that clergy can get ongoing supervision. The most common way is contracting with a counseling professional with whom clergy may discuss their work. Supervisors may be pastoral counseling specialists or mental health professionals who can be seen for an hour every two weeks or so. Another way that pastors may obtain supervision is through a peer group of fellow pastors with an interest in and practice of counseling. A bi-weekly "brown bag" supervision lunch group can be helpful and can provide a supportive fellowship as well.

12

Counseling for Solutions:
A Model for Parish Ministry in the
Third Millennium

James Sharp

ENDURING FAITHS throughout history have created and adapted ministries to meet the mutable needs of people and societies. As we enter a new millennium, only the accelerating speed of social change is new.[1]

The following are but a few examples of the extent and pace of the changes we face. In a recent National College Health Risk Behavior Survey, more female than male students (87.8 percent to 84.0 percent) reported having had sexual intercourse; 50 percent of men and 47.7 percent of the women surveyed had at some time used marijuana; and approximately 14 percent of men and women had tried some form of cocaine. Sixty-nine percent of all respondents reported having had six or more sex partners during their lifetimes so far.[2] Another survey questioned twenty-seven thousand twelve- through nineteen-year-olds from across the world and concluded that teens are mediavores: "Today's kids consume media at an accelerated pace. It is not uncommon for them to have the TV and radio on while they talk on the phone and do their homework. There is some evidence that they have developed the cognitive ability to possess multiple streams of information at the same time."[3]

Clearly, churches need to assess and plan for ministries that will meet the needs and challenges of a fluid, ever-changing age. Some traditional ministries will decrease and even disappear, while others will increase. New ministries already are developing to serve new populations and social conditions. Care and counseling ministries in particular must expand in order to meet the emotional, physical, and spiritual needs of communities of individuals. Specific approaches to pastoral counseling will continue to reflect the theological convictions and the practical resources of congregations. One of the great strengths of pastoral ministry in a rapidly changing age is its versatility of options and its ability to serve people in many areas of their lives (not just in Sunday worship or the traditional fifty-minute counseling hour). Pastoral counseling in the parish context is particularly fluid and adaptable to changing needs, for a great deal of it takes place in nontraditional ways, in a multitude of situations where pastors and parishioners come into contact with each other.

Of the many styles available, and for many reasons that have been put forth by other authors in this book, short-term[4] approaches to pastoral counseling provide an array of benefits uniquely suited to the pace and the problems of twenty-first-century life. For one thing, many people enter counseling in a state of emergency—an affair has endangered a marriage, a teenager has attempted suicide, a child has been molested, unemployment threatens the financial welfare of a family—and they desire an expeditious resolution to their crisis. Brief counseling methods also make it possible for lay ministers or caregivers as well as trained pastoral staff to share the ministry of wise counsel. Perhaps more important, it has been shown that most pastoral counseling encounters are limited to as little as one session and rarely more than a few. A brief and, more specifically, solution-focused model for counseling ministry confronts that reality and helps parishioners find solutions to their problems in the available time.

Carrie and her husband James were ending their fourth and final pastoral counseling session, and Carrie wanted to ask a departing question. "I heard from friends that marriage counseling would be long, hard, and very difficult. This has only been a month. Why has this been relatively pain free, and so positive?" Short-term, solution-focused counseling had invited James and Carrie to concentrate on alternative ways of interacting rather than on their anger, resentment, and their negative patterns of relating to each other. This couple's success was due in part to their willingness and readiness to work on their relationship; each made unique contributions to discovering solutions.

Such an outcome is the intent of solution-based couple, individual, or family counseling. In this chapter, *solution-focused counseling* (SFC) will be used as a general term for short-term, goal-oriented approaches to counseling.[5] Solution-focused counseling departs from traditional counseling methods that tend to be past-oriented, pathology-centered, speculative, caregiver-driven, and long in duration. Growing evidence supports the effectiveness of solution-focused counseling as a viable alternative for ministers, lay caregivers, and pastoral counseling specialists.[6] SFC meets the unique challenges of the local congregation, including time constraints, while providing a highly effective pastoral counseling approach. It draws upon parishioners' existing abilities and what they are already doing well in order to establish working goals, identify a hopeful outcome, and measure the effectiveness of behavioral changes. The objective of this chapter is to summarize the use of solution-focused counseling in the context of the local congregation.

Rapport and creative interaction—common threads in both traditional and solution-focused counseling—readily take on the distinguishing characteristics of the solution-focused genre. Counseling pastors utilize these two tools to help parishioners confront their self-limiting beliefs while broadening their awareness of possible solutions to their dilemmas. Parishioners are encouraged and supported to discover their own inner strengths and capabilities, resources that will facilitate personal recovery and long-term working outcomes.

Rapport Building

An essential ingredient in all effective caregiving, including counseling, is an ongoing exchange between parishioner and pastor of mutual respect, trust, and a willingness to work. Specific language and solution-directed steps initiated during rapport building launch the counseling relationship in a positive direction. Rapport begins to take shape from the moment of first contact, when ministers and those seeking help discuss their upcoming meeting. Good rapport establishes intent, attitude, and confidence as the counseling process begins.

The initial contact with counselees might include a statement affirming their willingness to secure help, an invitation to consider some preparatory action before the actual first session, a comment assuring them that every measure will be taken to ensure confidentiality, and/or questions concerning specific ways in which the caregiver might be of help. When the minister communicates caring, rapport ensues. It is fundamental to the pastoral counseling endeavor that follows.

During counseling sessions, a conscious effort at courtesy helps to establish rapport. For example, instead of assuming it is the counselor's prerogative to take notes, be sure to ask counselees if they object to notes being taken. Greet them warmly and courteously; provide an orderly room and a comfortable chair, a cup of coffee or glass of water, a box of tissues. The pastoral caregiver invites a parishioner's trust through intentional acts that convey the message: "You are a valuable person with meaningful strengths and skills." Courtesy keeps other persons in mind and seeks to serve them in caring and thoughtful ways.

Another example of extending courtesy is attentive listening. Charles Allen Kollar emphasizes that *intention* is the key distinguishing mark of attentive listening. While active listening offers parishioners a chance to express themselves fully, attentive listening goes a step further; it "has the quality of careful, alert listening; that is the ideal of active listening. Yet it is different in purpose. By it the counselor validates feelings while carefully listening for clues that may represent strengths and exceptions."[7]

Attentive listening includes taking an intentional posture—sitting up in the chair, facing counselees, interrupting periodically for clarification ("I hear you saying. . . . Is that accurate?"), and affirming progress ("Congratulations for reaching your goal between sessions.") An acrostic, SOFTEN, may help you remember the elements of intentional body language that facilitate attentive listening:[8]

> Smile
> Open posture
> Forward lean
> Touch
> Eye contact
> Nod

Utilizing these intentional postures and gestures strengthens the cords of rapport and stimulates a positive interaction in the counseling relationship. As rapport is established, the caregiver introduces solution-based counseling methods to draw the emphasis away from problems and toward solutions.

Counselee-Specific and Counselee-Driven Methods

Every person being helped is unique and ought to be treated as such. Counselee-specific methods do not label people or treat them as clinical categories but as singular human beings, unlike any other. Solution-focused pastoral counseling is also counselee-driven in that caregivers treat people as competent individuals, respect them for what they believe (while not necessarily agreeing with them), and cooperate with them to determine specific steps in the counseling process (see chapter 10).

Pastors are the experts on the counseling process, keeping the sessions focused on achieving parishioners' goals. Parishioners are the experts on their own problems, and the primary resource in determining solutions. By building up awareness of accountability and ability to produce working alternatives, pastors empower parishioners. At the same time, they are able to gauge parishioners' willingness to move forward toward beneficial change.

Readiness for Change

Along with the usual initial assessments of suicide lethality, mental and physical well-being, and faith concerns, it is important to assess the potential for behavioral change. Initial observations determine the intent and the readiness of parishioners to work toward changed behavior and appropriate outcomes.

In solution-focused pastoral counseling, ministers collaborate with parishioners to determine the optimum result that will fulfill their healthy and achievable aspirations.

A variety of questions can help determine readiness for change.[9] Is the person just looking, seeking information and investigating the possibility of counseling, like a shopper who has no intention of buying? Did this person come to complain, like the customer who is not satisfied with a purchase? Finally, like the man who goes to a clothing store ready to buy—knowing what kind of shirt he wants, picking it out, and completing the purchase—does this person acknowledge the problem with intent to work toward resolution? Determining troubled persons' readiness for behavioral change also will help determine subsequent steps in the solution-based counseling process.

When people are "just looking" or only want to complain, pastors can guide a transition into solid readiness for behavioral change. Asking solution-oriented questions, making goal-related statements, and seeking to establish exceptions to present problem behavior will reveal counselees' willingness to make that shift. If no movement toward readiness to change occurs, chances for real and lasting change are limited and ministers may want to consider some other form of caregiving such as listening, referral, or offering specific helpful advice.

Once parishioners are ready to make progress, they need to recognize their own abilities as a primary resource in solving their problem, to assist in setting goals, and to be affirmed in their efforts.

Exceptions to the Problem

Perhaps the most efficacious way to move toward action is to help parishioners discover what has been working for them already, and explore ways to repeat that success. The common-sense underlying principle is: If it didn't work in the past, don't do more of it. Do, however, capitalize and expand upon past behaviors that have yielded positive results (however small). These positive actions are exceptions to the problem. Often parishioners are unaware of such exceptions and they need to be ferreted out.[10]

One reason for the difficulty of discovering exceptions is that counselees tend to exaggerate their problems, especially in the initial counseling session. Anxiety about the problem has constricted their cognitive processes, creating the illusion that there are no answers or very limited choices available to them—that nothing can help. They may operate under the common but erroneous belief that no resolution is possible until a problem has been thoroughly discussed and analyzed. One excellent technique for breaking through cognitive barriers and self-limiting beliefs is the miracle question,[11] which asks: "If you awoke in the morning and by some miracle the problem was gone, what would you be doing differently?" or "What would (a significant other person such as wife, daughter, or boss) notice you were doing differently?" Such questions aim parishioners toward new, positive and beneficial actions. Consider the following dialogue:

> MINISTER: . . . So the problem is you fight with your daughter in the mornings and the rest of your day is a wreck.
>
> FATHER: Yes. That pretty well sums it up. I'm tired of the yelling and the disrespect.
>
> MINISTER: Do you mind if I ask you a question? It may seem a little strange. It's called the miracle question. You can use your imagination.
>
> FATHER: Sure.
>
> MINISTER: If you awoke in the morning and a miracle had taken place that removed the problem between you and your daughter, what would you notice right away that you were doing differently?
>
> FATHER: I would probably feel like fixing breakfast for the family.
>
> MINISTER: Good. What else? What would be your first response upon seeing your daughter?
>
> FATHER: With a miracle, I would probably say something for a change, like "Good morning."
>
> MINISTER: Excellent. Although I suggested it might take a miracle for these things to happen, tell me about a time when this happened even just a little.
>
> FATHER: Well. Well, several weeks ago, one Saturday morning I decided to cook pancakes, and she wasn't as bad as she usually is.
>
> MINISTER: Excellent. How did you do that?

Here the father identifies an exception to his usual style of interacting with his daughter. Often it takes more than one attempt to successfully discover an exception. With the helper's guidance, this father shifted his focus from the problems in his relationship with his daughter and paid attention to times when he had civil conversation with her. In solution-focused pastoral counseling, ministers bypass statements about the problem and concentrate on finding exceptions. The exceptions then lead directly to goal setting.

Goal Setting

When your parishioners establish their own goals for counseling, it proves intent and provides a way to measure results. However, sometimes they need guidance in crafting appropriate goals. Good goals are as simple as ABC:

Attainable, Believable, and Countable. A goal that is *attainable* is one that is positive without being overly ambitious, and makes sense for the person within the context of the problem. In the conversation above, cooking breakfast and saying good morning are attainable goals. A *believable* goal is one that will be acted upon. People need to believe that their actions are capable of bringing about changes that work for them. *Countable* goals are measurable. Action taken is evaluated for its potential to achieve a working, long-term outcome. Below is an example of goal setting in a short-term pastoral counseling session.

> MINISTER: With your response to the miracle question in mind, what first step are you willing to take this week?
>
> FATHER: Tomorrow I will say "Good morning" to my daughter; and Saturday I will get up early and fix breakfast for the family.
>
> MINISTER: That sounds great. Be sure and notice positive responses both mornings to what you have done. Also notice how you feel in doing them.

The goals set by parishioners have to be important to them; they need to be small, concrete, and behavioral. They should address the presence rather than the absence of something ("I will say 'Good morning' to my daughter" rather than "I will not ignore her"). At the same time, goals should be challenging, presented and perceived as hard but worthwhile work; after all, even the smallest task may be extremely difficult for people who are locked in negative patterns of behavior. Using time wisely and being clear about tasks lead to a sense of accomplishment.

Staying on Task

Since time is limited in counseling in the context of parish ministry, it is important to keep the counseling process from straying off the task at hand. Staying on task may involve a periodic assessment of time and a summary of what has been accomplished to that point in the session. Pastors can help by making a statement like, "In order to get the most out of our time together, I wonder if we could move on to. . . ." A way to keep focused on the task while enhancing rapport is to ask, near the close of the first session, "Has this been helpful?" If yes: "Can you share with me some ways that this has been helpful for you?" A negative response creates the opportunity for dialogue concerning a more helpful plan for the remaining time or future sessions. Like a compass being true to navigation, feedback guides the process toward productive outcomes.

Feedback

The feedback stage of solution-focused brief pastoral counseling begins with the second session, whether or not counselees have successfully completed their chosen goals. Feedback allows for discussion of the action taken, observation of the results, and evaluation of its benefits. What if a goal was not achieved, which is not unusual? Rather than label it a failure, reconsider the goal's appropriateness and the parishioner's readiness to work toward it. Reevaluate and progress accordingly. Following is one example of a feedback session:

> MINISTER: Welcome. I'm encouraged by your commitment to be here. It says a lot about your determination.
>
> FATHER: I know things can be different, and I know I have a part in bringing about change at home.
>
> MINISTER: If you don't mind, I'd like to start by asking you to help me with finding out how your homework task this past week turned out. Would you answer a question for me?
>
> FATHER: Sure, but let me say I think I blew it.
>
> MINISTER: Well, let's try this: on a scale of one to ten, with ten being the most effective resolution of the thing that brought you in here, and one being the least, where would you say you started?
>
> FATHER: Oh, I guess a one or two.
>
> MINISTER: Where are you today?
>
> FATHER: A three or four, I guess.
>
> MINISTER: Really? Wow. What has changed for you to make that kind of progress?
>
> FATHER: Well, I didn't realize it was progress, but I guess it was. I decided what I was going to do this week, and although it did not go as well as I had hoped, it did make a slight difference.
>
> MINISTER: Great. Tell me about the difference it made.

Feedback sessions are designed to encourage and affirm parishioners. They also clarify progress toward the counseling goal. When, for instance, the father begins to see his ability to effect positive change, it increases his impetus to discover more exceptions to his problem. As he discusses behavioral changes, he begins to realize that positive behavior invites a positive response from others, which encourages additional positive behavior. He gets a clearer understanding of what is working and what is not. In the following example, the feedback process also encourages the repetition of effective positive behavior.

FATHER: I said, "Good morning," and she just stared at me at first. Then she kind of smiled and said, "Good morning."

MINISTER: How did you feel when she smiled at you?

FATHER: Good, I think.

MINISTER: You stated when we first met that it had been weeks since you had exchanged kind words. How were you able to do it?

FATHER: I made up my mind that my actions toward her ought not to depend on what I thought she felt about me. I was going to do what I really wanted to do without any expectations. I really love my daughter, and I want her to know that.

MINISTER: (pause) Way to go. You were very intentional and very determined. That is great. What is another small step you could take using the same determination?

Through feedback, the process of goal setting and behavioral change continues while parishioners learn new ways of behaving that work for them. Succeeding at one small goal, they set new goals that will advance the changes they desire. Solution-focused brief counseling emphasizes doing; it works on the assumption that it is easier to behave your way into new feelings than it is to feel your way into new behavior.[12] Always, and especially when time is limited, solutions remain the focus of effective pastoral counseling.

Solution-Focused Conversation

In solution-focused brief pastoral counseling, goal-talk and solution-talk replace problem-talk. Words are important. Solution-talk (or change-talk)[13] moves the conversation from the problem to the many possibilities that exist beyond the problem. Examples of solution-talk include asking questions about changes that occurred before persons came in for counseling, highlighting the improvements they have made, identifying positive changes that parishioners have ignored, and asking them to brainstorm about actions they can take to improve their situation.[14]

Talking more about the problem only maintains the intensity surrounding it. Increasing efforts without making any changes inevitably leads to more of the same ineffective outcomes. The double of nothing is merely nothing. Increasing efforts around the problem multiplies problematic outcomes such as heightened anxiety, anger, and tension. (The more we talk about being angry, for example, the angrier we are likely to feel.)

Traditional counseling approaches that devote any significant time to problem-conversation may unwittingly exacerbate counselees' problems rather than resolve them.[15] Conversely, the majority of people in counseling willingly and gladly surrender their problems when they recognize exceptions to their problems and witness the positive results of their new behaviors.[16]

Creative Interaction

Creativity in counseling suggests that counseling is an art. As in other forms of art, the giver and the receiver contribute unique ingredients that mix and blend as no two others mix and blend. Parishioners bring with them considerable resources to aid in discovering solutions to their problems. Creative interaction allows for a free-flowing exchange of ideas and possibilities in the counseling relationship. It injects enthusiasm and even fun into the effort, while principles and methods of solution-focused counseling act as tools to shape and guide the proceedings. The potential for effective, long-term outcomes increases along with the parishioner's sense of self worth and capability.

Pastoral counseling ministry takes place within a faith context that strengthens the counseling relationship.[17] Knowing that God is already at work in the parishioner, the pastoral caregiver joins in that work. Within the Christian faith, it is believed that the Holy Spirit acts as an agent of creativity, providing discernment and guiding the pastoral caregiver's sensitivity to timing, verbal and body language, and other nuances that enhance the counseling endeavor.[18]

~

Enduring faith does not adjust its eternal truth, but it continually creates and reshapes its ministries to serve people in the current reality of their lives. Solution-focused counseling is one of these newly reshaped ministries for the third millennium. It offers congregational ministers a way of counseling that is equal to or greater than long-term strategies in effectiveness, yet takes far less precious time. Setting its sights on what is whole, on what works, solution-focused pastoral counseling can move troubled people away from bondage to their problems and their old ways of acting, and toward new life.

Notes

1.   Portions of this chapter are taken in modified form from my article "Solution-Focused Counseling: A Model for Parish Ministry" in the *Journal of Pastoral Care* 53, no. 1 (Spring 1999): 71–80.

2.   Reported by Todd Putnam, "Generation Y," *The Ivy Jungle Report: A Quarterly Newsletter for People Who Minister to Collegians* (Winter 1998): 1, 4.

3. Ibid.

4. For an overview of short-term approaches, see: W. O'Hanlon and B. Cade, *A Brief Guide to Brief Therapy* (New York: Norton, 1993); D. Benner, *Strategic Pastoral Counseling: A Short-Term Structure Model* (Grand Rapids: Baker, 1992); B. Childs, *Short-Term Pastoral Counseling* (New York: Haworth, 2000); H. Stone, *Brief Pastoral Counseling* (Minneapolis: Fortress Press, 1994); R. Fisch, J. H. Weakland, and L. Segal, *The Tactics of Change: Doing Therapy Briefly* (San Francisco: Jossey-Bass, 1982).

5. For an overview of this model, see: S. de Shazer, *Putting Difference to Work* (New York: Norton, 1991); S. de Shazer, *Keys to Solution in Brief Therapy* (New York: Norton, 1985); I. Berg and S. Miller, *Working with the Problem Drinker: A Solution-Focused Approach* (New York: Norton, 1992); J. L. Walter and J. E. Peller, *Becoming Solution-Focused in Brief Therapy* (New York: Bruner Mazel, 1992); S. Miller, M. Hubble, and B. Duncan, *Handbook of Solution-Focused Brief Therapy* (San Francisco: Jossey-Bass, 1996). Also see H. Stone, *Brief Pastoral Counseling* (Minneapolis: Fortress Press, 1994).

Among the distinctions of pastoral counseling from counseling in general is what Wayne Oates has called the God-in-relation-to-persons consciousness in counseling. "Regardless of a caregiver's professional identification, social role, and body of expertise, that person's counseling becomes *pastoral* when the counselee or the caregiver focuses their relationship upon the relation of God to the process of their lives" (W. E. Oates, "What Makes Counseling Pastoral," in *A Practical Handbook for Ministry*, ed. T. W. Chapman [Louisville, Ky.: Westminster/John Knox, 1992], 292). Pastoral counseling also relates faith to other areas of human development. James Fowler has written that a perspective of counseling that includes an understanding of religious experience "that is sensitive to the nuances of an evolving faith throughout the life of the person" allows the caregiver "to view the faith dimension as an essential feature of human experience that compliments other lines of development" (J. Fowler, "Pluralism and Oneness in Religious Experience: William James, Faith-Development Theory and Clinical Practice," in *Religion and The Clinical Practice of Psychology*, ed. E. P. Shafranske [Washington, D.C.: American Psychological Association, 1996], 1650). For additional commentary see also: Robert J. Lovinger, "Considering the Religious Dimension in Assessment and Treatment," in *Religion and The Clinical Practice of Psychology*, ed. E. P. Shafranske (Washington, D.C.: American Psychological Association, 1996), 347.

Solution-focused pastoral counseling is an outgrowth of the research and practice of solution-focused brief therapy as developed by de Shazer and others from the Brief Family Therapy Center in Milwaukee, Wis. See C. A. Kollar, *Solution-Focused Pastoral Counseling: An Effective Short-Term Approach for Getting People Back on Track* (Grand Rapids: Zondervan, 1997).

6. For example, see M. Weiner-Davis, *Divorce Busting* (New York: Simon & Schuster, 1992), 70–83. Weiner-Davis unfolds the beginnings of solution-oriented therapy and reveals the findings of research that lends support to its growing popularity. See also W. O'Hanlon and M. Weiner-Davis, *In Search of Solutions: A New Direction in Psychotherapy* (New York: Norton, 1989).

7. Kollar, *Solution-Focused Pastoral Counseling*, 109–10.

8. J. Drakford and C. V. King, *Wise Counsel: Skills for Lay Counseling* (Nashville: Convention Press, 1988), 87.

9. Berg and Miller, *Working with the Problem Drinker*, 45–79.

10. Weiner-Davis, *Divorce Busting*, 115; 117–40.

11. S. de Shazer, *Clues: Investigating Solutions in Brief Therapy* (New York: Norton, 1988).

12. Weiner-Davis, *Divorce Busting*, 199.

13. S. de Shazer, *Words Were Originally Magic* (New York: Norton, 1994).

14. Miller, Hubble, and Duncan, *Handbook of Solution-Focused Brief Therapy*, 258. For an examination of studies relating solution-talk to short-term and long-term outcome, see: W. J. Gingerich, S. de Shazer, and M. Weiner-Davis, "Constructing Change: A Research View of Interviewing," in E. Lipchik, ed., *Interviewing* (Rockville, Md.: Aspen, 1988).

15. Wiener-Davis, *Divorce Busting*, 88.

16. Ibid., 90.

17. Oates, *A Practical Handbook for Ministry*, 9–15; 482–83.

18. To quote Oates: "Jesus told his disciples that he was sending them forth as sheep among the wolves. He counseled them to have shrewdness in love. . . . He related this directly to the work of the Holy Spirit as Counselor. He told them that they should not be anxious, because the Holy Spirit would tell them in that hour what to say" (279). See also C. W. Brister, *Pastoral Care in the Church* (New York: HarperSanFrancisco, 1992), 69.

Part III

Pastoral Counseling Theory and Praxis

13

Theory Out of Context:
The Congregational Setting of
Pastoral Counseling

Howard W. Stone

TIME WAS, the need to consult with a psychotherapist or psychiatrist was a source of shame. You might talk to your pastor about a problem, but chances are you would avoid the disgrace of going to see a mental health professional. As recently as 1988 an American presidential candidate was knocked out of the race when his opponents revealed that he had been treated for depression.[1]

Today (Thomas F. Eagleton might note with some irony)[2] it is not unusual to hear people in urban restaurants, workplace lunchrooms, and fitness centers casually comparing notes about their dosage of Prozac or a new psychotherapist. Certain segments of our society, at least, are increasingly knowledgeable and sophisticated with regard to professional mental health care. Going to see a "shrink" has lost much of the stigma it once held for many people. Even so, clergymen and -women remain at the forefront when it comes to guiding their congregants through life's difficulties and crises.[3] Advice columnists still tell their readers to "talk to your pastor, priest, or rabbi."

Most of this pastoral counseling occurs not in the office suites of specialists but in the churches and synagogues where people also worship, study, socialize, and work together.[4] It takes place during pastoral visitation in people's homes, at the bedside of hospital patients, during chance encounters on the street or in the mall, after a church committee meeting, during preparations for a wedding or a funeral, in the odd quiet moment after a worship service or congregational dinner—in other words, in every arena of congregational life. A single pastoral counseling session, in this view, may last five minutes or several hours. The informal, unplanned pastoral encounter is every bit as vital and efficacious as the scheduled meeting in a pastor's office.[5]

William Hulme contends, "The congregation as a local community of faith is the most unused, undeveloped, and unorganized of all of the unique resources of the pastoral counselor." He refers to Eduard Thurneysen's definition

181

of pastoral counseling as "*extra*-ordinary ministry, dependent for its function in the church upon the ordinary ministries." Parishioners seek pastoral counseling, Hulme explains, when they need the pastor's ministry in a more specific and involved way—yet pastoral counseling is, by its definition, "a ministry associated with the worshipping community."[6]

Charles Kemp writes, "[T]he simple truth of the matter is that many people still go to their pastor for help. The parish pastor is in the front line of the mental health field whether he or she wants to be or not."[7] Wayne Oates adds, "The choice is not between counseling and not counseling, but between counseling in a disciplined and skilled way and counseling in an undisciplined and unskilled way."[8]

In this chapter I will report the findings of my recent research project that investigated whether theory in the field of pastoral counseling is congruent with its practice, most of which occurs in the context of the congregation. Is there a gap?

The Research

In recent years biblical theologians, systematic theologians, and pastoral theologians—I included—have criticized pastoral care and counseling for straying from its theological heritage.[9] Fortunately, theorists and practitioners alike increasingly show signs of returning to our theological foundation.

As pastoral care and counseling drifted from its theological roots, it appears also to have drifted from its congregational context—the place where most pastoral counseling occurs. As a result, underlying theory in the field of pastoral counseling may fail to take seriously the context of parish ministry and the brief nature of care offered in that setting.

In order to test this hypothesis, I undertook to examine the major authors in the field of pastoral counseling since 1950, with the goal of determining the degree to which pastoral counseling theory in the second half of the twentieth century has attended to the context of parish ministry. The guiding question, therefore, was this: Does the literature of pastoral counseling address the counseling situations typically encountered by parish pastors and offer methods well-suited to their context? Practice, after all, is most effective when it is in concert with theory. Ideally, practice and theory inform each other.

Method of Addressing the Problem

The study examined published works of the major theorists in the field of pastoral counseling from the second half of the twentieth century to determine each work's embedded psychology and theology as well as how seriously it considered and addressed the context of the parish. The decision to study only published books was purely functional and does not mean that I underestimate the importance of the development of the theory and practice of pastoral counseling by other means in which trends can be seen. Works in print are simply more accessible for study.

Criteria for Selection. Beginning with Seward Hiltner's seminal work *Pastoral Counseling,* published in 1949, the study covered all subsequent books with a distinctly pastoral counseling focus, omitting works that, though they may have discussed pastoral theology or pastoral care, did not address pastoral counseling specifically. It examined the writings of twenty-six pastoral counseling authors who are widely read by parish pastors, and who speak to mainline Christian ministers across Protestant and Catholic lines. These authors were selected through a poll of eight leading pastoral theologians/pastoral counseling specialists.

Each theorist selected has written at least one book; writers of edited or coauthored works were not studied unless they also have authored a work on their own. Some of the authors have written many books during their careers (for example, Howard Clinebell, Seward Hiltner, Wayne Oates) and their ideas on pastoral counseling may have evolved over the years; in those cases I chose a maximum of two representative works by each. The study excluded writers whose first book was published within the past five years, as it is too early to gauge their importance to the field. (Unfortunately, this criterion had the effect of omitting most women from the study because many of them are relatively new to the field and only recently have begun to publish works in pastoral counseling.)[10] For consistency, and to restrict the number of variables such as political and social influences, I limited the selection to American pastoral counseling literature.

Analysis. The study evaluated the theological and psychological resources cited by the chosen authors in order to cast light on their underlying assumptions; it also sought to determine how closely these writings addressed the context of congregational ministry (as opposed to the world of mental health professionals, pastoral counseling specialists, or chaplains) through analysis of their content. I will discuss the findings below, in the section headed "Results."

Theological and Psychological Influences

The study included a statistical tabulation of each work's references to other writers and theorists. (Appendix A includes the authors used in the study and describes the parameters of the research. Appendices C–G present the results of the theological and psychological resources cited. Appendices C–G included at the end of this book are in abbreviated form; for a complete listing of the results, see appendices C–G at www.fortresspress.com [search for *Strategies for Brief Pastoral Counseling*].) Every direct reference to a name or an authored work in the text (but not in an endnote or footnote) was counted; adjectives such as "Freudian" or "Jungian" were also considered to be a reference. The objective was to find trends, to get an overview of the field's orientation, and to discover whether in fact a particular viewpoint (or range of viewpoints) has driven the core of pastoral counseling theory and methodology.[11]

The Congregational Context

The study rated a writer's orientation to the congregational context according to several criteria. I asked: Does the author actually write about congregational ministry? Does the writer seem to have a "feel" for ministry in the parish? Does he or she describe a type of counseling that is applicable for the parish context, and is it described in enough specific detail that it can be carried out by the reader? Above all, can the author's methods and/or goals be readily accomplished in the context of parish ministry?

In other words, does the book offer practical, useful guidance for implementing the described method? Or does it insinuate that the described pastoral counseling approach is very difficult and that most readers working in the congregation will have difficulty doing it? Does the work present a style of counseling that can only be accomplished after extensive additional training? Is the counseling style long-term in duration (from the perspective of parish ministry, more than five or at most ten sessions)? Do the illustrative case histories extend well beyond the number of sessions that parish pastors typically can offer? If the answer to very many of these questions is yes, then my opinion is that the work does not take seriously the parish context of pastoral counseling. The purpose of the study and this chapter explaining and discussing it is not to find fault with any one author but rather to reveal a trend in pastoral counseling literature.

A few of these authors might object to being singled out for such analysis on the grounds that they were writing for pastoral counseling specialists rather than for parish clergy. Regardless of the author's preferred audience, however, publishers are in the business of selling books; for fiscal reasons they rarely target only a small, discrete population such as professional pastoral counselors or pastoral theologians. Presses routinely market books in the field of pastoral counseling to parish pastors and to seminaries that teach the parish pastors of the future.

What Parish Ministers Read

This study concerns itself not with authors' target audiences, therefore, but with what parish pastors (and seminarians training for ministry) actually read. Paul Engle carried out a national survey of 405 parish clergy in all areas of the United States to determine what they read and what types of books would help them most in their pastoral care and counseling.[12]

Only 6 percent of the respondents said that their counseling load was lower than in the previous year; 50 percent reported that they were doing more counseling. The survey asked them what they do if a parishioner needs more than five sessions; the overwhelming answer was that they typically see people for a maximum of five sessions and then refer.

Engle's research reveals striking information about the pastoral counseling literature pastors read. Engle comments, "If a pastor has limited time to read, he (or she) will likely opt for the book that promises more immediate practical help to face his (or her) upcoming counseling appointments that are probably squeezed between myriad other commitments."[13] He states that the "most important factor that pastors indicated they looked for in counseling books is that they are written to provide practical help rather than being technical books addressing issues faced in a clinical setting."[14] In other words, they wanted books that address a congregational, not a clinical, context. The ministers he surveyed generally see people in counseling for a maximum of two to five sessions and therefore seek out resources that provide practical help for the brief pastoral counseling they actually do.

Dissonance results when theory cannot be made to correlate to practice— that is, when it is out of context. If it is true that a majority of the pastoral counseling literature read by seminarians and parish pastors today does not seriously address the context of parish ministry and frequently is written by theorists who have adopted long-term psychotherapy as their model for care and merely recast it for ministers who do congregational ministry, the dissonance experienced by congregational ministers must be jarring indeed.

Results and Discussion

No works in the study were found to be overtly anti-parish. The pastoral counseling literature of the last five decades primarily treats congregational ministry with superficiality and silence. The problem is not antipathy toward counseling done in the congregation, but the apparent segregation of the discipline into a private venue reserved for pastoral care and counseling specialists or pastoral theologians.

Often the underlying assumptions of pastoral counseling books clash with the context of parish ministry. With a few exceptions, the pastoral counseling literature of the past five decades shows a significant long-term therapy bias; most of its theory and methods grow out of theoretical constructs and psychotherapeutic modalities of long-term clinical practice, even when written for pastors in the congregational context who primarily do short-term counseling. In the current study, this bias was evident both from the tabulation of resources cited and from content analysis of the texts, although the attention paid to the practice of pastoral counseling in the congregational context varied from book to book.

Tabulation of Sources:
Influential Psychotherapists and Theologians

A study of the authors cited by writers in the pastoral counseling field as resources for their ideas was suggestive. Such an examination of sources gives us an idea of the theory—theological and/or psychotherapeutic—that underlies the practice of pastoral counseling (see appendix A for a description of the parameters of this part of the study). The complete results are listed in appendices C–G, which catalogue references to those theorists The present section discusses the results of the part of the study that tabulated the twenty-six pastoral counseling authors' references to other theorists.

In all, 550 different writers in the fields of theology and psychotherapy were cited by these key authors of the pastoral counseling literature over the last five decades. Of them, 277 were in the field of psychology/psychotherapy, 159 in classical fields of theology (biblical theology, systematic theology, historical theology, ethics, etc.), 14 in marriage and family therapy, 92 in pastoral theology/pastoral counseling, and 8 writers in the field of spirituality. (See appendices C, D, E, F, and G respectively.)

Writers in the field of pastoral counseling naturally refer to one another (17 percent of sources referred to were those already in the field—see appendix F). Anton Boisen, Howard Clinebell, Seward Hiltner, and Wayne Oates each were cited by nine of the twenty-six pastoral counseling authors in the study. Aside from that, on the whole, pastoral counseling theorists give more authority and space to authors in the field of psychology than to the pastoral tradition from which they come. In fact, half of all references were to psychological sources (50 percent). In the works studied, Sigmund Freud (cited by 17 out of 26 authors), Harry Stack Sullivan (14), Erik Erikson (13), Carl Jung (11), and Erick Fromm (10) received the most frequent mention in the pastoral counseling literature of the last five decades (see appendix C).

Clearly the field of pastoral counseling owes a debt to Freud and to those closely associated with him, but the influence of Carl Rogers is greater than that of Freud or any other psychotherapeutic theorist or theologian. Pastoral counseling writers make more references to Rogers (cited by 19 of the 26 pastoral counseling authors studied) than to any other theorist no matter what the field. Boisen, Clinebell, Hiltner, and Oates are cited by only half as many authors as Rogers. The heavy reliance of an entire field on the thinking of one person—Carl Rogers—is astonishing.

Although the writers studied make extensive references to psychological theorists, none of them seems to draw to any extent upon the resources of spiritual direction and spirituality (only 1 percent of all works referred to; see appendix G). Ironically, in recent years a number of writers in the field of psychology have "discovered" spirituality and seem to make more spiritual references than do the pastoral counselors—though with a somewhat different understanding of spirituality than exists in the Christian tradition.

In the present study, references to spiritual resources and disciplines tend to be generalized and somewhat vague. Some of the writers mention prayer; most of them quote scripture. A few write about worship, although regular participation in the local congregation is rarely if ever suggested. (Don Capps addressed the integration of preaching and pastoral counseling in one of his books, as did several early writers covered by the study.) But there is no significant space devoted to how these resources can be helpful as an intervention in pastoral counseling. No author in the study discussed specific exercises and interventions such as *lectio divina*, the Jesus Prayer, or icons. It became apparent during the course of the research that authors of the last half century of pastoral counseling literature are not grounded in spiritual/ascetic theology—which, therefore, has little influence on the field.

The field of pastoral counseling has been dominated by Protestants, although Roman Catholics have had somewhat more presence in the area of hospital chaplaincy. Roman Catholic theorists tend to address spirituality and the resources of the Christian spiritual traditions more frequently than do the Protestant writers. Still, one might wonder if the shaping of Roman Catholics who have entered the field has led them to leave behind most of their training in spiritual direction and spirituality. One pastoral counselor puts it this way: "There has been quite a tradition of anti-spiritual resources and anti-prayer. I experienced it when I first went into the field."[15]

One surprising discovery emerged from the reading of all of these pastoral counseling authors together. Although there was a time when pastoral counseling seemed to be drifting from its moorings of theology, the drift proved to be more subtle than I had expected; this is especially true in the last decade or so. To read some recent writers in the field of pastoral theology, one might wonder if pastoral counseling has any relationship to the church and its theology; yet 29 percent of all the writers referred to were from the classical fields of theology, second only to psychology. Pastoral counseling theorists refer to classical theologians more than they do to each other (29 percent versus 17 percent).

To some extent at least, every author in the study wrestled theologically with the task of pastoral counseling. To be sure, some of them might come under criticism for being too simplistic, for using biblical quotes to "proof-text" their underlying psychological theory, or for narrowly wedding their thought to a single theological or denominational tradition—but most did try to tie their particular slant on pastoral counseling to theology. It may be that voices raised in recent years decrying the theological drift of pastoral counseling served a purpose to help establish pastoral theology as a distinct specialization in its own right, a new fenced-in arena of expertise.

The influence of psychology on writings in pastoral counseling has shifted during the period studied. Recent writings have more references to theology and exhibit less reliance upon psychology. It is a positive movement; pastoral counseling is more in touch with its theological roots. There is a negative: with less obvious reliance upon psychology for its writings, there is less ongoing assessment of the psychology that is endemic to the field. As a result, the influence of Rogers and psychodynamic psychology lives on, its existence hardly examined or reassessed. Therefore, the dominant understanding of psychotherapy of the field implicit within its writings continues to have a long-term therapy bias, which is theory ignoring the context of the congregation.

To a degree the field of pastoral counseling is theologically incestuous. Until recently its writers repeatedly cited the same thinkers, such as Paul Tillich, Martin Luther, and Søren Kierkegaard (referenced by 13, 12, and 9 of the 26 pastoral counseling theorists, respectively; see appendix D). Augustine, Jürgen Moltmann, Karl Barth, and Martin Buber are the next most common theological/philosophical writers referenced by the pastoral counseling literature of the last five decades. Some recent authors have drawn heavily upon process theology, but many theological strains and movements (liberation theology and feminist theology, to name two) seem not to have made a great impact upon the theory and practice of pastoral counseling. Also, there is little dialogue with other faith traditions—a critical oversight for these days and times.

Over the last twenty years a greater number of women have specialized in pastoral counseling and pastoral theology. The significant influence of womanist and feminist theologians upon theology and pastoral theology unfortunately has not carried over into pastoral counseling to a similar degree. Few women authors in pastoral counseling have addressed the context of the parish; most write about pastoral theology. Pastors who look for pastoral counseling books written by feminist and womanist authors that address the parish will be disappointed. Given that context has been central to these theologians, one might hope that they will soon give more attention to counseling in the context of the congregation.

Content Analysis: Relevance for the Parish Context

Most pastoral counseling theorists are not particularly sensitive to the context of the parish. As pastoral counseling has moved toward specialization in its practice, authors in the field increasingly address issues endemic to these specialty fields and devote less attention to the congregational context—where, in fact, the majority of all pastoral counseling is carried out.

As a result, most authors pay heed to such issues as the importance of advanced training in a pastoral care specialty—certainly a worthy endeavor in itself—but frequently offer little to ministers who do not have the opportunity to participate in an advanced training program yet wish to develop their pastoral counseling skills. Sometimes it almost seems as if the specific details of how to go about pastoral counseling are deliberately locked away from readers, to be opened only upon entering a seminary degree program, clinical pastoral education, or perhaps extensive personal psychotherapy.

A number of the authors in the study communicate the implicit position that pastoral counseling is a daunting task and that many or most parish pastors are unlikely to successfully use the techniques they recommend—even though congregational ministers have been doing pastoral counseling in one shape or form for centuries. Some explicitly warn that the counseling approach they describe is only possible in a specialized context. These writers cite lack of time as the primary reason why parish pastors are unable to do a particular style of counseling yet, incongruously, fail to incorporate into their thinking the many emergent counseling strategies that address people's problems in a limited number of sessions. Time-efficient models of psychotherapy appeared first in crisis intervention, and more recently in the new field of brief therapy. Most pastoral counseling writers, unfortunately, have eschewed these new methods and pursued seemingly endless variations of early twentieth century therapeutic approaches.

Although pastoral counseling has long been a vital task of parish ministry, at times it seems as if theorists in the specialized fields of pastoral theology and counseling are fencing off pastoral counseling from the rest of parish ministry and subtly (or not so subtly) alleging that parish pastors cannot or should not undertake it. This, of course, is a concomitant danger of specialization in any field. You get yourself inside the fence, which gives you the opportunity and authority to do what you want, and then you try to keep others outside the arena.

The majority of the authors studied either fail to demonstrate a good grasp of the kind of counseling that occurs in parish ministry, or they show little interest in it. Many writers in pastoral counseling seem more in tune with classical theology, psychotherapy, or specialized pastoral counseling than with the counseling that happens in local congregations. A professor at Union Theological Seminary, presupposing a technical, long-term orientation, describes the aim of counseling as follows:

> Increased consciousness is not the goal at all, nor any measurement of
> behavior that such a goal might suggest, but rather a pervasive and

subtle, yet really quite thorough rearrangement of the place of consciousness in the psyche. In such an understanding of psychological
process, consciousness loses its function as the defining center of inte-
rior events and comes to recognize instead its pivotal relation to an
ever-present unconscious.[16]

The writer appears to be addressing psychoanalysts rather than those who
are engaged in congregational ministry. Parish pastors reading these lines
could find little insight or understanding (and certainly no practical tools) to
aid them in counseling troubled parishioners who come to them for help.

Many of the authors in the study do a good job of relating to the helper-
helpee context, but not to the parish context. They talk about the other person—the counselee (and if they are influenced by family systems theory, those
immediately related to the counselee)—but they rarely address the person(s)
seeking help in the context of a local church or a faith community. The counseling process, for them, is very individualized; as a result, it becomes cut off
from the community, the fellowship of believers.

One obvious clue to a writer's lack of parish orientation is the choice of
words to identify the pastoral caregiver and the person receiving help: *therapist*,
pastoral counselor or *pastoral psychotherapist* may designate clergy, for example,
and *patient* or *client* frequently identify the parishioner/counselee.

When authors do make references to parish ministry, they primarily
describe large and/or multiple-staffed churches. The fact is, most parishes in
the United States are small and are served by a single minister. The Christian
Church (Disciples of Christ), to cite only one denomination, has an average
parish membership of less than 150 persons, and the majority of its churches
are estimated to have 50 or fewer members. To describe pastoral counseling
ministry primarily in terms of large urban parishes is to be out of touch with
the context of ministry in many of America's churches.

What is more, the parish of much pastoral counseling literature appears to
be the parish of a previous era, having congregants of many years' standing
who are lifelong members of the denomination and a male pastor who entered
seminary directly out of college. Among the important changes in today's
churches is the rising incidence of second-career pastors and the increased
authority of women—who not only take on more positions of power as lay
persons but also, at many seminaries, comprise the majority of those entering
ordained ministry. Life goes by at a faster pace than it did fifty years ago. Families now move at least once every five years (and at least once every three years
in the western part of the United States). Today's congregations are multicultural. People change their church affiliations readily. There is greater diversity
in churches, with members coming from various denominations, religions,
cultures, and countries of origin.

To be fair, as the period studied covers a half century, some of these books were indeed written in a different era. Others were written by authors who have not performed congregational ministry for many years and write out of their experience in an earlier era. Nevertheless, many of the changes cited above were already in effect in 1950, at the start of the period studied.

It is important to note exceptions. Although most writers in pastoral counseling merely nod toward the parish—if they acknowledge its existence at all—a few take seriously the care and counseling that originates in congregational settings. C. W. Brister, Howard Clinebell, William Hulme, Charles Kemp, Wayne Oates, David Switzer, and Charles Taylor show in at least some of their works a sensitivity for the needs of pastors who work in the real world of contemporary congregations. The final section of this chapter will discuss their contributions to pastoral counseling in the parish context.

Thinking Long, Doing Brief Counseling

Rogers and Freud were in vogue during the birth of the contemporary movement in pastoral counseling. Their influence still dominates. (A cursory review of the list of psychotherapy theorists in appendix C will suggest the extent to which the field of pastoral counseling has relied on this theory.) Today the discussion may revolve around Kohut rather than Freud, but the field remains tied to second- or third-generation Freudian psychodynamic theory and the relationship methods of Rogerian therapy, especially Carl Rogers's early work. While theory and practice in psychology, psychotherapy, and marriage and family therapy since that time have evolved to reflect new research and changing social conditions, it almost seems that the pastoral counseling field has "fixated" (if I may use a Freudian term) on its beginnings, its theory developmentally stuck, as it were, in the therapeutic model of an earlier era. Unlike most mental health specialties, pastoral counseling has not to any significant extent diversified its early psychological base.

The situation reminds me of the lingering influence of Scandinavian culture on third-generation Swedish and Norwegian Americans raised in the upper Midwest. Our family still eats lutefisk and lefse at Christmas. (Although lefse is a lovely potato griddle bread, lutefisk is dried codfish soaked in lye, to my taste virtually inedible.) When I lectured in Norway a few years ago, my host and I discussed foods of our respective countries over lunch. I told him about the Scandinavian foods we have at Christmas, and he replied that he had never tasted lutefisk in his life. Late nineteenth- and early twentieth-century Scandinavian immigrants brought their traditions to America along with their trunks of belongings. Common foods, along with other customs and attitudes, evolved or disappeared in the "old country" while many Scandinavian Americans continue to observe traditions as they existed on the day their ancestors boarded a ship for the new world.

When pastoral counseling carved out its separate identity from the field of practical theology, it embraced the prevalent psychological theory of the time. Though time passes by, to a great extent it retains that embedded theory much as third-generation Americans hold onto the traditions of the old country. It is understandable why those who first wrote on pastoral counseling in the second half of the last century based their work on the ideas of Freud and psychodynamic psychology. There were not many other options—although to be fair, other psychological theories did exist. The embedded theological anthropology and etiology in psychoanalytic thought that are no longer dominant in either contemporary psychology or theology still exist in pastoral theology. It seems that the field of pastoral counseling has not revisited the issue.

In the new country of the dawning millennium, the vast majority of congregational counseling practice is brief—a fact borne out by statistics as well as by common sense—and tends to fall somewhere between pastoral care/visitation and pastoral counseling. I frequently refer to it as *pastoral conversation,* a style of purposeful interaction with parishioners that can be used in the fifty-minute hour counseling session as well as in the unplanned chat after a church meeting about a problem occurring. Most pastoral counseling theorists recognize that counseling in the parish rarely lasts more than a few sessions, but they continue to base their theory on long-terms models that rarely apply in such a setting. What is the sense of a theory that does not fit the circumstances of its practice? Long-term psychotherapy is a square peg to the round hole of the congregational context. Perhaps many congregational ministers can relate to Howard Clinebell's experience: "During the early years of my ministry, I attempted to use the Rogerian and neo-Freudian approach, which I had studied in graduate school. It gradually became clear to me that the relatively passive, long-term model of psychotherapy that I had learned was not particularly effective with many persons who came for pastoral counseling."[17]

Even when the authors do provide examples of ministers doing counseling, frequently they illustrate their discussions with case histories of individuals seen for a long time. To give only a few examples: Charles Gerkin refers to a counseling case that lasted for a year; Paul Johnson cites one case going on for eleven sessions and another for twenty-five sessions; John Patton describes a counseling relationship that lasted several months and another for more than one year.[18] What is most disturbing are authors who merely make reference to other people's cases or to novels, apparently not having enough recent practice of pastoral counseling to write from their own experience.

Wayne E. Oates was one of the first writers who, at least to some extent, attempted to correct the long-term therapy bias in pastoral counseling. In his 1959 book, *An Introduction to Pastoral Counseling,* he noted that much of the counseling in the parish is done in a single interview and that the number of people served as well as the many other roles and duties of ministry make it important that clergy "know how to use one-interview opportunities to the fullest possible advantage."[19]

The Journey

In psychotherapy, especially the long-term variety, practitioners believe it is their task to accompany individuals along the entire journey from the beginning, when they first recognize and address a problem, until change has occurred and even beyond. A psychiatrist I know once proudly announced, "I have never terminated a patient in my entire career." She sees herself as a companion on the patient's journey of self-discovery and change, all the way to the end. It is no surprise that along the way she often discovers issues other than the one that brought the person into counseling, and encourages the patient to address those as well. The result is a life of unending therapy—at least until her clients decide at some point to terminate the care before it is "completed."

This travel-guide model of psychotherapy is not suitable in the context of the congregation. The entire ministry of the church accompanies people on their lifelong journey of faith; the appropriate goal of pastoral counseling within that context is much more modest and limited. It shepherds individuals through a tough passage or a steep turn but does not continue the therapeutic assistance beyond that point. It helps those who are bound up with a particular problem or face a crisis. Pastoral counseling is a brief point on the journey, a refocusing of energies and perspective. Other ministries continue when pastoral counseling has done what it can do; the journey of faith is the task of the whole church. In addition, the understanding of "health" found in psychodynamic thinking is to some extent inconsistent with an understanding of finitude found in a Christian anthropology: healing is never complete, and many wounded people function competently and are faithful to the call of the gospel without ever approaching anything resembling "health."

In this regard it seems, once again, that many pastoral counseling theorists have patterned themselves after the caregiving model found in psychotherapy, which lacks such a built-in community, and have lost sight of the care offered by the many other ministries of the church. Psychotherapists do not—or are not supposed to—see their clients outside the therapy session. In contrast, congregational ministry offers care in many settings and ways other than counseling (including preaching, worship, teaching, care groups, spiritual direction, and so on). The entire ministry of the church helps to strengthen individuals and ultimately prepare them for their own ministries of care, peace, and justice.

Insight and Depth

Many pastoral counseling specialists and theorists have subscribed to the view that insight (defined by Carroll Wise as "a result of an emotional relationship and process with another person that permits the communication of life experience, the release of negative feelings, and the growth of positive feelings")[20] should be the ultimate goal of counseling. Most of the pastoral counseling writers in this study speak of insight being the primary or only goal of counseling. Some would echo Freud that insight should lead to action, but most of the attention in their writing is given to insight, and to the necessity of exploring the past in depth with counselees in order to achieve that insight. Theorists who even mention change in behavior do so briefly, as something that follows insight.

A number of the works in this study are heavily laced with the language of depth and insight. Seward Hiltner, for example, once defined pastoral counseling as "the attempt by a pastor to help people help themselves through the process of gaining understanding of their inner conflicts," and wrote that conduct "can be understood only if we look both at conscious awareness and at the deeper levels which influence personality and affect its acts, but which are not ordinarily recognized in consciousness."[21] He no doubt was relying to some extent upon the thinking of Freud as well as Carl Rogers who described counseling as entering "deeply with this man into his confused struggle for selfhood."[22]

The two-step model of change (insight first, then action) is not the understanding of change typically found among those who write about brief pastoral counseling. In brief counseling change normally occurs by *acting* or *believing* one's way into it. Insight happens after behavioral or cognitive change already has started; it is the result of change rather than a necessary step to change. Parishioners achieve insight sometimes during the counseling process, sometimes after the formal sessions have ceased, and sometimes not at all—but they still change.

The metaphor of depth as a model for pastoral counseling in the congregational context has several fatal flaws. It is a hierarchical term containing an imbedded value judgment. (Shallow is bad; deep is good; deeper, better; deepest, best.) The depth metaphor also is hierarchical to the degree that it assumes the pastor or therapist knows best what parishioners need, places parishioners in a dependent mode, and robs them of the power or authority to act on their own benefit. The effort to dig below successive layers of counselees' psyches and their past may needlessly delay their active movement in the future and forestall concrete efforts to resolve problems. If counselees do not stay in counseling for many sessions, actual change of behavior may never happen.

Furthermore, as a metaphor in general usage, depth can imply stillness ("still waters run deep") rather than the sometimes strenuous activity that is required to repair and renew troubled lives. Another, more important reason to replace the depth/insight model in pastoral counseling with a more proactive and immediate approach is that insight does not of itself produce change. Oates writes: "One naïve assumption of some insight therapy is that if a person *sees* what a problem is, he will automatically do something about it of a constructive nature. This is not necessarily so."[23] Indeed, in my personal and professional experience, achieving insight often does not result in positive change and may even hinder it, because it gives the illusion that we have accomplished something. For that reason I suggest we talk about the *facets* of situations or personalities rather than their depth, because that term connotes characteristics of a phenomenon rather than a hierarchy of levels or values.

Problems versus Solutions

Much of long-term-oriented pastoral counseling could be characterized as *problem talk*. Problem talk focuses on people's difficulties and tries to find explanations for their bad feelings and unhealthy behaviors. It delves deeper and deeper into their experience of the problem. It attempts to discover more and more facts about the problem. But, as Ludwig Wittgenstein points out, all of "the facts belong only to the problem, not to its solution."[24] Long-term, problem-oriented counseling assumes a causal link between the problem and the solution. This leads to the idea that an underlying problem, deeper than the presenting problem, must be worked on before counselees can tackle their other difficulties.

Solution talk does not assume this causal link between problem and solution. It recognizes that solutions are commonly encountered outside of the facts.[25] Solutions are constructed from pastoral conversation. Together pastor and parishioner envision a new future, one not dominated by the problem; through language they clarify a picture of this new future and discuss what specific things the parishioner will do (and think) when the solution begins to be achieved. This is not an insight about the problem but a careful attention to the future where change will occur.

Passive Pastoral Caregivers, Active Social Reformers

What can brief pastoral counseling accomplish? According to Seward Hiltner, it should follow the advice of Hippocrates and do no harm. "And if it does not harm—that is, if the parishioner can say something about his situation and how he feels, not becoming worse thereby but having the feeling that he is understood—then it is fair to say that something positive has happened."[26] These are disturbingly modest expectations for the pastoral counseling enterprise.

Wayne Oates also commented on this passive approach to pastoral counseling: "[I]n the early to middle-1950's pastoral counseling emphasized listening, empathy, and responsive counseling to such an extent that a whole generation of exceptionally passive pastors was produced."[27] John Patton believes that the most prevalent difficulty encountered by ministers learning pastoral counseling is "listening rather passively while a counselee dumps a problem on him/her and then feeling the demand to come up with an 'answer' to it."[28]

The emphasis in pastoral counseling upon listening and empathy, *à la* Rogers, created a whole generation of pastors who were passive in their counseling ministry. Incongruously, many of the same ministers actively worked to remediate injustices in society. Racism, nuclear war, sexism, and other issues propelled them to make bold statements from the pulpit and to take strong steps for social change. Their ministry took on a split personality: passive in pastoral counseling, active in social change. There was no consistent model of ministry. Even today, many pastors are trained to be passive, empathetic listeners but assertive—even aggressive—prophetic leaders in other areas of their ministry. It must be confusing for parishioners.

Much of the pastoral counseling literature offers a one-word response to this active/passive dissonance: *referral*. William Oglesby writes: "[O]n many occasions parishioners bring problems to the pastor which are within the scope of his skill and resources but for which he simply does not have sufficient time."[29] Most writers applying their embedded long-term therapy orientation to the parish conclude that parish pastors do not have enough time to take active steps to bring about "real" change and therefore must refer. They assume that change is a long, complicated task. They do not encourage ministers to learn brief counseling methods that can help people to make small yet significant changes, enabling them to live productively and faithfully to God's call. They do not relate the process of change to many ministries of the church, but only to therapy. Instead, they urge, pastors ought to empathize, listen, and then refer.

Certainly parish pastors can and should refer when a situation is beyond their scope, but even before the referral they can do more than merely listen and empathize. Small but important changes often result from a single solution-focused (rather than problem-oriented) visit, and in many cases, a referral may not be necessary.

Methods in Pastoral Counseling

Many of the authors in the present study seem to assume that the reader already knows how to enact the pastoral counseling they write about only in theory. They discuss at length the importance of the pastor-counselee relationship but too frequently omit what pastors actually do once a counseling session begins.

"Technique" and "method" are almost dirty words that many of the authors disregard altogether—perhaps assuming that parish pastors lack the ability or time to do what they describe, and therefore should refer their parishioner-counselees to professional therapists. In *Widening the Horizon*, for example, Gerkin claims that he writes for parish and community contexts and seems to understand and respect the diverse demands on the pastor as well as the tension between what is ideal and what is realistic. He provides a hermeneutic schema for the parish pastor—but accompanies it with little direction in terms of actual practice.[30] Herb Anderson devotes a mere seventeen of 123 pages of *The Family and Pastoral Care* to practical ways of carrying out marriage and family care.[31]

The movement from theory to practice is not automatic, intuitive, or magical. Ministers working in the parish need and deserve not only theory, but practical schooling in effective methods that will facilitate the doing of pastoral counseling in their real-world context.

Thinking Individual, Caring for Systems

It is understandable why some of the early writers in the contemporary pastoral counseling movement such as Seward Hiltner, Paul Johnson, Carroll Wise, or Russell Dicks do not refer to marriage and family therapy theorists; not much was written on it at the time. What is astounding is the absence of references from more recent pastoral counseling authors (see appendix E). In the study on sources referenced by pastoral counseling authors, only 2 percent of all authors cited were theorists writing on couple and family therapy. Since over half of all counseling cases seen by pastors involve marriage and family issues, one might have hoped that pastoral counselors would have been among the first counseling professionals to use the theory and methods of this burgeoning field.

The parish is a system. As such, it has a unique mix of spiritual, social, educational, and helping relationships, to name only a few. Unlike the majority of institutional systems in society (such as schools, government offices, businesses, and most clubs), the parish system incorporates entire families. "Ministers are in a more strategic position to do family care and counseling than any other professional," writes Howard Clinebell. "The context within which they function as leaders of congregations provide frequent and natural entrees to many family systems."[32] Charles Kemp observes that ministers are with people during important family occasions—that they perform weddings, for example, and are present in the home during times of celebration and sadness—and thus people quite naturally think to go to them when family problems arise.[33]

Similarly, Herb Anderson points out, "No other helping professional has the kind of access to people in families that pastors do," and there are "an infinite variety of ordinary moments in our pastoral care with families in which an appropriate response may help effect change."[34] Despite his enthusiasm about the access pastors have to families, however, Anderson describes a care and counseling process that is both difficult and time consuming and goes to great lengths to warn readers of its attendant dangers. Indeed, Anderson writes: "[O]rdinary prior pastoral relationships may preclude the kind of distance that is necessary for effective family counseling," and most clergy have "neither the time nor the training to do therapy with families."[35] (Russell L. Dicks earlier made the same point: "Marriage counseling is an extremely difficult art and the local pastor has neither the time nor the skill to do much with people in serious marital difficulties."[36])

Of course, ministers do confront marriage and family issues, and yet the field of pastoral counseling remains decidedly oriented toward individual counseling (see appendix E).[37] In the present study only seven of the twenty-six pastoral counseling theorists made *any* reference to marriage and family theorists. Indeed, while pastoral counseling theorists made reference to 277 theorists who write primarily about individual therapy, they made reference to only 14 writers whose expertise was in the field of couple and family counseling.

Seward Hiltner's conception of pastoral counseling reflected the individual bias of his underlying psychological theory; he wrote: "Some may object to the definition of counseling as a process occurring between an individual and a helper and suggest that there is such a thing as family counseling and group counseling. . . . But the ordinary connotation of the term counseling is, and with justification, the relationship of the person who seeks help and a helping person. . . ."[38] His attitude has dominated the field ever since.

The lack of attention to systems of couple and family counseling theory may be the result of an antiquated theological anthropology that views humans individualistically, rather than an anthropology that takes seriously the web of relationships and constructs that shape all of us. If pastoral counseling theorists view human beings as limited and alone, bounded by their bodies and made up of discrete entities of body, soul, and mind, the individual-oriented counseling that most of them propose is consistent with that view. It is interesting to note that two of the three theologians referred to most by pastoral counseling theorists (Tillich and Kierkegaard) are existential theologians. It is possible that existential theological thought concerning the person has contributed to pastoral counseling's tardiness in adopting a systems perspective to counseling.

This deficiency also may be traceable to the individual orientation of psychotherapeutic theorists at the onset of modern pastoral counseling. Given those theorists' presupposition that human change must first occur intrapsychically, a focus on the single client quite logically follows. The comments by Hiltner above certainly bear this out. Clearly the movement from an intrapsychic, individual orientation to a systems approach is not a simple matter of adopting new ideas—it requires a massive shift in one's basic underlying assumptions. John Patton tells how hard it has been to alter his psychoanalytic background: "I have difficulty integrating some of the structural and systematic interventions described in the family-therapy literature into my understanding of the pastoral relationship and with the norm of relational humanness. . . ."[39]

Convinced nonetheless, Patton cites God's covenant with individuals as well as communities as a model for pastoral care; ministers, in his view, "must respond both to the person who asks for help and to the system of which he or she is a part—even when the person asking for help seems to be leaving out the marital partner or other members of the family." He presents it as a clear ethical issue: "[T]he pastor who fails to take a marital system seriously enough to make every effort to have both spouses involved in the counseling may naïvely be providing an emotional affair for the spouse who is involved. He or she is contributing to the counselee's disloyalty to the marital system in a way that is ultimately destructive."[40]

Given that many of the proponents of brief counseling have come from marriage and family therapy, it may be that pastoral counseling theorists have tended not to embrace brief counseling because of their ties to individual rather than systems-oriented theory and methods. For parish pastors this means that, though they care for couple and family difficulties more than any other type of problem, the pastoral counseling books they read are primarily individual in orientation. Once again, the literature of pastoral counseling is out of touch with the context of congregational ministry.

Brief Pastoral Counseling in the Congregational Context

When I worked in the parish, often before services began I would peer at the assembled congregation through a cracked door in the sacristy. It helped me to notice and attend to the variety of needs and concerns of those in worship.

On one particular morning that stands out in my memory, I saw not only the whole body of one hundred people or so in the pews, but many diverse individuals and concerns. A teenage couple who had recently eloped sat with the groom's mother and father; the bride's parents would not speak to them and were absent from church. A woman, caretaker for her mother in the advanced stages of cancer, displayed exhaustion in her face and body. Two married couples were experiencing strain in their marriages; in one case both husband and wife were present but sat noticeably apart from each other, and in the other only the wife sat before me (if this weekend was like others, her husband was home nursing a hangover with Bloody Marys). A lonely widower who eight months earlier had lost his wife of forty-six years looked off into the distance. A Norman Rockwell family filled a back pew, clean-cut and well-dressed, one boy, one girl, showing no evidence that the mother recently had reported the father for sexually abusing their eleven-year-old daughter. A man who was rumored to have been charged with white-collar crime hunkered with lowered eyes at the end of a pew. A retired army sergeant sat on the aisle, veins visibly pulsating in his temples, angry not only at the modern army and the government, but increasingly at everything in his life—including his wife beside him and his estranged, incarcerated son.

I had already made pastoral calls to some of them; several had or were now coming for counseling; others were as yet only in my prayers while I looked for a time to have a pastoral conversation with them. All were there for worship. Certainly there were many untroubled folks in the congregation that morning, but I was struck by the number, in a group so small, who came burdened with problems and concerns.

Although the demographics of that particular rural/suburban church probably heightened the range of experiences and lifestyles within its membership, it was by no means atypical of congregations in cities, towns, and suburbs throughout the Western world. With such a vast diversity of needs, some of them serious, ministers serving congregations need resources to guide and support them as they offer counsel to their troubled parishioners.

Addressing the Parish Context: Notable Exceptions

We have seen, as shown by the study, that a slow drift away from the parish context began early in the evolution of pastoral counseling as a distinct field. Early authors attempted—sometimes with considerable success—to pay attention to the counseling that went on in the congregation. A number of later writers appear at best to nod in the direction of the parish while speaking primarily to specialist issues that would little concern those who minister in the congregational context. Edward Wimberley's words echo the findings of the study: "[H]istorically pastoral counseling has functioned in a manner that has alienated it from the local church." He goes on to say that the pastoral counseling movement has limited itself by failing to speak to the needs of parish ministry.[41]

However, the want of parish orientation in pastoral counseling literature is a deficiency, not a vacuum. Not every pastoral counseling writer has disregarded the congregational context. Some have taken seriously the care and counseling that originates in parish ministry, showing in at least some of their work a sensitivity for pastoral counseling ministry in the context of the congregation. They may write at times for pastoral care or pastoral theology specialists, but they devote significant attention to the congregational setting where most pastoral counseling is carried out.

In *An Introduction to Pastoral Counseling*, Wayne E. Oates underlines the importance of context: "Counseling of any kind is shaped and directed by the context in which it takes place. The native environment of pastoral counseling is the fellowship of believers, the gathered community of Christians, the church."[42] Oates understood that parish pastors, while carrying out their many other ministries, are already beginning the task of helping that may in the future make the transition to counseling. He pointed out that it "often begins in some seemingly insignificant, everyday event, far removed from a formal request for help on the part of the person who needs it. . . . The pastor and other religious workers, therefore, can never become so professional in their pictures of themselves that they underestimate the importance of informal relationships both as powerful ministries in and of themselves, and as points of vital contact for beginning more formal counseling relationships."[43]

Charles Kemp also believed that context was important to counseling. He submitted, "The setting itself makes a difference." He cited the study by Seward Hiltner and Lowell Colston suggesting that people enter a church with different perspectives from those with which they go to a counselor in independent practice, a hospital, a family service agency, a school, or medical arts building, adding:

> The pastor also has a relationship with the ones he or she counsels that is different from that of other professionals. The pastor participates in a continuing relationship that begins before the specific problem occurs and continues after the counseling is discontinued. The relationship of other professionals to someone they counsel begins with the occurrence of the difficulty; they have no previous background knowledge of the person. Their relationship is terminated when the counseling is terminated. . . . the pastor has a background to begin with and knows when relapses occur and whether counseling should be activated again.[44]

Kemp was a pastoral counseling theorist who always taught and wrote about pastoral counseling from the perspective of the parish. Indeed, it seems as if all his work—whether in the congregation, the counseling office, the hospital or the seminary classroom—was carried out as a parish pastor. He gently urged students who became overly enamored with the clinical setting to look again at ministry in the congregation. He reminded his readers that pastoral counseling began in the parish: "Even some pastors may doubt their place and tend to feel somewhat inferior to those in the other professions who have such extended training and specialized skills. . . . The pastor is a professional, too, with specialized training and with the availability of spiritual resources that have been proven over the centuries as means of health and strength."[45]

Howard Clinebell has published two revisions of his now-classic *Basic Types of Pastoral Care and Counseling*.[46] It is *the* best-selling book on pastoral care and counseling written for mainline Protestants and Roman Catholics (for one reason, I believe, because he directly addresses the care and counseling that ministers do in the context of the congregation). In *Basic Types*, Clinebell seeks "to highlight those types of caring and counseling that are essential and therefore normative in a persons-oriented, general (non-specialists) ministry"— short-term, grief, marriage/family, referrals, education/small group, and lay caring are examples of this ministry. For Clinebell these constitute the "heart of a parish minister's caring and counseling."[47]

Like Kemp, Clinebell believes that the congregational context of pastoral counseling is vital. "The *setting* and *context* of a pastor's counseling," he writes, "give it uniqueness in profound ways. The setting is the life of a gathered community of faith, a congregation. The context is pastoral care and the other functions of the general ministry through which pastoral care can occur. The fact that ministers counsel within an ecclesial setting, a complex network of relationships where many people know each other and see their pastor in non-counseling situations, influences what happens in counseling significantly."[48] Clinebell recognizes the importance of context to pastoral counseling. The parish setting gives a unique perspective to counseling because of its unusual access to families and to individuals and to a relationship with them across the lifespan.

Turning the Corner:
The Brief Nature of Counseling in Congregational Ministry

Even though the pastoral counseling literature of the past five decades shows a significant long-term therapy bias with theory and methods evolving from theoretical constructs and psychotherapeutic modalities of long-term clinical practice, as early as 1949 Steward Hiltner recognized that ministers' time limitations call for brevity in most of their counseling. According to him, the principal purpose of brief counseling is to help parishioners "turn the corner," or make a minor course correction: "Even brief counseling can often do just enough to bring a slightly new perspective, hence altering the approach to the situation and giving a chance for spontaneous successful handling of it by the parishioner."[49]

"Turning the corner" is in contradistinction to the more insight-oriented long-term approach that Hiltner himself favored. Even though he recognized that virtually all counseling in the parish is brief, to the field's great loss Hiltner did not put his efforts toward refining an approach to counseling that parish pastors could use as they assist parishioners to turn the corner, to make those small changes necessary for engendering hope. Instead, like so many that followed him, he focused on a theory of psychotherapy that could rarely be used in counseling in congregational ministry.

Fortunately, brief pastoral counseling has become much more finely tuned than when Hiltner wrote those lines, and its methods are better designed to help people make a change of direction in a few sessions. Turning the corner, in fact, is the primary goal of brief pastoral counseling. The other ministries of the church will care for people as they continue the task of addressing a problem, making the necessary changes and moving into the future. Charles Taylor describes well the goal of brief pastoral counseling: "This problem-solving or problem management model is designed to respond to the one-time conversations and very brief counseling (up to six weekly sessions that are focused on a specific problem or situation) that characterize the majority of pastoral contacts."[50]

In *Mental Health Ministry of the Local Church*, Howard Clinebell adds to our understanding of pastoral counseling when he writes that, it "does not aim at radical changes in personality. It deals mainly with contemporary relationships and problems rather than exploring childhood relationships. Its aim is to help persons mobilize their inner resources for handling a crisis; for making a difficult decision; for adjusting constructively to an unalterable problem; or for improving their interpersonal relationships, including their relationship with God."[51] Clinebell recognizes that brief pastoral counseling, unlike long-term psychotherapy, has a minimalist perspective. It helps set persons on a path of change or growth and then gets out of the way while they continue their journey supported by the other ministries of the church.

Wayne Oates comments on brief pastoral counseling's limited perspective: "Much of the help which a pastoral counselor renders to his people is given in a single interview. He should have the ability, the consecration, and the training to deal with people on a more intensive basis. However, the great number of people whom he serves and the many other ways he has of serving them make it important that he know how to use one-interview opportunities to the fullest possible advantage."[52] C. W. Brister makes the same point when he suggests that "the individual's need for ordering his existence, for spiritual strength, and for clarification of direction may be as urgent in a single-interview contact as in multiple-interview counseling. He will not minimize such conversations, for from the person's perspective they are usually most significant."[53]

David Switzer, like Clinebell and Oates, has given thoughtful consideration to how one goes about actually doing brief pastoral counseling. The focus of much of his work is upon individuals in crisis situations, but his ideas have proved useful in many other situations. In *The Minister as Crisis Counselor*, he relates his experiences as a minister of pastoral counseling in a local parish, when only 15 people out of 154 came to him for more than six sessions, but adds that the parish pastors whom he polled had seen not even one parishioner during the year for six or more consecutive weeks. He notes that even psychotherapists, faced with new challenges, are adopting short-term approaches to therapy that call for fewer sessions with greater intensity, and that ministers need skills to help people address "a number of painful, frustrating, anxiety-producing, problematic situations by means of a variety of approaches that will take only a few sessions. . . ."[54]

Switzer goes on to describe his understanding of brief pastoral counseling as a focus on "the decision-making process and the carrying out of the decisions at the time the needs arise makes an immediate contribution to the reduction of confusion, stress, and anxiety, and opens up new vistas in people's lives."[55] He believes that ministers need skills to help people work through "painful, frustrating, anxiety-producing, problematic situations by means of a variety of approaches that will take only a few sessions." In recent years, Switzer adds, "new approaches to the resolution of many personal problems have been offered by professionals in the fields of pastoral counseling, psychology, and community and emergency psychiatry. More and more, the inadequacy of traditional methods of long-term individual psychotherapy to deal with the constantly increasing mental-health needs of the nation has become apparent."[56]

Research findings, articles, and books that set forth brief pastoral counseling theory and methodology are beginning to correct these inadequacies and provide needed skills for ministers who counsel in the congregational context. (See appendix B for an annotated list of additional readings on brief pastoral counseling.)

The Future of Brief Pastoral Counseling

The principal strength of every long-enduring culture and faith is an ability to meet the evolving needs of its people. One might hope that other voices will soon join these few, that more and more pastoral counseling theorists will begin the new millennium with a fresh and useful body of work that reflects the real-life congregational context of pastoral counseling, the real-life situations of people who do not wish to spend endless weeks or years in therapy, and parish pastors' real-life need for a theory and practice of counseling ministry that is responsive to the present.

Neither I nor any author in this book would claim that the parish is the only place for ministry to take place. Surely there is real ministry in the work of specialist pastoral counselors. Pastoral counseling ministry occurs in hospitals, nursing homes, hospices, prisons, offices, and clinics, and much of what is discussed herein is useful in these various contexts as well. However, it is time to correct the disregard for the congregational context and the lack of attention given to pastoral counseling ministry in the parish setting by so many pastoral counseling theorists in the half-century past. Context is important. It is my hope that the entire field of pastoral counseling will give the context of the congregation its due. The field needs to focus on finding new ways to do counseling in a short period of time.

Pastoral counseling can be done both skillfully and expeditiously. Fitted out with the tools of brief pastoral counseling, ministers in the congregational context can meet the diverse needs of a wide variety of parishioners without sacrificing the other functions of ministry. I am convinced that brief pastoral counseling is the best known way of coping with the complexity and limitations of our vocation, the best stewardship of our time and talents, the best way to help our parishioners work through their difficulties so that they can regain hope and be faithful to God's call.

Notes

1.   The research project described in this chapter was supported by a grant from the Louisville Institute, for which I am very grateful.

2.   Thomas F. Eagleton was George McGovern's vice presidential running mate in 1972 and was replaced when it was discovered that he had been treated for emotional problems in his past.

3.   Joseph Veroff, Richard A. Kulka, and Elizabeth Dorran, *Mental Health in America* (New York: Basic, 1981).

4.   Ibid.; also see Howard Clinebell, *Basic Types of Pastoral Care and Counseling*, rev. ed. (Nashville: Abingdon, 1984); and idem, *The Mental Health Ministry of the Local Church* (Nashville: Abingdon, 1972).

5.   Clinebell, *Basic Types*, 35–36.

6.   William E. Hulme, *Pastoral Care and Counseling: Using the Unique Resources of the Christian Tradition* (Minneapolis: Augsburg, 1981), 153, 155.

7.   Charles Kemp, *The Caring Pastor: An Introduction to Pastoral Counseling in the Local Church* (Nashville: Abingdon, 1985), 12.

8.   Wayne Oates, *An Introduction to Pastoral Counseling* (Nashville: Broadman, 1959), vi.

9.   Don S. Browning, *The Moral Context of Pastoral Care* (Philadelphia: Westminster, 1976) and *Practical Theology* (New York: Harper & Row, 1982); Alastair Campbell, *Rediscovering Pastoral Care* (London: Darton, Longman & Todd, 1981); William A. Clebsch and Charles R. Jaekle, *Pastoral Care in Historical Perspective* (Northvale, N.J.; Jason Aronson, 1964); Deborah van Deusen Hunsinger, *Theology and Pastoral Counseling* (Grand Rapids: Eerdmans, 1995); Charles Gerkin, *The Living Human Document: Re-Visioning Pastoral Counseling in a Hermeneutical Mode* (Nashville: Abingdon, 1984); Andrew Lester, *Hope in Pastoral Care and Counseling* (Louisville: Westminster/John Knox, 1995); Thomas Oden, *Pastoral Theology* (New York: Harper & Row, 1983); Thomas Oden, *Classical Pastoral Care: Pastoral Counsel*, vol. 3 (Grand Rapids: Baker, 1987); John Patton, *Pastoral Counseling: A Ministry of the Church*, (Nashville: Abingdon, 1983); Howard W. Stone, *Theological Context for Pastoral Caregiving*, (New York: Haworth, 1996); Friedrich Schleiermacher, *Christian Caring: Selections from Practical Theology*, ed. by James O. Duke and Howard W. Stone (Philadelphia: Fortress Press, 1988).

10. Women have been writing for some time in the field of pastoral theology but have only recently started to write to any extent in pastoral counseling.

11. Although the complete texts of all of the books in appendix A were reviewed for the study, in order to insure uniformity of response, only the first hundred pages of one book per author (noted with an asterisk) were analyzed for the tables furnished in appendices C–G. For a complete description of how the study was carried out, see appendix A.

12. Paul Engle, "National Survey of Selected Pastors on Pastoral Counseling," survey for Baker Book House, Grand Rapids, Mich., 1990.

13. Ibid., 41.

14. Ibid., 2.

15. Duane R. Bidwell, letter to author, 19 November 1999.

16. Ann Belford Ulanova, *Picturing God* (Cambridge, Mass.: Cowley, 1986), 8–9.

17. Howard Clinebell, *Basic Types*, 9.

18. Gerkin, *The Living Human Document*, 124; Paul Johnson, *Person as Counselor* (Nashville: Abingdon, 1967), 88, 136; Patton, *Pastoral Counseling*, 30, 34. See also Oates, *An Introduction to Pastoral Counseling*.

Oates wrote a chapter on "The Exploratory or Short-Term Interview." In it he states, "We find two extremes among pastoral counselors today: those who try to accomplish everything in one-interview contacts and those who think nothing really constructive can be done unless an extensive series of therapeutic sessions can be arranged. Both of these approaches miss the real values of one-interview counseling because they do not perceive accurately the goals and the limitations of this kind of service to needy people. The goals of one-interview counseling must be set strictly within the limitations of such work" (110). Or, "Much of the help which a pastoral counselor renders to his people is given in a single interview. He should have the ability, the consecration, and the training to deal with people on a more intensive basis. However, the great number of people whom he serves and the many other ways he has of serving them make it important that he know how to use one-interview opportunities to the fullest possible advantage" (108).

19. Oates, *An Introduction to Pastoral Counseling*, 108–9.

20. Carroll A. Wise, *Pastoral Counseling: Its Theory and Practice* (New York: Harper, 1951), 116.

21. Seward Hiltner, *Pastoral Counseling* (New York: Abingdon, 1949), 19, 73.

22. Carl Rogers, *Client-Centered Therapy* (New York: Houghton Mifflin, 1951), 45.

23. Wayne Oates, *Pastoral Counseling* (Philadelphia: Westminster, 1974), 76.

24. Ludwig Wittgenstein, *Lectures and Conversations on Aesthetics, Psychology, and Religious Belief* (Berkeley: Univ. of California Press, 1972), no. 6.4321.

25. Peter DeJong and Insoo Kim Berg, *Interviewing for Solutions* (Pacific Grove, Calif.: Brooks/Cole, 1998).

26. Hiltner, *Pastoral Counseling*, 84.

27. Oates, *Pastoral Counseling*, 65.

28. Patton, *Pastoral Counseling*, 163.

29. William Oglesby, *Referral and Pastoral Counseling* (Philadelphia: Fortress Press, 1968), 36.

30. Charles V. Gerkin, *Widening the Horizon: Pastoral Responses to a Fragmented Society* (Philadelphia: Westminster, 1986).

31. Herb Anderson, *The Family and Pastoral Care* (Philadelphia: Fortress Press, 1984).

32. Clinebell, *Basic Types,* 243.

33. Kemp, *Caring Pastor,* 108.

34. Ibid., 18.

35. Anderson, *The Family and Pastoral Care,* 118–19, 122.

36. Russell L. Dicks, *Principles and Practices of Pastoral Care* (Englewood Cliffs, N.J.: Prentice-Hall, 1963), 99.

37. Clinebell, *Basic Types,* 198.

38. Hiltner, *Pastoral Counseling,* 95.

39. Patton, *Pastoral Counseling,* 219.

40. Ibid., 110, 112.

41. Edward Wimberley, *Prayer and Pastoral Counseling: Suffering, Healing, and Discernment* (Louisville: Westminster/John Knox, 1990).

42. Oates, *An Introduction to Pastoral Counseling,* 2.

43. Ibid., 59.

44. Kemp, *Caring Pastor,* 30–31.

45. Charles Kemp, *The Caring Church: An Introduction to Pastoral Counseling in the Local Church* (Nashville: Abingdon, 1985), 27.

46. Clinebell, *Basic Types.*

47. Ibid., 19.

48. Ibid., 68–69.

49. Hiltner, *Pastoral Counseling,* 82.

50. Charles W. Taylor, *The Skilled Pastor: Counseling as the Practice of Theology* (Minneapolis: Fortress Press, 1991), 11.

51. Clinebell, *Mental Health Ministry,* 213.

52. Oates, *An Introduction to Pastoral Counseling,* 108.

53. C. W. Brister, *Pastoral Care in the Church* (New York: Harper & Row, 1964), 171.

54. David K. Switzer, *The Minister as Crisis Counselor,* rev. ed. (Nashville: Abingdon, 1986), 23.

55. Ibid., 24.

56. Ibid., 23.

Appendix A

Pastoral Counseling Authors
in Study

THE MAJOR AUTHORS in the field of pastoral counseling were examined with the goal of determining the degree to which pastoral counseling theorists in the second half of the twentieth century have attended to the context of parish ministry. The guiding question, therefore, was this: Does the literature of pastoral counseling address the counseling situations typically encountered by parish pastors and offer methods well-suited to their context?

Beginning with Seward Hiltner's *Pastoral Counseling,* published late in 1949, the study covered subsequent books with a distinctly pastoral counseling focus, omitting works that, though they may have discussed pastoral theology or pastoral care, did not address pastoral counseling specifically. It examined the writings of twenty-six pastoral counseling authors who are widely read by parish pastors, and who speak to mainline Christian ministers across Protestant and Catholic lines. These authors were selected through a poll of ten leading pastoral theologians/pastoral counseling specialists.

Each selected theorist has written at least one book on pastoral counseling; authors who only wrote edited or coauthored works were not included. Some have written many books during their careers, and their ideas on pastoral counseling may have evolved over the years; in these cases a maximum of two representative works by each was chosen. The study excluded writers whose first book was published within the past five years, as it is too early to gauge their importance to the field. For the purpose of consistency, and to restrict the number of variables such as political and social influences, the selection was limited to American pastoral counseling literature.

The study included a statistical tabulation of each work's references to other writers and theorists in order to cast light on their underlying assumptions (see appendices C–G). Each time an author made a direct reference to a name or an authored text in the book selected for study (but not those names listed in an endnote) they were counted; references such as "Freudian" or "Jungian" were also considered a reference. Although the complete texts of all of the books in appendix A were reviewed for the study, in order to ensure uniformity of response only the first hundred pages of one book per author (noted with an asterisk) were analyzed for the tables furnished in appendices C–G. The objective was to find trends, to get an overview of the field's orientation, and to discover whether in fact a particular viewpoint (or range of viewpoints) has driven the core of pastoral counseling theory and methodology.

Pastoral Counseling Theorists

*Herbert Anderson, *The Family and Pastoral Care* (Philadelphia: Fortress Press, 1984).

_____ et al., eds., *The Family Handbook* (Louisville: Westminster/John Knox, 1998).

*William V. Arnold, *Introduction to Pastoral Care* (Philadelphia: Westminster, 1982).

*James B. Ashbrook, *Minding the Soul: Pastoral Counseling as Remembering* (Minneapolis: Fortress Press, 1996).

David W. Augsburger, *Anger and Assertiveness in Pastoral Care* (Philadelphia: Fortress Press, 1979).

*_____, *Pastoral Counseling across Cultures* (Philadelphia: Westminster, 1986).

C. W. Brister, *Pastoral Care in the Church* (New York: Harper & Row, 1964).

*_____, *The Promise of Counseling* (San Francisco: Harper & Row, 1978).

*Don S. Browning, *Atonement and Psychotherapy* (Philadelphia: Westminster, 1966).

_____, *The Moral Context of Pastoral Care* (Philadelphia: Westminster, 1976).

*Donald Capps, *Living Stories: Pastoral Counseling in Congregational Context* (Minneapolis: Fortress Press, 1998).

_____, *Pastoral Counseling and Preaching: A Quest for an Integrated Ministry* (Philadelphia: Westminster, 1980).

*Howard Clinebell, *Basic Types of Pastoral Care and Counseling: Resources for the Ministry of Healing and Growth* (Nashville: Abingdon, 1984).

_____, *Growth Counseling: Hope-Centered Methods of Actualizing Human Wholeness* (Nashville: Abingdon, 1979).

*Russell L. Dicks, *Principles and Practices of Pastoral Care* (Englewood Cliffs, N.J.: Prentice-Hall, 1963).

*Charles V. Gerkin, *The Living Human Document: Re-Visioning Pastoral Counseling in a Hermeneutical Mode* (Nashville: Abingdon, 1984).

_____, *Widening the Horizons: Pastoral Responses to a Fragmented Society* (Philadelphia: Westminster, 1986).

*Larry Kent Graham, *Care of Persons, Care of Worlds: A Psychosystems Approach to Pastoral Care and Counseling* (Nashville: Abingdon, 1992).

*Seward Hiltner, *Pastoral Counseling* (New York: Abingdon-Cokesbury Press, 1949).

_____ and Lowell G. Colston, *The Context of Pastoral Counseling* (New York: Abingdon, 1961).

*William E. Hulme, *How to Start Counseling: Building the Counseling Program in the Local Church* (New York: Abingdon, 1955).

_____, *Pastoral Care and Counseling: Using the Unique Resources of the Christian Tradition* (Minneapolis: Augsburg, 1981).

*Paul E. Johnson, *Person as Counselor* (Nashville: Abingdon, 1967).

_____, *Personality and Religion* (New York: Abingdon, 1957).

*Charles F. Kemp, *The Caring Pastor: An Introduction to Pastoral Counseling in the Local Church* (Nashville: Abingdon, 1985).

_____, *A Pastoral Counseling Guidebook* (Nashville: Abingdon, 1971).

*James N. Lapsley, *Renewal in Late Life through Pastoral Counseling* (New York: Paulist, 1992).

_____, *Salvation and Health: The Interlocking Processes of Life* (Philadelphia: Westminster, 1972).

Andrew D. Lester, *Coping with Your Anger: A Christian Guide* (Philadelphia: Westminster, 1983).

*_____, *Hope in Pastoral Care and Counseling* (Louisville: Westminster/John Knox, 1995).

Wayne E. Oates, ed., *An Introduction to Pastoral Counseling* (Nashville: Broadman, 1959).

*_____, *Pastoral Counseling* (Philadelphia: Westminster, 1974).

Thomas Oden, *Contemporary Theology and Psychotherapy* (Philadelphia: Westminster, 1967).

*_____, *Kerygma and Counseling: Toward a Covenant Ontology for Secular Psychotherapy* (Philadelphia: Westminster, 1966).

*William B. Oglesby Jr., *Referral in Pastoral Counseling* (Englewood Cliffs, N.J.: Prentice-Hall, 1968).

John Patton, *Is Human Forgiveness Possible? A Pastoral Care Perspective* (Nashville: Abingdon, 1985).

*_____, *Pastoral Counseling: A Ministry of the Church* (Nashville: Abingdon, 1983).

*David Switzer, *The Minister as Crisis Counselor* (Nashville: Abingdon, 1974).

_____, *Pastoral Care Emergencies: Ministering to People in Crisis* (New York: Paulist, 1989).

* Charles W. Taylor, *The Skilled Pastor: Counseling as the Practice of Theology* (Minneapolis: Fortress Press, 1991).

*Ann Belford Ulanov, *Picturing God* (Cambridge, Mass.: Cowley, 1986).

_____ and Barry Ulanov, *Religion and the Unconscious* (Philadelphia: Westminster, 1975).

*Edward P. Wimberly, *Pastoral Counseling and Spiritual Values: A Black Point of View* (Nashville: Abingdon, 1982).

_____, *Prayer in Pastoral Counseling: Suffering, Healing, and Discernment* (Louisville: Westminster/John Knox, 1990).

*Carroll A. Wise, *Pastoral Counseling: Its Theory and Practice* (New York: Harper, 1951).

_____, *Pastoral Psychotherapy: Theory and Practice* (New York: Jason Aronson, 1983).

Appendix B

Suggested Readings for Congregational Ministers

These readings have a very specific focus: brief pastoral counseling in the context of the congregation. They do not cover writings in other areas of pastoral counseling, pastoral care, or theology.

Berg, Insoo Kim and Scott Miller. *Working with the Problem Drinker: A Solution-Focused Approach* (New York: Norton, 1992). The authors provide a clear description of how to do brief counseling whether it is applied to problem drinking or any other problem.

Childs, Brian H. *Short-Term Pastoral Counseling.* Rev. ed. (New York: Haworth, 2000; 1st ed. (Nashville: Abingdon, 1990). Childs expands on the chapter in this book.

Clinebell, Howard. *Basic Types of Pastoral Care and Counseling* (Nashville: Abingdon, 1984). This is a good, basic text on pastoral care and counseling; it is a must for every pastor's bookshelf.

De Jong, Peter, and Insoo Kim Berg. *Interviewing for Solutions* (Pacific Grove, Calif.: Brooks/Cole, 1998). This is the best book on the basics of doing brief counseling and is highly recommended.

Gorsuch, Nancy. *Pastoral Visitation* (Minneapolis: Fortress Press, 1999). This is a good book on how to do pastoral visitation.

Kollar, Charles Allen. *Solution-Focused Pastoral Counseling: An Effective Short-Term Approach for Getting People Back on Track* (Grand Rapids, Mich.: Zondervan, 1997). Kollar expands upon his chapter in this book.

O'Hanlon, William, and Michele Weiner-Davis. *In Search of Solutions* (New York: Norton, 1989). A useful book on the basics of brief counseling.

Stone, Howard. *Brief Pastoral Counseling: Short-Term Approaches and Strategies* (Minneapolis: Fortress Press, 1993). Stone provides the basics of doing brief pastoral counseling.

_____. *Crisis Counseling* (Minneapolis: Fortress Press, 1994). *Crisis Counseling* discusses the pastoral care and counseling of parishioners who are experiencing a crisis.

_____. *Depression and Hope* (Minneapolis: Fortress Press, 1998). This book expands upon *Brief Pastoral Counseling,* applying it to individuals who are depressed.

Switzer, David K. *Pastoral Care Emergencies: Ministering to People in Crisis* (Minneapolis: Fortress Press, 2000). Switzer addresses brief care and counseling for parishioners who are experiencing personal or family emergencies.

Taylor, Charles W. *The Skilled Pastor: Counseling as the Practice of Theology* (Minneapolis: Fortress Press, 1991). This is a good, basic book on pastoral counseling.

Thomas, Frank and Jack Cockburn. *Competency-Based Counseling* (Minneapolis: Fortress Press, 1998). The authors help readers base their pastoral counseling on parishioners' strengths (competencies) rather than on their liabilities.

Weiner-Davis, Michele. *Divorce Busting: A Revolutionary and Rapid Program for Staying Together* (New York: Simon & Schuster, 1993). Weiner-Davis's book is very good on marriage counseling based on solution-focused brief therapy and is especially useful for counseling couples who are on their way to divorce.

Appendix C

Psychotherapy Theorists

	Herbert Anderson	William Arnold	James Ashbrook	David Augsburger	C.W. Brister	Don Browning	Donald Capps	Howard Clinebell	Russell Dicks	Charles Gerkin	Larry Kent Graham	Seward Hiltner	William Hulme	Paul Johnson	Charles Kemp	James Lapsley	Andrew Lester	Wayne Oates	Thomas Oden	William Oglesby	John Patton	David Switzer	Charles Taylor	Ann Belford Ulanov	Edward Wimberly	Carroll Wise	Total
Adler, A.					2	4						3			8			2	4								23
Allport, G.		1		2	5							1		4													13
Bateson, G.			2					8																			10
Beck, A.															2	9											11
Butler, J.					8																						8
Cabot, R.									15																		15
Caplan, G.																	1						6				7
Carkhuff, R.			1		1		2														1	7	7				19
de Shazer, S.								7																			7
Doan, R.								10																			10
Egan, G.							2																		5		7
Ellis, A.		1													3	1									11		16
Erickson, M.							201																				201
Erikson, E.		6	1	6			3		8						2		3	9	1		4	1			3	1	48
Frank, J.			2	4														1									7
Frankl, V.				4	1									4	2		5								2		18
Freud, S.	1		3	1	35	2	2			50	11	16		16	19	4		7	13			2			22	4	208
Fromm, E.				1			2		1	2	1	1		1	1										1	17	28
Gergen, K.																		9									9
Gergen, M.																		9									9
Glasser, W.		1		1											3				2								7
Horney, K.						2					9			1	1										1	1	15
Hudson, P.								16																			16
James, W.	1			2							2			12	3	1		1									22
Jourard, S.																				10		2					20
Jung, C.		1		10			1				6	10		11	1			1			1				25	22	89
Kernberg, O.									19																		19
Kohut, H.			6					1	20		1						3										31
Laing, R. D.																								14			14
Maslow, A.		1		2	7	2	1										3										16
May, R.					1	1	1										2	1									6
Menninger, K.				10				1						1				2				1				1	16
O'Hanlon, W.								20																			20
Parry, A.								10																			10
Pruyser, P.		1			5		1									5	1	1	4								18
Rice, L.						6																					6
Roberts, J.								36																			36
Rogers, C.	1	1	8		9	40	22	4	1	4	1	5		18			2	1	112			4	7		1	3	244
Rosen, S.								32																			32
Sue, D.				4								3															7
Sullivan, H.S.		1		2	1		1				1	1		4	2	1		10	2			4	1		1		32
Watzlawick, P.								18																			18
Weakland, J.								6																			6
Winnicott, D.W.			2						35																8		45
Yalom, I.	2																			4							6
Other		4	20	31	40	21	10	5	10	14	8	7	2	18	19	66	21	33	14		7	26	12	15	19	1	423
																									GRAND TOTAL		1848

Appendix D

Writers in the Classical Theological Fields

	Herbert Anderson	William Arnold	James Ashbrook	David Augsburger	C.W. Brister	Don Browning	Donald Capps	Howard Clinebell	Russell Dicks	Charles Gerkin	Larry Kent Graham	Seward Hiltner	William Hulme	Paul Johnson	Charles Kemp	James Lapsley	Andrew Lester	Wayne Oates	Thomas Oden	William Oglesby	John Patton	David Switzer	Charles Taylor	Ann Belford Ulanov	Edward Wimberly	Carroll Wise	TOTAL
Abelard, P.					5																						5
Augustine			1											1	2		1	5	4						5		19
Aulen, G.					12																						12
Anselm					72																						72
Barth, K.				3						1				3					27	11				1			46
Baxter, R.						1								1	3												5
Bonhoeffer, D.				1	1	3												1	3								9
Breuggemann, W.	1	1															1				1						4
Brooks, P.														1	6												7
Buber, M.					1		1				1			1				3	3								10
Bushnell, H.					89	1									1						1						92
Calvin, J.		8			15												9				1			4			37
Campbell, M.					6																						6
Chodorow, N.											7																7
Cobb, J.			3								1															1	5
de Chardin, T.	2				1	1															1						5
Drummond													5														5
Fosdick, H.					1		1	1										2									5
Frei, H.																				4							4
Hauerwas, S.		1															6										7
Iraneus						92															1						93
Kierkegaard, S.			1	2		1										1	21	2	1		1			7			37
Koyama, K.				4	1																						5
Lawson, J.					4																						4
Lewis, C.S.				6									1														7
Luther, M.	3	2	2		1		7	2					4		3	1					1				1	4	31
Lynch, W.																	12										12
Macquarrie, J.			1	1													7										9
Moltmann, J.	1				1						25	1					5				6						39
Navone, J.																	5										5
Niebuhr, H. R.							1				3						1	1									6
Niebuhr, R. R.								1			5						1										7
Nouwen, H.		1	2		1		1											1									6
Pannenberg, W.					1						1						2										4
Roberts, D.																		3	1								4
Schleiermacher, F.			1	3							8																12
Spencer, I. S.																	4										4
Tertullian					2																1			1			4
Tillich, P.	1		1	2	4		5	1	19				4				4	4	1		25	3					74
Tittle, E.								4																			4
Tracy, D.			4																								4
Wesley, J.		1			1								1								1						4
Williams, D. D.				4	13		4												1								22
Wingren, G.					4																						4
Other	3	1	8	22	16	15		9	6	9	6		2		1	3	11	25	10		7				6	2	162
																					GRAND TOTAL						925

214

Appendix E

Couple and Family Systems Theorists

	Herbert Anderson	William Arnold	James Ashbrook	David Augsburger	C.W. Brister	Don Browning	Donald Capps	Howard Clinebell	Russell Dicks	Charles Gerkin	Larry Kent Graham	Seward Hiltner	William Hulme	Paul Johnson	Charles Kemp	James Lapsley	Andrew Lester	Wayne Oates	Thomas Oden	William Oglesby	John Patton	David Switzer	Charles Taylor	Ann Belford Ulanov	Edward Wimberly	Carroll Wise	TOTAL
Ackerman, N.																		4									4
Beavers, R.																	4										4
Bowen, M.	1																								4		5
Brown, D.						1																					1
Burgess, E.					1																						1
Haley, J.							16																				16
Hoffman, L.							2																				2
Jackson, D.							2																				2
Mace, D. R.																							1				1
Minuchin, S.							1				2														3		6
Mudd, E.																									1		1
Nichols, M.							1																				1
Satir, V.							1																1		5		7
Whitaker, S.							1																				1
																							GRAND TOTAL				52

215

Appendix F

Pastoral Care/Counseling/Theology Theorists

	Herbert Anderson	William Arnold	James Ashbrook	David Augsburger	C.W. Brister	Don Browning	Donald Capps	Howard Clinebell	Russell Dicks	Charles Gerkin	Larry Kent Graham	Seward Hiltner	William Hulme	Paul Johnson	Charles Kemp	James Lapsley	Andrew Lester	Wayne Oates	Thomas Oden	William Oglesby	John Patton	David Switzer	Charles Taylor	Ann Belford Ulanov	Edward Wimberly	Carroll Wise	TOTAL
Adams, J.					2																						2
Andrew, W.									2																		2
Bianchi, E.																3											3
Boisen, A.			4		1			3	11	43						3		1				7				1	74
Bonthius, R.																			3								3
Browning, D.	2				1							1		1	1										7		13
Burkhart, R.																			3								3
Cabot, R.								1														1					2
Capps, D.			6												1												7
Carrigan, R.																	7										7
Clebsch, W.					1			2							2										4		9
Clinebell, H.	2		2		3					3	7				2			6			1		1				27
Cole, T.					2																						2
Colston, L.			1		1									5	3												10
Dicks, R.					1			2														1					4
Gerkin, C.			2							4						9	4								3		22
Guiles, P.								1	5																		6
Hitner, S.			1						1	4		7		2	4			9			5	1					34
Howe, R.				13																							13
Hulme, W.					1																				2		3
Jaekle, C.					1			2							2										4		9
Johnson, P.								1		6																	7
Keuther, F.									3																		3
Kemp, C.					2													1									3
Kimper, F.				2																							2
Madden, M.					1													3									4
Mitchell, K.		1			1													2									4
Neuger, C.			9																								9
Oates, W.	2				5			2		7					1	2	2	6	1								28
Oden, T.				1	2					4														7			14
Oglesby, W.					7													1									8
Patton, J.		1			2						3																6
Roberts, D.					1			1																			2
Schneider, C.				2																							2
Smith, A.											2														2		4
Stone, H.								1								2											3
Switzer, D.					1												1										2
Taggert, M.					2													1			1				1		5
Thornton, E.					2																						2
Thurneysen, E.														3					1								4
Tinker, G.											3																3
Van Dusen, H.									2																		2
Whitehead, E.										2																	2
Winter, G.																					3						3
Wise, C.			3		1				1	14				1	2	1		2									25
Other	2	3			7			2	5		5	1	1	2	1	6	1	4			2	2				3	47
																					GRAND TOTAL						449

216

Appendix G

Writers in Spirituality and Spiritual Direction

	Herbert Anderson	William Arnold	James Ashbrook	David Augsburger	C. W. Brister	Don Browning	Donald Capps	Howard Clinebell	Russell Dicks	Charles Gerkin	Larry Kent Graham	Seward Hiltner	William Hulme	Paul Johnson	Charles Kemp	James Lapsley	Andrew Lester	Wayne Oates	Thomas Oden	William Oglesby	John Patton	David Switzer	Charles Taylor	Ann Belford Ulanov	Edward Wimberly	Carroll Wise	TOTAL
Barry, W.																1											1
Brother Lawrence													1														1
Connolly, W.																1											1
Kelsey, M.																								1	3		4
May, G.																									6		6
Merton, T.																1											1
Sanford, J.																								1			1
Steere, D.		1																									1
																								GRAND TOTAL			16

Index